Praise for the first edition of *Steal This Comp*

"*If ever a book on cyberculture wore a fedora and trench coat and leaned against a lamppost on a foggy street, this is the one.*"
—AMAZON.COM

"*[Wang's] philosophical banter makes his computer guide read like a novel.*"
—CIO WEB BUSINESS

"*. . . a delightfully irresponsible primer on how to spam one's friends and foes, how to get Internet dirt on fellow citizens via government Web sites, how to encrypt one's own files and read somebody else's and other hypertext hijinks.*"
—CHICAGO TRIBUNE

"*This book is not going to make a lot of people very happy—and it's going to make a lot of others very nervous.*"
—HOUSTON CHRONICLE

"*If you are a frequent user of the Internet you won't be able to put this book down.*"
—THE TAMPA TRIBUNE

"*Don't go online without it!*"
—THE MIDWEST BOOK REVIEW

"*If this book had a soundtrack, it'd be Lou Reed's Walk on the Wild Side.*"
—INFO WORLD

"*If you're smart, and you work on the Internet, you'll get [Steal This Computer Book] before that teen-aged computer geek down the block does.*"
—THE SARASOTA HERALD-TRIBUNE

STEAL THIS COMPUTER BOOK (2)

What They Won't Tell You About The Internet

Wallace Wang
Wally

 no starch press

San Francisco

STEAL THIS COMPUTER BOOK 2

Publisher: *William Pollock*
Project Editor: *Karol Jurado*
Assistant Editor: *Nick Hoff*
Editorial Production Assistant:
  Jennifer Arter
Cover and Interior Design: *Octopod Studios*
Compositor: *Magnolia Studio*
Copyeditor: *Karen Lamoreux*
Proofreader: *Ruth Stevens*

Distributed to the book trade in the
United States and Canada by Publishers
Group West, 1700 Fourth Street, Berkeley,
California 94710; phone: 800-788-3123 or
510-528-1444; fax: 510-528-3444

For information on translations or book
distributors outside the United States,
please contact No Starch Press directly:

No Starch Press
555 De Haro Street, Suite 250
San Francisco, CA 94107
phone: 415-863-9900
fax: 415-863-9950
info@nostarch.com
www.nostarch.com

Library of Congress Cataloging-in-Publication Data

Wang, Wallace.
        Steal this computer book / Wallace Wang.--2nd ed.
             p. cm.
        Includes index.
        ISBN 1-886411-42-5 (pbk.)
            1. Computer hackers--Handbooks, manuals, etc. 2. Internet (Computer
      network)--Handbooks, manuals, etc. 3. Subculture--Computer network resources.
        I. Title.
HV6773.W35 2000
306'1--dc21   00-030737

DEDICATION

This book is dedicated to truth, justice, honesty, and the
American Way—which are too often mutually exclusive ideas.

BRIEF CONTENTS

CONTENTS IN DETAIL

PART 4: DESTRUCTIVE THREATS ON THE INTERNET

ACKNOWLEDGMENTS

If it weren't for the wonderful people at No Starch Press, this book would still be just another good idea floating around the publishing industry. The most important person involved in the creation of this book is William Pollock, who provided guidance for the book and gently nursed it from a rough idea to a completed manuscript. Two other extremely important people include Nick Hoff and Karol Jurado, both of whom worked tirelessly to ensure that the manuscript was as complete and error-free as possible.

Many hackers deserve credit for their work that directly or indirectly influenced this book. While I have never met many of these people, their books, text files, Web sites, and software creations have helped influence my thoughts about the "underground" aspect of the computer industry.

I'd also like to thank David Hakala, Jack Rickard, and Todd Erickson of *Boardwatch* magazine (http://www.board-watch.com) for giving me the chance to write a monthly column that covers the world of computer hacking. Much of the material in this book originally came from these columns, dubbed "Notes From the Underground."

Additional thanks go to Steve Schirripa and Don Learned for giving me my break in performing at the Riviera Comedy Club (http://www.theriviera.com) in Las Vegas. Also a big thanks go out to all the stand-up comedians I've had the pleasure of working with over the years including Willie Barcena, Larry Omaha, Kip Addotta, Bob Zany, Gerry Bednob, and Patrick DeGuire.

Final thanks go to stand-up comedians Barry Crimmins, Jimmy Tingle, Bill Hicks, and Will Durst for their delightfully insightful and biting political humor. If you want to know the truth about our governments, foreign policies, and the motives behind our world leaders, listen to any comedy album from these four comedians. I guarantee you'll learn more about world news and politics from their stand-up comedy acts than you ever could from *Newsweek*, *The New York Times*, the *Wall Street Journal*, the *CBS Evening News*, or CNN.

"Another Presidential election is coming up and I think you'll all agree that the biggest problem is that someone will win."

—BARRY CRIMMINS

"It was said during the 1994 elections there wasn't one candidate that could be elected to national office unless they supported the death penalty. Which got me to thinking, if Jesus Christ were here and running for elected office, would the Christian Coalition vote for Him?"

—JIMMY TINGLE

"The Supreme Court defines pornography as 'anything without artistic merit that causes sexual thought.' Hmm, sounds like every commercial on television, doesn't it?"

—BILL HICKS

"This country (America) is so racially divided that it's only a matter of time before South Africa slaps sanctions on us."

—WILL DURST

Introduction

This book won't turn you into a hacker any more than reading a military manual can turn you into a soldier. But what this book will do is open your eyes to the darker side of the Internet that most people never see, read, or hear about—the world of hackers, virus writers, unwholesome Web sites, censorship, racism, and government propaganda.

Not surprisingly, some people will find the information in this book distasteful, disturbing, and downright dangerous. Yet others will see this same information as an excuse and a reason to cause havoc and make trouble for others. But neither side is correct.

The purpose of this book is to challenge you to think about your own preconceived notions about right and wrong, and how you've been trained to think by your culture no matter what part of the world you may live in. Computers and the Internet can help open your mind to new worlds that you never dreamed could possibly exist—or it can shut off your mind and funnel your thinking down the narrow confines of the fantasy world you choose to see. The choice is up to you.

So if you want to use your computer as a tool to expand your awareness rather than substitute for it, keep reading. We need you more than ever before. But don't get me wrong. This book isn't advocating the overthrow of your government or the development of a radically different one.

YOUR OWN REVOLUTION

Instead, this book advocates a more personal form of revolution—the revolution within your own head. Instead of

It would take only one generation of forgetfulness to put us back intellectually several thousand years.

—DEAN TOLLEFSON

2

blindly blaming national governments, international corporations, ethnic groups, sexual preferences, multi-cultural
organizations, ideological beliefs, religious institu-
tions, or political parties for all the world's problems,
this book suggests that:

→ If you change the way you think, you'll change
the way you act.

→ If you change the way you act, you'll be able
to change the way others act and think.

→ If you change the way others act and think, you
can help change the world—one person at a time.

But it all begins with you.

That's why this book advocates changing your own way
of thinking first, because none of us can be correct 100%
of the time, and the first step toward true change is
admitting that neither you nor I—nor your parents, your
boss, your spouse, your family, your government, or your
church—know everything.

There's no shame in not knowing everything, but there
is shame in pretending that we do. We can and must learn
from each other, regardless of what we look like, where we
live, what gods we worship, or who our parents might be.
Open, honest communication is the only way we can change
this world for the better, and that's where this book and
your personal computer come into play.

Communication's the thing

Although computers are still notoriously difficult, confusing, and downright frustrating to use, they represent a
quantum leap in communication similar to the inventions of
the alphabet or the printing press. With personal computers and the Internet, people can send and receive email,
research information through the World Wide Web, and purchase items from anywhere in the world.

But don't be fooled by the marketing hype designed to
suck you into the computer revolution. The world of computers is fraught with hidden dangers that the computer
marketing departments don't mention, such as Trojan

Horses, electronic espionage, remote computer monitoring, hate groups, con artists, pedophiles, pornography, and terrorism—all just a mouse click away.

This book not only reveals these dangers, but will also help you understand how people create them in the first place. The more you know about anything, the better you can avoid or fight it. Besides exploring the underground nature of the Internet that television and magazine ads conveniently ignore, this book also exposes the darker side of the computer industry itself.

Want to find and trade X-rated pictures on commercial online services like America Online and CompuServe? Want to know how anti-virus companies often cooperate with the very virus programmers they are purportedly fighting against? Think your company may be spying on you and need to know how you can protect yourself (or even fight back)? If this is the type of information you're looking for, then this is the book for you.

Buckle up

Although this book won't pretend to be a comprehensive resource for every possible legal and illegal activity you might run across on the Internet, keep in mind that the information provided in this book can help or hurt others. The information itself is neutral. Crash your government's computer network, and you may be labeled a terrorist. Do the same thing to an enemy's computer network, and your government may proclaim you a hero. Good and evil depend solely on your point of view.

So welcome to the side of computers that the computer industry doesn't want you to know about, a world where slickly printed tutorials and training classes don't exist.

This is the underground of the real computer revolution, where everyone is encouraged to question, explore, and criticize, but most importantly, to learn how to think for themselves.

And to some organizations, people who know how to think for themselves can be more dangerous than all the weapons in the world.

PART 1

INFORMATION OVERLOAD

Finding What You Need:
The Magic of Search Engines

PROPAGANDA DOESN'T ALWAYS PROVIDE SKEWED FACTS AND SLANTED INFORMATION. Sometimes the most effective propaganda omits facts and information altogether. By inviting you to "choose" from incomplete information, this subtle form of propaganda allows you to believe that you're actually thinking for yourself, keeping you from realizing that you're really being duped. Just remember that Internet search engines, like all media (including this book), selectively choose which facts and information to display and omit.

SEARCH ENGINES

If you ask different search engines to find the same information, each one will find a number of Web sites not found by the others. So rather than limit the information you find by the tunnel vision of a single search engine, visit and experiment with some of the different search engines listed below. For example, the Ditto.com search engine allows you to search the Internet by clicking on pictures, rather than by typing words (see Figure 1-1). The following list includes some of the more powerful search engines:

About	http://about.com
AltaVista	http://www.altavista.com
Ask Jeeves	http://www.askjeeves.com
Ditto	http://www.ditto.com
Google	http://www.google.com
Hotbot	http://www.hotbot.com

If you can get people to ask the wrong questions, they'll never find the right answers.

—THOMAS PYNCHON

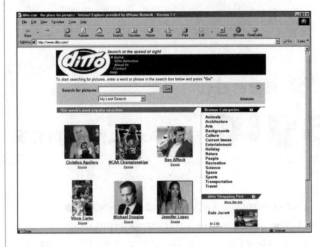

FIGURE 1-1:

The Ditto.com Web site allows you to search the Internet by using pictures.

LookSmart   http://www.looksmart.com

WebCrawler   http://www.webcrawler.com

Yahoo!   http://www.yahoo.com

Meta-search engines

Rather than visit multiple search engines yourself, you
can save time by using a meta-search engine, which simultaneously sends your query to two or more general-purpose
search engines and eliminates duplicate results. Here are
some popular meta-search engines: All-In-One Search Page
(http://www.allonesearch.com), DogPile (http://www.
dogpile.com), MetaCrawler (http://www.metacrawler.com),
and SavvySearch (http://www.savvysearch.com).

Specialized search engines

Finally, don't ignore specialized search engines designed
to search only for Web sites pertaining to a particular
topic. Specialized search engines often find obscure Web
sites that the larger search engines might overlook. There
are specialized search engines for everything from caring
for fish to the latest crafting fads. Here are a few interesting ones:

AvatarSearch
Finds occult information about witchcraft, vampires, pagan rituals, astrology, tarot cards, and other topics that often panic right-wing conservatives (http://www.avatarsearch.com).

Black Web Portal
Finds Web sites of particular interest to Blacks (http://www.blackwebportal.com).

Business Seek and Business Web Source
Provides links to various business Web sites. If you need to find the Web site of a particular company, try these search engines first (http://www.businesseek.com and http://www.businesswebsource.com).

Crime Spider
Searches for Web sites providing information about various crimes including bank robbery, domestic violence, and cybercrime (http://www.crimespider.com).

Disinformation
Conspiracy theory—laden search engine that helps you uncover Web sites offering the "real truth" behind the pyramids of Mars, the sightings of black helicopters over America, film footage of Bigfoot, and the government secrets hidden in Area 51 (http://www.disinfo.com).

Education World
Finds Web sites that can help students, teachers, and parents learn more about education (http://www.education-world.com).

Federal Web Locator
Searches through all U.S. government information posted on the World Wide Web. Maybe you can use it to find out where all your hard-earned tax dollars are going (http://www.infoctr.edu/fwl).

GovSearch
Collection of government search engines for finding information about the US Government: IRS documents, Customs

Services, NTIS, U.S. Law Code, legislative information, OSHA regulations and many other agencies and departments (http://www.nwbuildnet.com/nwbn/govbot.html).

InfoJump
Provides links to Web sites of magazines you've probably never heard about before (http://www.infojump.com).

Law Enforcement Links Directory & Search Engine
Helps you find Web sites related to law enforcement so you can find a policeman when you need one (http://www.leolinks.com).

NerdWorld
Search engine dedicated to computer and technology fanatics (http://www.nerdworld.com).

Public Safety Search
Lists public safety-related Web sites, dealing with topics such as law enforcement, fire departments, and medical research. Learn how your city government is planning to protect you from terrorist attacks or flu epidemics (http://www.policeworld.net/search).

Que Pasa!
A bilingual search engine geared towards Hispanics and Latinos, available in both English and Spanish (http://www.quepasa.com).

Searching Satanism
A search engine dedicated to finding Web sites related to Satanism (http://the600club.com/satanic-search).

Women.com and WWWomen
Two search engines geared toward helping women find information and resources on the Internet (http://www.women.com and http://www.wwwomen.com).

Kid-safe search engines
If you leave your children unsupervised, it's likely that they'll eventually find bomb-making instructions and pornog-

raphy on the Internet. While keeping children isolated from such information may be impossible, you can at least limit their searching to kid-safe search engines. Unlike general-purpose search engines, kid-safe search engines won't accidentally display links to pornographic or bomb-making Web sites. Try one of the following: Ask Jeeves for Kids (http://www.ajkids.com), Fathead Search (http://fathead.net/search), Super Snooper (http://snooper.com), or Yahooligans (http://www.yahooligans.com).

Regional search engines

Search engines often include Web sites from all over the world. If you'd rather limit your search to a specific region or country, try using one of the following regional search engines instead:

TABLE 1-1: INTERNATIONAL SEARCH ENGINES

COUNTRY	WEB SITE	URL
International		
	GloboSeek	http://www.globoseek.com
	International Search Engine Links	http://www.aaa.com.au/
Asia		
General	GlobePage	http://www.globepage.com
Hong Kong	HK Search Engine	http://www.websearch.com.au/hk
India	123India	http://www.123india.com
	IndiasWeb	http://www.indiasweb.com
Japan	Search Desk	http://www.searchdesk.com
Philippines	G-Spot	http://www.gsilink.com/gspot
Singapore	Catcha.com	http://www.catcha.com.sg
South Korea	Kor-Seek	http://kor-seek.com/cgi-bin/korea.cgi
Africa		
General	Mosaique	http://www.mosaique.net
	Orientation Africa	http://af.orientation.com

TABLE 1-1 (CONTINUED): INTERNATIONAL SEARCH ENGINES

COUNTRY	WEB SITE	URL
Africa (continued)		
South Africa	Ananzi	http://www.ananzi.co.za
	Max	http://www.max.co.za
Europe		
General	Search Europe	http://www.searcheurope.com
France	Francité	http://www.francite.com
	Lokace	http://www.lokace.com
Iceland	Iceland on the Web	http://www.vefur.is/iceland
Italy	Ragno Italiano	http://ragno.plugit.net
Malta	Search Malta	http://www.searchmalta.com
Netherlands	Search NL	http://www.search.nl
Russia	Russian Internet Search	http://www.slavophilia.net/russia/search.htm
Scandanavia	Absolutt Internett	http://www.sol.no/sws/absolutt/absolutt.html
Switzerland	Swiss Search	http://www.search.ch
U.K.	UKMax	http://www.ukmax.com
	Lifestyle.co.uk	http://www.lifestyle.co.uk
	WebSearch UK	http://www.websearch.com.au/uk
Middle East		
General	ArabNet	http://search.arab.net/arabnet/search
Egypt	Egypt Search	http://www.egyptsearch.com
Israel	HaReshima	http://www.hareshima.com
North America		
Canada	Canada.com	http://www.canada.com
Mexico	Radar	http://www.radar.com.mx
South America		
Bolivia	Bolivia Web	http://www.boliviaweb.com
Brazil	Cade	http://www.cade.com.br
Chile	ChilNet	http://www.chilnet.cl/index.htm

TABLE 1-1 (CONTINUED): INTERNATIONAL SEARCH ENGINES

COUNTRY	WEB SITE	URL
South Pacific		
General	South Pacific Search	http://www.southpacificsearch.com
Australia	Matilda	http://www.aaa.com.au
	WebWombat	http://www.webwombat.com.au
	WebSearch AU	http://www.websearch.com.au

Searching for more search engines

New search engines seem to appear almost daily (Figure 1-2). The following sites will help you find the latest and best Internet search engines: AllSearchEngines (http://www.allsearchengines.com), The Front Page (http://www.thefrontpage.com/search), Search Engine Watch (http://www.searchenginewatch.com), and Search Engines on the WWW (http://wang.pimpin.net/search.html).

TIPS FOR USING SEARCH ENGINES

Search engines can help you find specific information on the Internet, but they also flood you with large amounts of irrelevant information. With a little bit of extra effort

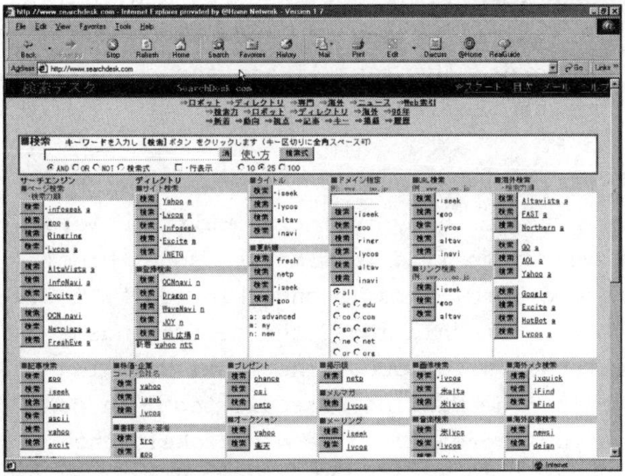

FIGURE 1-2:

You can find a search engine in any language.

on your part, though, you can make sure that a search engine finds exactly what you want as quickly as possible. The next time you use a search engine, try some of the following tips.

Search within categories

Many search engines, such as Yahoo!, display categories, such as Computers & Internet or Business & Economy. If you click on a category and then use the search engine, you'll have the option of searching the entire Internet or narrowing your search just within the currently selected category. Obviously searching within a selected category will take less time and avoid irrelevant Web sites. Still, you might like to search the entire Internet just for the surprise of seeing what the search engine might uncover that you might not have found if you had only limited your search to a specific category.

Use specific words

If you want to find all Web sites that focus on birds, you could type in the word "bird" into a search engine. Unfortunately, the search engine might return thousands of irrelevant Web sites that talk about badminton birdies or different ways to cook game birds. Instead of searching for general words, use more specific words such as "ornithology" (which is the zoological branch of studying birds). The more precise your words, the less likely the search engine will be to uncover irrelevant Web sites.

Use multiple words

You can also narrow your search by typing in multiple words. For example, if you wanted to find information about Miami, Florida, type in the two words "Miami" and "Florida." If you just searched for "Miami" or "Florida," the search engine might bombard you with Web sites about the Miami Dolphins football team or the Florida Marlins baseball team. In general, the more words you search for, the more likely the search engine will be to find exactly what you want.

Use boolean operators

Many search engines allow you to focus your search by using two different Boolean operators: AND and OR.

   If you wanted to search for all Web sites that contain both the words "hot" and "dog," you would simply type the following:

   hot AND dog

   This search would find Web sites devoted to hot dogs, but could also turn up Web sites that talk about ways to cool down a dog on a hot day.

   If you wanted to search for all Web sites that contain either the word "hot" or "dog," you would type the following:

   hot OR dog

   This could turn up Web sites that talk about dogs, different ways air conditioning can cool you down on a hot day, hot chili sauces, or dog food.

REMEMBER THE LIMITATIONS OF SEARCH ENGINES

Search engines may not find everything that you need. Some search engines are better at finding specific topics (such as computer information) than others, while some search engines will miss Web sites that other search engines uncover with ease. Just remember that search engines rarely show you everything available on the Internet. So try different search engines until you find the one that you like the best.

2

Alternative Sources of **News** and **Information**

THINK YOU CAN BELIEVE EVERYTHING YOU READ IN THE PAPER, HEAR ON THE RADIO, OR SEE ON TV? Think again. Newspapers tend to contain detailed information about local events but relatively little historical background or contextual information about international events. If you rely solely on local newspapers for information, your knowledge of national and international news is likely to be incomplete at best, one-sided, or completely wrong at worst.

Reading publications from other countries is one way to get a more balanced view of world events. Try looking at how newspapers from similar countries, such as England and the United States, cover a particular event, compared to how a newspaper from the Middle East or Asia covers that same event.

This chapter lists online newspapers, magazines, and other sources to get you started, but remember that these selections reflect the author's point of view. So be sure to spend some time searching for different newspapers and magazines on your own as well.

NEWSPAPERS ONLINE

Newspapers don't report facts; they report information filtered through the eyes and opinions of the reporters, writers, editors, and news services that provide the information in the first place. Even worse, many newspapers find it more profitable and easier to tranquilize the public

There has never been an objective being. Knowing this, the rest is known.

—UPANISHADS

with shallow sensationalism, local stories, and trivia in order to capture the largest market share possible for their advertisers.

If you begin reading newspapers from different cities and countries, you may be surprised to find that African, European, and Asian newspapers report international events that American newspapers do not choose to cover. Furthermore, even when foreign and American newspapers do cover the same event, the overseas newspapers often provide completely different points of view based on facts that American newspapers gloss over or completely ignore. Browsing through multiple newspapers can give you a much wider exposure to news and a greater appreciation of a newspaper's inherent bias. Try reading an Iraqi newspaper to get a better understanding of how the Iraqi media portrays the feelings of their people toward America. Or read a Brazilian or Australian newspaper to learn about events affecting the Southern Hemisphere that North American newspapers routinely ignore.

The following links point to some of the more prominent English-language newspapers (with the exception of the French newspaper, *Le Monde*). Remember that English-language newspapers may offer information that differs slightly or dramatically from newspapers in other languages, and that the following links aren't the only newspapers available on the Internet.

AfricaNews
Since news about Africa is often scarce, visit the AfricaNews site to read the latest information about a continent that most of the world still ignores (http://www.africanews.com).

Bahrain Tribune
News about the Middle East from Bahrain (http://www.bahraintribune.com/home.asp).

Bangkok Post
News from Thailand (http://www.bangkokpost.net).

Buenos Aires Herald

Get information about South America from an Argentinean newspaper that's been in business since 1876 (http://www. buenosairesherald.com).

China News

English-language Web site providing news about and from China (http://www.china.org.cn/wcm/expe).

Christian Science Monitor

A highly respected newspaper that maintains its own news bureaus in 13 countries, including Russia, Japan, Germany, France, the U.K., South Africa, and Mexico, as well as throughout the United States (http://www.csmonitor.com).

Financial Times

Covers financial news from around the world (http://news. ft.com).

Gulf News

News from the United Arab Emirates (http://www.gulf-news. com).

Ha'aretz

Daily newspaper from Tel Aviv, Israel (http://www. haaretzdaily.com).

International Herald Tribune

A well-respected newspaper edited in Paris and published in conjunction with the *Washington Post* and the *New York Times* (http://www.iht.com).

Investor's Business Daily

A financial newspaper that covers international events with an obvious emphasis on money and how the news affects different stock markets (http://www.investors.com).

Irish Times

Keep up with the latest business, sports, and politics of Ireland, and use this Web site as a search engine for Irish topics as well (http://www.ireland.com).

Japan Times

Provides the latest news of interest about Japan and Asia
(http://www.japantimes.co.jp).

Le Monde

France's leading newspaper (http://tout.lemonde.fr) covering world events from a uniquely French point of view
(written in French).

Moscow Times

Read news from a Russian perspective in this English-
language newspaper (http://www.themoscowtimes.com/).

NetIran

Provides links to four sources of news from Iran: IRNA
(Islamic Republic News Agency), *Iran News*, IRIB (Islamic
Republic of Iran Broadcasting), and the *Tehran Times*
(http://www.netiran.com).

The New York Times

Get the latest news from one of the most respected newspapers in the world (http://www.nytimes.com).

The New Zealand Herald

News from New Zealand's major newspaper
(http://www.nzherald.co.nz).

The Norway Post

Learn the latest news from Norway and the rest of Europe,
as seen through the eyes of a country that most people
never think about (http://www.norwaypost.com).

The Paperboy

Provides links to the most popular international newspapers—see Figure 2-1 (http://www.thepaperboy.com).

Pravda

Once the political mouthpiece of the Soviet Union, Pravda is
now a national newspaper covering all aspects of political
and social life throughout Russia (http://www.pravda.ru).

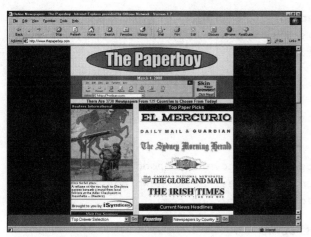

FIGURE 2-1:

The Paperboy Web site provides links to major newspapers from around the world.

Russia Today

The Russian equivalent of *USA Today*, this newspaper provides information about daily activities in Russia (http://www.russiatoday.com).

South China Morning Post

The *South China Morning Post* is Hong Kong's English-language newspaper, covering financial, political, and technological news about Hong Kong, China, Thailand, Japan, and Singapore. Read this to get a better idea what the Asian public thinks about Europe, America, and the rest of the world (http://www.scmp.com).

The Sydney Morning Herald

Read the latest news from down under (http://www.smh.com.au).

The Telegraph (London)

Major British newspaper providing news about England, Europe, and the rest of the world (http://www.telegraph.co.uk).

The Times of India

One of India's major newspapers, covering national and world events (http://www.timesofindia.com).

The Times (London)
International news from a distinctly British point of view (http://www.the-times.co.uk).

Toronto Star
News from one of Canada's largest daily newspapers (http://www.thestar.com).

USA Today
An American newspaper that covers a broad range of news from around the United States. Best known for its colorful weather maps (http://www.usatoday.com).

The Wall Street Journal
Provides financial news from all over the world, emphasizing Europe, Asia, and North America (http://www.wsj.com).

The Washington Post
News from another well-respected American newspaper, most commonly known as the newspaper that helped break open the Watergate scandal in the early '70s (http://washingtonpost.com).

The Weekly World News
The leading tabloid of nonsensical news stories ranging from Elvis sightings and UFO abductions of movie stars to yearly psychic predictions of Doomsday and impossible health diets for losing weight without changing your eating habits—see Figure 2-2 (http://www.weeklyworldnews.com).

By opening your mind to the wealth of newspapers available through the Internet, you can be as fully informed (or ignorant) about world events as you wish to be. Once you start reading a British, Egyptian, or Japanese newspaper (or even a newspaper from another American city) on a regular basis, you may never look at your own world the same way again.

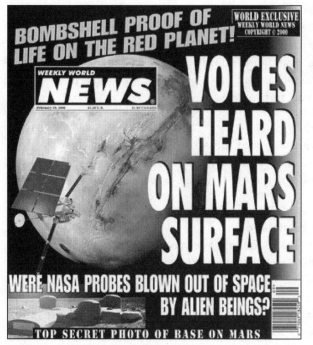

FIGURE 2-2:

The Weekly World News proves that sometimes illiteracy can be a blessing in disguise.

MAGAZINES ONLINE

Whereas newspaper coverage is pretty much confined to stories that are deemed acceptable by the paper's corporate owners, magazines usually have more freedom to target specific audiences and advocate specific opinions and beliefs. As a result, two different magazines will often reach completely different conclusions about the same topic.

Although it's tempting to read only those magazines that support your own opinions, take some time to learn what people who have different political views or are from another country or continent might have to say. For foreign magazines, visit one of the Web sites listed below, or visit your favorite search engine and try to hunt up some different magazines not listed in this book.

Arastar Internet News Page

Lists newspaper and magazine Web sites throughout the
United States, Africa, Asia, South America, Europe, and the
Middle East. Also includes publications focusing on business, computers, law, politics, science, and society
(http://www.arastar.net/news).

The Economist

Comprehensive magazine that provides news about events
from around the world, including places most American
high school graduates can't find on a map (http://www.
economist.com).

The Electronic Newsstand

Offers plenty of links to various magazines, including
Soldier of Fortune (http://www.sofmag.com), Mother
Jones (http://www.mojones.com), and Skeptic Magazine
(http://www.skeptic.com). If you read both conservative and
liberal magazines, you can't help but learn the issues that
concern both sides, as well as the solutions proposed by
each (http://www.enews.com).

Monday Morning

Lebanon's English-language weekly news magazine (http://
www.mmorning.com).

The National Review

Conservative magazine providing its own unique point
of view on American politics and international events
(http://www.nationalreview.com).

New American Magazine

An ultra-conservative magazine that takes American patrio-
tism to the extreme. Reading this magazine will certainly
open your eyes to the way people can interpret world events
(http://www.thenewamerican.com).

Philippine News Link

Links to an enormous range of newspapers and magazines
that cover the Philippines, including The Manila Times,

Filipinas Magazine, Asiaweek, and The Manila Bulletin
(http://www.philnews.com).

ZMag
Magazine available in English, French, Spanish, and Swedish,
billing itself as a magazine for people concerned about
social change (http://www.zmag.org).

NEWS SERVICES ONLINE
Newspapers and magazines often get their information from
national and international news services, which often get
the information directly from people at the scene of the
event itself. Local writers, unable to attend the news event
in person, simply embellish, exaggerate, or expand on the
information from these news services to create their own
newspaper or magazine articles. So, rather than wait for
news to appear in your favorite newspaper or magazine, go
directly to the source by visiting a news service Web site.

ABC News, CBS News, and MSNBC
News from the three largest television news networks in
North America (http://abcnews.go.com, http://cbsnews.cbs.
com, http://www.msnbc.com).

Agence France-Presse
French news service that offers news in English, French,
Spanish, German, and Portuguese (http://www.afp.com).

Associated Press
One of the most popular wire services, AP provides stories
to newspapers throughout the United States including the
Los Angeles Times, the *Detroit News*, and the *Washington
Times* (http://wire.ap.org).

Baltic News Service
The largest news agency in the Baltic states. Distributes
news in Estonian, Lativian, Lithuanian, Russian, and
English (http://www.bns.ee).

Business News Americas
Financial news about Latin America (http://www.bnamericas.com).

China Daily
News from mainland China covering Chinese and international news (http://www.chinadaily.net).

CNN
You can't ignore the only news service that can get inside countries like Iraq and Cuba and interview world leaders like Saddam Hussein and Fidel Castro (http://www.cnn.com).

Fox News
News from the fast-growing Fox Network (http://www.foxnews.com).

Intelligence Online
This news service is especially designed for diplomats, military and political officials, heads of company security services, or academics interested in intelligence matters, business intelligence, and international political issues. Find news on money laundering, terrorist activities, weapons smuggling, and other types of crimes that are occurring at this very moment (http://www.intelligenceonline.com).

Inter Press Service
This non-governmental organization delivers daily news from around the world in English, Finnish, Dutch, German, Norwegian, Spanish, and Swedish (http://www.link.no/IPS/eng).

Korean Central News Agency
The official news service of North Korea. Learn about world events as seen from communist North Korea's point of view (http://www.kcna.co.jp).

Nando Global
Another news service providing information from around the world (http://www.nando.net).

One World

Provides news from over 150 global organizations, from such groups as Save the Children, ActionAid, UNICEF, and Christian Aid. One of the few sites that presents news from a brutally honest point of view with headlines such as "Brazil to celebrate date that meant genocide for 5 million" (http://www.oneworld.org).

Reuters

Read information from one of the most popular and famous news services in the world (http://www.reuters.com).

Stratfor.com

Analyzes global events to offer the general public access to information normally reserved for governments (http://www.stratfor.com).

FINDING MORE NEWS SOURCES

Because space permits only a select listing of news sources and since the number of newspapers, magazines, and news services present on the Internet keeps growing, you can get a more complete listing of sources by visiting one of the following Web sites that list news services by region, continent, or country: Discovery Channel (http://www.discover.co.uk/NET/NEWS/news.html), Editor & Publisher Online (http://www.mediainfo.com), News Directory (http://www.ecola.com), Newspapers Online (http://www.newspapers.com), or News Resource (http://newo.com).

READING TO LEARN

Whatever your background, reading news from different countries and political viewpoints can open your eyes—especially if you've never previously gone beyond the readily available information around you. Reading something different every day will undoubtedly expose you to opposing, conflicting, and possibly confusing information. How you decide to react to information that contradicts your own way of thinking is (of course) up to you.

3

Censorship Online

WITH SO MANY SEX PERVERTS, STALKERS, PEDOPHILES, SERIAL KILLERS, AND JUST PLAIN WEIRDOS ROAMING THE WEB AT ALL HOURS OF THE DAY AND NIGHT, PEOPLE ARE PUSHING FOR GOVERNMENT REGULATION OF THE INTERNET. While regulation may sound like a good idea to some, it's virtually impossible because the Internet is a global network and not under any jurisdiction. Also, any form of censorship is completely against the spirit of the World Wide Web. Nevertheless, many people continue to insist that Internet censorship is necessary—just as long as they're the ones who get to pick and choose. Apparently, some people are as eager to practice censorship as some governments.

FIGHTING GOVERNMENT-SPONSORED CENSORSHIP

Since some countries do censor their ISPs, activists sometimes set up anti-government Web sites outside these countries to bypass censorship. Cuba and China are often targets of such Web sites.

Cuba

One of the more prominent anti-Castro groups is the Cuban American National Foundation (CANF) (http://www.canfnet. org). CANF provides firsthand reports of Cuban human rights violations (written by Cuban refugees), as well as reports of religious repression and debates about U.S. foreign policy toward Cuba.

CubaNet posts information it receives from Cuba's underground democracy movement to http://www.cubanet.org

Censorship always defeats its own purpose, for it creates, in the end, the kind of society that is incapable of exercising real discretion . . . In the long run it will create a generation incapable of appreciating the difference between independence of thought and subservience.

—HENRY STEELE COMMAGER

(which it hosts outside of Cuba), and regularly emails into Cuba so the Cuban dissidents there can spread their message to the rest of the world.

China

China regulates the use of the Internet by controlling the national telecommunications system, which all Chinese Internet providers must use. Thus, it can permanently block access inside China to the Web sites of foreign newspapers (like *The New York Times*) and sites deemed pornographic (like *Playboy* magazine).

Despite these restrictions, a few Chinese citizens still manage to access forbidden sites. A New York–based site, Human Rights in China (HRIC—http://www.hrichina.org), claims dozens of hits each week from people inside China. Founded by Chinese scientists and scholars in March 1989, HRIC monitors the implementation of international human rights statutes in China. It also supports human rights and is an information source for Chinese people both inside China and abroad (see Figure 3-1).

While the Chinese government can restrict access to particular sites from inside China, it can't screen the vast amount of Internet email that crosses the Chinese borders every day. Exploiting this weakness, Chinese dissidents write and edit a weekly electronic magazine called *Tunnel* (http://www.geocities.com/SiliconValley/Bay/5598), sending their articles from inside China to a U.S. email account from which the magazine is then distributed via email to readers in China. Using this method, the magazine hopes to prevent the Chinese government from identifying the writers and blocking the magazine's distribution in China.

Another newsletter, dubbed VIP Reference (http://www.bignews.org), provides information about human rights and pro-democracy movements inside China. Recently the Chinese government jailed a software engineer named Lin Hai (http://www.linhai.org) for giving VIP Reference over 30,000 email addresses of people inside China.

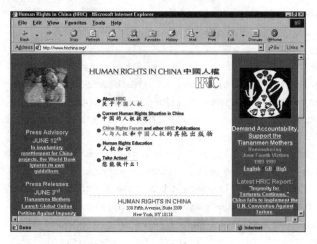

FIGURE 3-1:

The American-based site, Human Rights in China, offers information to people living inside communist China.

Censorship elsewhere

The Index on Censorship Web site (http://www. indexoncensorship.org) has up-to-date information about censorship in many countries around the world. If you're specifically interested in Eastern Europe, visit the Radio Free Europe (http://www.rferl.org) Web site. By promoting free speech in any available form (Internet, newspapers, radio, etc.), Radio Free Europe hopes to create a well-informed citizenry that will act as a foundation for democracy.

PARENTAL CONTROL SOFTWARE

Just as national governments use filtering software to block certain Web sites, parents can use parental control software to monitor and filter their children's Internet use. These programs allow parents to block access to a list of URLs of their choosing, or to limit access to certain content by *content scanning*—blocking access to URLs or Web pages that contain specific words.

When content scanning is in use, if your child enters a URL with a word like "love," "sex," or "nude," or she tries to access a page that contains similar words, the parental control program refuses to grant access. But URL scanning does have limitations since the program does not distinguish between, for example, scientific and pornographic use of the word "sex."

The databases of banned Web sites used by parental control programs are controversial. Most of the banned Web sites in these databases are no-brainers, like Condom Country, Playboy, or Hustler. But since new pornographic Web sites appear every day, the publishers of parental control software must constantly update their lists of banned sites to maintain their programs' effectiveness, which presents a problem of time versus resources. Publishers of parental control software can't afford to hire enough people to visit and check suspect Web sites, so most publishers use programs that automatically scan Web sites and search for keywords.

When these programs determine that a site contains too many banned keywords, they store that site's address in their updated list of banned Web sites. The result is that parental control programs often block many innocent Web sites. Even worse, many blocked sites have no knowledge that they're being blocked by a particular parental control program.

Blocking political and educational sites

While parental control software publishers clearly have the right to create proprietary filtering programs and databases of banned Web sites, the criteria they use can be questionable. Rather than simply blocking obviously pornographic sites, many parental control programs also venture into the shady area of political censorship. Here are some examples:

→ Net Nanny (http://www.netnanny.com) has blocked the Banned Books page at Carnegie Mellon (http://www.cs.cmu.edu/People/spok/banned-books.html).

→ I-Gear (http://www.symantec.com) has blocked The Wisdom Fund (http://www.twf.org), an Islamic non-profit organization that provides information about Islam and opposes anti-Islamic bias in the media, and the Human Rights Campaign (http://www.hrcusa.org), an organization working to protect lesbian and gay rights.

→ Cyber Patrol's Cyber Spyder (http://www.cyberpatrol.com/) has blocked such "dangerous" sites as Envirolink (http://www.envirolink.com), an animal rights Web site; the Ontario Center for Religious Tolerance (http://www.religioustolerance.org), an organization devoted to promoting religious diversity and acceptance; and the MIT Student Association for Freedom of Expression (http://www.mit.eduactivities/safe/home.html).

To see whether a site is blocked by a parental control program, visit the following sites:

SurfWatch's Test A Site	http://www1.surfwatch.com/testasite
Cyber Patrol's CyberNOT search engine	http://www.cyberpatrol.com/cybernot
WebSENSE's site lookup	http://database.netpart.com/site_lookup
SmartFilter's SmartFilterWhere	http://www.securecomputing.com/cgi-bin/filter_where.cgi
Net Nanny's check a site form	http://www.netnanny.com/CheckURL.asp

Parental control software gone really bad: CYBERsitter

Perhaps the most controversial parental control program is CYBERsitter (http://www.cybersitter.com), which has blocked both NOW (The National Organization for Women) and the Human Awareness Institute site (http://www.hai.org), which promotes workshops for personal growth focusing on love, intimacy, and sexuality.

While most parental control programs allow sites to appeal a block, CYBERsitter seems to have constructed a wall of self-righteousness. For example, when NOW appealed its ban by CYBERsitter, Brian Milburn, the CEO of Solid Oak Software (CYBERsitter's publisher) replied, "If NOW doesn't like it, tough . . . We have not and will not bow to any pressure from any organization that disagrees with our philosophy."

CYBERsitter on the offensive

A heated battle has occurred between CYBERsitter and Bennett Haselton, cofounder of Peacefire (http://www.peacefire.org), an Internet anti-censorship site for teenagers. After Bennett posted information on the Peacefire site criticizing CYBERsitter, along with instructions for disabling various parental control programs including CYBERsitter, Peacefire was promptly added to the CYBERsitter banned Web site database.

Peacefire also claimed that during installation of the trial version, CYBERsitter scans the Internet Explorer cache and aborts the installation with a cryptic error message if it finds evidence of visits to the Peacefire site (such as the files peacefire.html or peacefire.gif).

Brian Milburn defended his software by saying, "We reserve the right to say who gets to install our software for free. It's our software—we own it, we publish it, we have an absolute legal right to protect our software from being hacked in any way, shape or form."

Cyber Patrol vs. cphack

In a dispute similar to the Peacefire.org vs. CYBERsitter debate, Microsystems Software, the publisher of Cyber Patrol, recently filed a lawsuit against two computer programmers, Eddy L.O. Jansson and Matthew Skala, for creating the cphack program, which allows children to uncover their parents' passwords and view Cyber Patrol's entire list of more than 100,000 banned Web sites.

"I oppose the use of Internet filtering software on philosophical grounds," Skala said. "The issue here was to see what does Cyber Patrol actually block. Parents have a right to know what they're getting and without our work they wouldn't know."

To avoid a drawn-out legal debate, Microsystems announced that Jansson and Skala, the original authors of the cphack program, had settled with the company and granted them all rights to their cphack program. Microsystems now claims that Web sites that post the cphack program are violating the Microsystems copyright.

Decrypting the CYBERsitter database

Every parental control program encrypts its database of banned Web sites to protect its work from competitors and to make sure children can't see the banned URLs. Unfortunately, by encrypting banned Web sites databases, they prevent parents from knowing exactly what the programs are blocking.

To unencrypt the CYBERsitter database, visit the Peacefire site, choose "Censorship," then download their CYBERsitter codebreaker software. Note that if CYBERsitter detects the CSDECODE.ZIP file on your hard disk, it will refuse to install, so install CYBERsitter before copying the CSDECODE.ZIP file to your hard disk.

Project Bait and Switch: Revealing the double standard of censorship

To show beyond a doubt that many parental control software publishers are using questionable tactics, Peacefire.org ran an experiment to see if parental control programs would block certain content if hosted on a personal Web page while not blocking the same content on the Web site of a large, well-funded and well-known organization. (Read more about it on their site.)

They collected anti-gay quotes from the Family Research Council (http://www.frc.org), the Concerned Women for America (http://www.cwfa.org), Focus on the Family (http://www.family.org), and Dr. Laura's Web sites (http://www.drlaura.com). Then they posted these anti-gay quotes on free Web page sites and submitted the pages anonymously to the publishers of SurfWatch, Cyber Patrol, Net Nanny, Bess, SmartFilter, and WebSENSE.

All of the companies agreed to block some or all of the "bait" pages (since they met their criteria for "denigrating people based on sexual orientation"), at which point Peacefire.org revealed the sites that were the source of these quotes. Surprisingly, none of the publishers agreed to block any of the four originating Web sites, yet they continued to block the "bait" pages, even though both sites contained identical homophobic quotes.

Other users of parental control software

Unfortunately, libraries, public schools, and corporations often use parental control software without notifying their users. You can read about some of them at The Censorware Project's Hall of Shame at http://www.censorware.org/shame.

The Hall of Shame lists both the organization using parental control software and the program they're using. While you may not be surprised that the right-wing Bob Jones University uses parental control software, you may be surprised to learn that Gateway Computers, Coca-Cola, Fidelity Investments, and Lockheed-Martin have also installed these programs.

Even more surprising is Australia's recently passed Broadcasting Services Amendment to the Online Services Act of 1999, a law that requires all Australian ISPs to offer filtering software that restricts access to X-rated Web sites or sites that have been refused classification by an Australian government agency. While this censorship may seem justified to protect children, there's still the question that always surrounds censorship of any form: Who decides what can and cannot be seen?

DEFEATING PARENTAL CONTROL SOFTWARE

To help you disable various parental control programs, Peacefire.org provides a list of instructions on their Web site. Disabling some of these programs is surprisingly simple, as described below.

Defeating CYBERsitter

To disable CYBERsitter 97, you just need to rename two files:

1. Rename the file c:\windows\system\wsock32.dll to something like wsock32.bak

2. Rename the file c:\windows\system\wsockc97.dll to wsock32.dll

This simply reverses the changes that CYBERsitter made when it initially installed itself. When CYBERsitter installs, it renames the original wsock32.dll file as wsock97.dll and inserts its own version of wsock32.dll in its place.

Alternatively, you can download a program from http://www.fortunecity.se/kista/virus/9/cs97hack.zip, which can display the master CYBERsitter 97 password on your computer.

Defeating Cyber Patrol

To allow Cyber Patrol to run without blocking any Web sites (to give the illusion that it's still doing its job), just follow these steps:

1. Back up the files C:\patrol\cyber.bin and C:\patrol\cyber.not to some other location on the computer. Or just rename them by adding ".bak" to the end of their names, although this will make it easy for other people to find them.

2. Create a zero-byte file called cyber.not in the C:\patrol\ directory by running Notepad and saving the blank file as cyber.not in the C:\patrol\ directory. Notepad usually adds ".txt" to the end of a file, so if this happens, be sure to rename the file from cyber.not.txt to cyber.not.

3. Restart Windows without restarting your computer by choosing **Shut Down** from the Start Menu, selecting **Restart the computer**, and holding SHIFT when you click **OK**. You can also

restart your computer the usual way, but this is faster.

4. When you return to Windows, you will not be able to access the Internet because Cyber Patrol will think that "tampering" has occurred. A new cyber.bin file will have been created automatically in C:\patrol, slightly smaller than the old one.

5. Restart Windows again as in Step 3. You will now be able to access the entire Internet.

To permanently uninstall Cyber Patrol, follow these steps:

1. Remove the shortcut to Cyber Patrol, if there is one, from the StartUp folder, usually located at C:\Windows\Start Menu\Programs\StartUp\.

2. Open the C:\windows\win.ini file and replace the line

   load=c:\patrol\cp.exe ic.exe

   with

   load=

3. Right-click on the file C:\windows\win.ini, select **Properties**, and check the box for "read-only."

4. Right-click the file C:\windows\system\system.drv, select **Properties**, and un-check the boxes for "hidden", "system," and "read-only."

5. Right-click the file C:\windows\system.386, select **Properties**, and un-check the boxes for "hidden," "system," and "read-only."

NOTE Steps 6, 7, and 8 only apply to versions of Cyber Patrol downloaded after November 1998. If you try this step and you don't find what you're looking for, don't worry about it—you probably just have an older version of Cyber Patrol on your machine.

6. Run Regedit (go to the Start Menu, select **Run...** and type **REGEDIT.EXE**). Moving around in RegEdit is a lot like moving around in Windows Explorer; think of values as files and keys as folders, with sub-keys stored inside other keys.

7. Find the "FltProcess" value (labeled msinet. exe) in the key HKEY_CURRENT_USER\Software\ Microsoft\Windows\CurrentVersion\Run. Delete this value by clicking **FltProcess** and pressing **DELETE**.

8. Find the "FltProcess" value (labeled msinet.exe) in the key HKEY_LOCAL_MACHINE\Software\Microsoft\ Windows\CurrentVersion\Run and delete it.

9. Restart the computer in DOS mode, change to the C:\windows\system\ directory and type **move system.drv system.bak**, then press **RETURN**. Now type **move ..\system.386 system.drv** and press **RETURN** again.

10. Type **win** to start Windows again. If it tells you "Windows is still running one or more MS-DOS based programs..." try typing **exit**.

Now the next time you start Windows, you'll be free to roam the Internet without the restrictions of Cyber Patrol hampering your curiosity.

Defeating SurfWatch

To disable SurfWatch, you can use the SurfKey program to permanently uninstall SurfWatch without knowing the Surf-Watch password (peacefire.org), or uninstall SurfWatch by following these instructions:

1. Remove the shortcuts to SurfWatch (and possibly SurfWatch Updater) from the StartUp folder.

2. Open the win.ini file and replace the line

   load= C:\CO_RO_NT\surfctl.exe

   with

   load=

3. Run regedit.exe to edit the Windows Registry and delete the "GraphicsFilter" key (labeled C:\CO_RO_NT\surfctl.exe) which is a subkey of HKEY_LOCAL_MACHINE\SOFTWARE\Microsoft\Windows\CurrentVersion\RunServices\.

4. Restart the computer in DOS mode. Change to the C:\windows\system\ directory and type:

```
attrib -h -r -s system.drv

attrib -h -r -s net.drv

move system.drv system.bak

move net.drv system.drv
```

5. Type **win** to start Windows again. If it tells you "Windows is still running one or more MS-DOS based programs..." try typing **exit**.

You should now have successfully defeated SurfWatch.

Defeating Net Nanny

To disable Net Nanny temporarily, follow these steps:

1. Press **CTRL**, **ALT**, and **DELETE** simultaneously to display the Task Manager window.

2. Highlight **Wnldr32** and click **End Task**.

This disables Net Nanny until you restart your computer. To permanently disable it, follow these steps:

1. Open the file C:\windows\system.ini. Find the line labeled "drivers=" (with some text after it) under the section marked [boot].

2. Remove the word wndrv16.dll from the "drivers=" line.

3. Save changes to the file and restart your computer.

ACCESSING BANNED WEB PAGES

If you can't visit a Web site because of parental control software or other filtering tools and can't defeat the filtering program, try retrieving the Web page by email using a Webmail server. Although this is time-consuming, it will allow you to avoid parental, office, or government restrictions. And, unless someone takes the time to examine every email you receive, no one will know that you've been accessing forbidden Web sites.

To use a Webmail server, email it with the URL of the Web page you would like to see, and within a few minutes, hours, or days (depending on the server) the server will send you the page as HTML code. Once you have the HTML, you can view the Web site's text (but not always the graphics) on your computer. If the server returns only a site's text, you can view the site's graphics by telling the server to follow the URLs for the various graphics.

For example, to retrieve text from a Web site, you could send email to the webmail@www.ucc.ie site with the following message:

    To: webmail@www.ucc.ie

    Subject: none

    GO http://www.cnn.com

This tells the server webmail@www.ucc.ie to send you the Web page at http://www.cnn.com. Of course, half the fun of visiting Web sites is viewing their graphics. To retrieve the text and graphics from a Web site, use the w3mail@gmd.de server, which can send you text and images as UUencoded text. To use the w3mail server, send a message like this:

    To: w3mail@gmd.de

    Subject:

    get -img http://www.unitedmedia.com/comics/
    dilbert/

When you decode the file you receive (using the uudecode program, which you can find at many shareware Web sites or at http://www.neosoft.com/~pane), create an HTML file and several GIF files. You can then open the HTML file with your favorite Web browser and see the Web page exactly as it would appear with a "live" Web connection.

Here are some Webmail servers and the syntax to put in the body of your message. Leave the Subject blank in all cases.

WEB MAIL ADDRESS	SYNTAX TO USE
agora@dna.affrc.go.jp	SEND \<URL\>
agora@kamakura.mss.co.jp	SEND \<URL\>
getweb@usa.healthnet.org	GET \<URL\>
getweb@unganisha.idrc.ca	GET \<URL\>
webmail@www.ucc.ie	GO \<URL\>
w3mail@gmd.de	GET \<URL\>
Web-mail@ebay.com	\<URL\>

NOTE   For the agora, getweb, and w3mail servers, you only get the text from a Web page. If you want the actual HTML source code, you need to replace the SEND or GET command with SOURCE instead.

READING BANNED BOOKS ONLINE

→ In 1993, the school districts in Fairbanks, Alaska and Harrisburg, Pennsylvania, came close to banning its students from reading the Bible, claiming that it contains "language and stories that are inappropriate for children of any age, including tales of incest and murder. . . . There are more than three hundred examples of 'obscenities' in the book."

→ In 1986, Gastonia, North Carolina, burned *The Living Bible*, by William C. Bower, claiming it was "a perverted commentary on the King James Version."

→ Harper Lee's novel, *To Kill a Mockingbird*, has been considered "dangerous" because of profanity. Parents throughout the years have claimed that the plot of a white lawyer defending a black man undermines race relations, at least according to school districts in Eden Valley, Minnesota, 1977; Warren, Indiana, 1981; Waukegan, Illinois, 1984; Kansas City, Missouri, 1985; and Park Hill, Missouri, 1985.

You can use the Internet to read the books that your parents, teachers, or government authorities consider harmful to your intellectual and spiritual development. Project Gutenberg offers famous works such as *The Adventures of Huckleberry Finn*, *Dracula*, and *A Tale of Two Cities* as plain ASCII text files that any computer can display and print. Their goal is to give away one trillion text files by December 31, 2001.

To find banned books online, visit Banned Books Online (http://www.cs.cmu.edu/People/spok/banned-books.html), MIT Press Bookstore (http://mitpress.mit.edu/bookstore/banned.html), On-Line Books Page (http://digital.library.upenn.edu/books), or Project Gutenberg (http://www.promo.net/pg).

Of course, you still need to access the Internet to download a free e-book. But once you've downloaded it, you can share it with others. By copying and sharing e-books with others, you can preserve your right to read certain books that other people (your parents, boss, or government) don't want you to see.

Secretly reading a banned book in broad daylight

Most Web sites that offer banned books as ASCII text files assume you're going to read the book using your computer. Of course, you could still get in trouble if someone catches you reading a banned book on your computer screen.

To disguise what you're reading, use a reading program like Vortex (http://www.vallier.com/tenax/tenax.html) or AceReader (http://www.stepware.com). Both programs display the entire text of an ASCII document across your screen in large letters, one word at a time, at speeds up to 1,000 words per minute, so that it's virtually impossible for anyone to see what you're reading at a glance. With these programs you can read the ASCII text of a book that your parents, school officials, or government authorities don't want you to read, right in front of their eyes without them ever knowing it.

No matter what obstacles people may use to block your access to information, there will always be ways to defeat or avoid them if you just exercise a little bit of creativity.

4

Pledging Allegiance:
Hatred as Patriotism

WHILE NEWSPAPERS AND MAGAZINES HERALD THE INTERNET AS THE CURRENT REVOLUTION IN COMMUNICATIONS, THEY OFTEN IGNORE ANOTHER ASPECT OF ITS LOW-COST, WORLDWIDE AVAILABILITY: Hate groups have flocked to the Internet to use it as an inexpensive and easy way for recruiting new members and communicating with existing ones.

As early as 1995, Don Black, the ex-Grand Dragon of the Ku Klux Klan and owner of the white supremacist home page Stormfront (http://www.stormfront.org), said that the ". . . Internet has had a pretty profound influence on [the white supremacist] movement whose resources are limited. The access is anonymous and there is unlimited ability to communicate with others of a like mind." (*New York Times*, March 13, 1995)

I am free of all prejudices. I hate everyone equally.

—W.C. FIELDS

MONITORING HATE GROUPS

Because so many hate groups use the Internet to spread their messages, the organizations Anti-Racist Action (http://www.aranet.org), HateWatch (http://www.hatewatch.org), and the Southern Poverty Law Center (http://www.splcenter.org) were founded to keep track of the different hate groups and their activities. HateWatch provides links and background information on different hate groups so that concerned individuals, academics, organizations, and media can study and fight back against hate group activities in an informed way. The idea is that it's better to know what different hate groups are doing and hold them responsible for their actions, rather than to ignore their plotting and scheming. After browsing through HateWatch's links to hate-mongering white supremacists, skinheads, black radicals, neo-Nazis, Holocaust deniers, Christian nationalists, anti-gay activists, anti-Christian groups, and anti-Arab groups, you may wonder if people will ever learn to live together in peace.

While there are people who might use these links to find the nearest hate group to join, existing hate groups can also browse through these same links to find groups that hate them just as much as they hate others.

White supremacy

Perhaps the most well-known white supremacy group in the United States is the Ku Klux Klan (http://www.kkk.com), an organization that outrageously claims to be built on the foundations of Jesus Christ. Its Web site even claims that "The Fiery Cross is used as a Klan symbol representing the ideals of Christian Civilization. The Klan Crosslighting represents the Light of Jesus Christ, who died for the White Aryan Race."

Like other groups that promote apartheid, the Klan claims that it does not hate non-whites. For example, it claims that "The Knights of the Ku Klux Klan does not consider itself the enemy of non-Whites. The only way all races can develop their full potential and culture is through racial separation. For example, we promote protectionism in foreign trade, closing our southern border, laws prohibiting foreigners from purchasing American property and industry and drug testing for welfare recipients." Apparently the KKK prefers to forget who the original "landowners" of North America were.

You can get a look at the white racist view of world events from the Web site of the monthly white racist publication, *The Nationalist Observer* (http://www.whiteracist.com), which proudly posts its message of hate without the aid of a spell-checker:

> *In 1999, we are White Aryans living in a country*
> *that has been usurped by the very racial enemies*
> *that have threatened our Race and Europe many,*

46

innummberable times. The nonwhite racial aliens
are exploding in numbers, sometimes by immigra-
tion, sometimes by high-birth rates and, most
abhorantly, by the interracial race treason by
whites who have defiled themselves with mud.

If you think that all white racists are men, visit
SIGRDRIFA Publications (http://www.sigrdrifa.com) or Women
for Aryan Unity (http://www.front14.org), two groups that
promote the woman's role in the white pride movement. The
Women for Aryan Unity Web site is no less outspoken than
its male counterpart:

Often, it is asked "Why Do We Hate Non Whites?"
It is unknown why the people that ask this really
wonder. Every day we are surrounded by the filth
that the mud races have created, whether in middle
class, predominantly white neighborhoods that are
fastly [sic] rotting into ghetto slums by the one
or two blacks that live down the street, or the
lack of education our children receive in the pub-
lic schools. So tell us, Why Should We Love Races
That Bring Down Our Society? I have noticed when
this is asked, they usually do not have a very
intelligent or plausible answer. They refuse to
acknowledge the fact that non whites really do
bring down our society. Rather, they are intent on
complaining how much we are 'evil nazis', and how
we are 'so ignorant'.

One of the more devious tricks of white supremacy
groups is to snatch up domain names that appear to belong
to legitimate organizations. For example, the domain names
MartinLutherKing.org and MLKing.org are actually owned by
the two white supremacy groups Stormfront and National
Alliance. Both domain names point to the same Web site,
which deride Martin Luther King as "Just a sexual degener-
ate, an America-hating Communist, and a criminal betrayer
of even the interests of his own people." Ironically, much
of the negative information about Martin Luther King comes

from declassified FBI documents from the 1960s when the FBI organized a smear campaign against King. Although the FBI's propaganda has been largely discredited, it does show how the FBI, at one time, discriminated against blacks.

For more exposure to white supremacy ideas, visit these Web sites: Heritage Front (http://www.freedomsite.org/hf), National Alliance (http://www.natvan.com), The Nationalist Movement (http://www.nationalist.org), or White Aryan Resistance (http://www.resist.com). Or browse these select Usenet newsgroups: alt.politics.white-power, alt.skinheads, alt.politics.nationalism.white, alt.music.white-power, or alt.flame.niggers.

Neo-Nazis

Unlike the white racists who claim they aren't necessarily enemies of non-whites, neo-Nazis advocate violence against non-whites in support of Adolf Hitler's Third Reich. One of these organizations is the American Nazi Party (http://www.americannaziparty.com), based in Michigan. After reading their message of hate and blaming non-whites for all the problems of society, you have to wonder why so many neo-Nazis live in countries that their leader, Adolf Hitler, had bombed during World War II.

To get the inside scoop on two more American organizations that probably didn't know which side to root for in *Saving Private Ryan*, visit the National Socialist Movement (http://www.nsm88.com—see Figure 4-1) or The New Order (http://www.theneworder.org). The New Order site proclaims:

> We are the Movement of Adolf Hitler. We are His heirs. He has given us a commission, which it is our duty to discharge. For it was Adolf Hitler who came into the world to remind modern man of Nature's eternal laws, and to make them the basis for a miraculous regeneration in human affairs. That is why we proudly recognize Him as the greatest figure of the age, and why we regard His cause as the one great hope of Aryan mankind on this Earth.

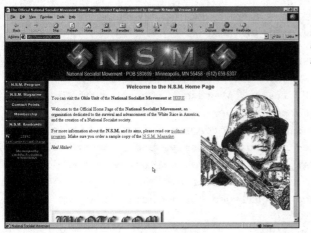

To learn about other groups that combine white
supremacy attitudes with a socialist political twist, visit
the following: American Front (http://www.americanfront.
com), American Nationalist Union (http://www.anu.org),
ProPatria (http://www.propatria.org), or ThuleNet
(http://www.thulenet.com). Or try the alt.flame.jews or
alt.fan.ernst-zundel Usenet newsgroups.

Holocaust deniers

While many Holocaust deniers do not claim to be Nazis (or
neo-Nazis, if there's any difference), they still upset
many people by their persistent claims denying that the
slaughter of six million Jews ever took place. The Adelaide
Institute (http://www.adelaideinstitute.org), for example,
asks for proof of the Holocaust:

> *People who claim that during World War II, the
> Germans gassed millions of Jews are leveling three
> allegations at the Germans:*
>
> *1. They planned the construction of huge chemical
>   slaughter houses;*
>
> *2. They constructed these huge chemical slaughter-
>   houses during the middle of WWII; and*

*3. They used these huge slaughterhouses to exter-
minate millions of Jews.*

*Any normal person familiar with bureaucratic red
tape will now ask: What proof is there to back up
these claims? Firstly, where are the plans of this
enterprise? Secondly, where is the budget needed
to finance the massive enterprise? Finally, it is
inconceivable that such a massive undertaking would
get past first base without an executive order. To
date, we have been led to believe that "a wink and
a nudge" began the alleged extermination project.*

*We at Adelaide Institute believe that those who
level the homicidal gassing allegations at the
Germans owe it to the world to come up with
irrefutable evidence that this happened.*

For another denial of the Holocaust, visit the Air
Photo Evidence Web site (http://www.air-photo.com), which
claims that aerial and ground-based photographs prove that
the Holocaust could not have happened, even to the point of
stating that "ground photos show happy well-fed inmates" at
the Plaszow Camp. Of course. Naturally, this Web site fails
to include any supporting testimonials from all these
happy, well-fed inmates.

To probe further into the bizarre and dangerous world
of Holocaust deniers, try visiting the following sites:
Institute for Historical Review (http://www.ihr.org),
The National Journal (http://www.nationaljournal.org),
Revisionism.com (http://www.revisionism.com), or The
Zundelsite (http://www.zundelsite.org). Or share your
thoughts with others in the alt.revisionism Usenet newsgroup.

Black racists

Not all racists are white. Blacks can be racists too,
and their favorite targets are usually whites and Jewish
people. Visit the Blacks and Jews Newspage Web site
(http://www.blacksandjews.com) and you'll find the following curious claim:

*President Clinton's Initiative on Race has been
presented as a serious effort to address America's
intractable problem of race, but the form that the
Initiative has taken and the circumstances of its
birth raises suspicions about the Initiative's
actual purpose. We will suggest that the Initiative
is a front for anti-Black Jewish interests and its
real focus is to severely restrict Black progress
and to outlaw the Nation of Islam.*

The Blacks and Jews Newspage twists nearly every bit
of information and converts it into "proof" that the Jewish
people are conspiring against blacks:

*There are 100 Black colleges and universities in
this country but only 41 are members of the United
Negro College Fund presided over by William H.
Gray, III, the ex-congressman. And he is the
"secret weapon" of Israel, the country whose goal
has been development, also of an ethnic diplomacy.
And Black scholars, intellectuals and students are
the new Israeli target group.*

While black racists attack whites and Jews for prof-
iting off the slave trade, they ignore any evidence that
many black Africans sold their own people into slavery for
profits as well.

To learn more about how blacks can be just as racist as
whites, visit alt.politics.nationalism.black or alt.flame.
whites. As an extra challenge, ignore all references to
skin color and try to determine the difference between a
white racist and a black racist.

Anti-Semitism

While you might expect neo-Nazis to be anti-Jewish, it is
surprising how many other groups also have no qualms about
attacking the Jews, usually accusing them of conspiring to
control world governments. The Politics and Terrorism Web
site (http://myweb.flinet.com/~politics/) offers this
insight into common anti-Semitic thinking:

We Americans have allowed ourselves to be placed between a rock and a hard place, the Jews and the Arabs. It is a very uncomfortable place, it is a meat grinder. We have allowed this to happen by our own apathy, we have allowed the Jews to seize control of our government. They are using us to further their own agenda of taking over the land of Palestine. When Israel has a disagreement with the U.S. Z.O.G., it is just one Jew arguing with another, often the disagreement is over means, not ends.

Despite the teachings of the Bible to "love thy neighbor," an organization calling itself the Bible Believers (http://biblebelievers.org) has somehow reached the following conclusion:

The Jew however, is bound in fear to his people. He exercises the fear of the curse throughout the sphere of religion — "I will curse them that curse thee." He only comprehends works by his own strength and knows nothing of the grace of God. At the slightest provocation they claim persecution and misrepresentation. They have not entered God's rest. This policy succeeds because the Gentiles have been improperly instructed in the Bible and feel somehow the Jews are the "chosen people."

If you want to explore the minds of people who believe that all Jewish people are secretly conspiring to control the world and all non-Jews in the process, you might find the following Web sites interesting: First Amendment Exercise Machine (http://www.faem.com), Holy War (http://holywar.org), or The Tangled Web (http://www.codoh.com/zionweb/zionweb.html).

Anti-Arab groups

The radical Jewish Defense League (JDL) (http://www.jdl.org) has taken what it calls self-defense to the extreme in the following statement: "It has always been a JDL priority to encourage as many Arabs as possible to leave Israel to make new homes in America or wherever they wish to live." Hmmm. Sounds strangely similar to the Ku Klux Klan's belief that non-whites can live anywhere they want just as long as they live outside America.

Although the Jewish Defense League claims not to be anti-Arab, its attitude towards certain Arab organizations is less than civil:

> We see those in the Muslim communities (American Muslims For Jerusalem, American Arab Anti-Discrimination Committee, to name just two) who hate the state of Israel and want to see another Muslim country occupy the Jewish Homeland. These anti-Israel forces are on the march again and this time they're attempting to thwart two pieces of legislation that support the U.S. Embassy in Jerusalem and U.S. recognition of Jerusalem as Israel's Undivided Capital.

The Kahane Web Page (http://kahane.org), another extreme Jewish group, tows a similar line:

> It is a central tenet of Judaism that G-d wished the Jew to create a unique, total, pure and complete Jewish life, society and state in Eretz Israel. This being so, who can honestly believe that He then sanctioned the democratic right of a non-Jew, who is totally alien and outside the Jewish society and who is free of its religious obligation, to have the slightest say in its workings?

To see that there is little unique or new in the rhetoric of hate groups, try this exercise: The next time you read or hear anything from radical Jewish groups or the Ku Klux Klan, substitute the name of a new villain in the dia-tribe, such as the word "Arab" for "black" (or vice versa). Then see if you can still tell which group is talking.

Anti-Christians

While Muslims and Jews take the brunt of most anti-religious attacks, a few people have decided that Christians shouldn't be exempt from hatred. Some anti-Christian groups target Christianity as the source of everything wrong in society, as shown in this message found on the Black Plague Web site (http://www.blackplague.org):

> The Christian Holocaust movement founds its kinetic potential upon the simple discovery of how language, culture, and social inculcation dictate individual human intellectual precepts, forming the filter which the individual uses to process the world. Christianity believes heavily in that filter with its duty-centric justification-based system of moral logic and its karmic work ethic, the primary elements of control in society today.

> For this reason there came about a movement which realized that the shared cultural understanding of this filter permits the brutal abuse of environment, human rights, and human value as we are abused in jobs designed to leave us four waking hours of free time. Society has brought us many good things and the addiction of their continued expense; Christianity believes this is progress and conveniently denies the importance of death with its explanation of the afterlife.

The Fuck God Web site (http://www.fuckgod.com) offers its own anti-Christian sentiment by stating:

> When on a Sunday morning we hear the bells ringing we ask ourselves: is it possible! this is going on because of a Jew crucified 2000 years ago who said he was the son of God. The proof of such an assertion is lacking. — In the context of our age the Christian religion is certainly a piece of antiquity intruding out of distant ages past, and that

the above-mentioned assertion is believed — while
one is otherwise so rigorous in the testing of
claims — is perhaps the most ancient piece of
inheritance. A god who begets children on a mortal
woman; a sage who calls upon us no longer to work,
no longer to sit in judgement [sic], but to heed
the signs of the imminent end of the world; a justice which accepts an innocent man as a substitute
sacrifice; someone who bids his disciples drink
his blood; prayers for miraculous interventions;
sin perpetrated against a god atoned for by a god;
fear of a Beyond to which death is the gateway; the
figure of the Cross as a symbol in an age which no
longer knows the meaning and shame of the Cross —
how gruesomely all this is wafted to us, as if out
of the grave of a primeval past! Can one believe
that things of this sort are still believed in?

If you want to read more from anti-Christian groups,
try The Altar of Unholy Blasphemy (http://www.anus.com/
altar) or Worldwide Blasphemy (http://freedom.gmsociety.
org/~god) Web sites.

Anti-gay activists

When people use the Bible to rationalize attacks on homo-
sexuals, they ignore that same Bible that tells people to
practice forgiveness. One of the most prominent anti-gay
hate groups is the God Hates Fags Web site (http://www.
godhatesfags.com), run by the Westboro Baptist Church in
Topeka, Kansas. Its FAQs Web page is insightful into their
way of thinking:

Why do you preach hate?

Because the Bible preaches hate. For every one
verse about God's mercy, love, compassion, etc.,
there are two verses about His vengeance, hatred,
wrath, etc. The maudlin, kissy-pooh, feel-good,
touchy-feely preachers of today's society are

damning this nation and this world to hell. They are telling you what you want to hear rather than what you need to hear, just like what happened in the days of Isaiah and Jeremiah.

Do you ever pray for the salvation of those who you feel are condemned?

Of course not! For, if we follow (as we ought) the example of our Saviour and the clear commandment of God, we would not dare to do so.

And here's more from the anti-gay sermon of the Westboro Baptist Church:

The only true Nazis in this world are fags. They want to force you by law to support their filth, and they want to shut you up by law when they hate what you say. They would be perfectly happy to make it a crime to preach that "God hates fags" under the guise of "hate speech legislation." Likewise, baby-killers support the genocide of millions of innocent babies, and then act indignant that Hitler killed a few million innocent Jews.

The only true Jews are Christians. The rest of the people who claim to be Jews aren't, and they are nothing more than typical, impenitent sinners, who have no Lamb. As evidence of their apostacy [sic], the vast majority of Jews support fags. Of course, there are Jews who still believe God's law, but most of them have even departed from that.

In case this Web site hasn't opened your eyes to the way people can turn religion into a forum of hatred, there's even more evidence in the God Hates America (http://www.godhatesamerica.com—see Figure 4-2) and Bob Enyart Live (http://www.enyart.com) sites.

Or try joining the alt.flame.fucking.faggots Usenet newsgroup and share your thoughts with others.

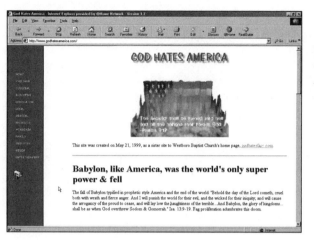

FIGURE 4-2:

The God Hates America Web site is an example of a site that uses religion to justify its hatred of others.

LEARNING FROM HATE GROUPS

Anytime you join an organization based on race, religion, or nationality, it's easy to target people outside the organization as the enemy. Hatred can come in all colors, religions, and nationalities; so rather than blindly condemn entire groups of people, ask yourself what you really fear or what you're angry about, and then decide if the destruction of an entire group of people will really help you achieve it.

After browsing through various hate group Web sites, you may notice a common denominator: Hate groups want the freedom to blame others while preventing others from exercising the same rights that they enjoy. If you look beyond the surface distinctions (skin color, national citizenship, religious affiliation, etc.) that hate groups use to identify their members, you'll see that hate groups are often more similar to each other than they are to the people they're trying to recruit.

5

Where the Hackers Are

PERHAPS THE MOST UNUSUAL SOURCE OF ALTERNATIVE INFORMATION COMES FROM COMPUTER HACKERS. Although the term "hacker" often conveys an air of mystery and intrigue, hackers are simply people who are very skilled at using technology. To differentiate between "good" and "bad" hackers, the media has created a variety of terms such as "white-hat hackers" (the "good" ones) and "black-hat hackers" (the "bad" ones). Other terms for a "bad" hacker include "malicious hacker" or "cracker."

Whatever you call them, the fact is that hackers are people, and, like any group of people (Americans, police officers, athletes, Christians), some will be good and some will be bad. But unlike most other groups, hackers rely exclusively on computers and the Internet to communicate with each other.

Finding a hacker on the Internet is fairly easy if you know where to look. Just as you can quickly find a drug dealer or policeman if you know where to look in a city, you can also find good and bad hackers if you know where to look on the Internet.

Vice is its own reward.

—QUENTIN CRISP

HACKER WEB SITES

Many hackers have banded together to post and advertise their own Web sites. Most hacker sites provide information about the hacker world told from the hacker's point of view, which mainstream media typically ignores. On hacker Web sites you'll find the latest security holes found in the more popular operating systems, and even hacker programs for invading other computers.

One of the more controversial hacker Web sites is AntiOnline (http://www.antionline.com), which not only provides hacker news, virus source code, and Trojan Horse programs (see Chapter 16), but also maintains a comprehensive profile of hackers for use by law enforcement agencies. Naturally, AntiOnline's cooperation with the police has upset many hackers, many of whom retaliate by breaking into AntiOnline's computers on a regular basis. In fact, attempts to hack into AntiOnline are so common that AntiOnline now posts real-time logs showing the latest hacker attacks, attempted method of attack, target, and (when possible) the hacker's Internet address (see Figure 5-1).

FIGURE 5-1:

AntiOnline's real-time log of hacker break-in attempts.

To learn more about hacking from the hacker's point of view, take a look at AntiOnline or visit any of the following sites:

Attrition.org
News and archives of hacker text and program files (http://www.attrition.org).

Cult of the Dead Cow
Infamous hacker group responsible for releasing the Back Orifice remote administration tool that can also be used

as a Trojan Horse to hijack another computer (http://www.cultdeadcow.com).

Hack Canada
Unique Web site focusing on hacking, phone phreaking, and anarchy from a Canadian point of view (http://www.hackcanada.com).

Hacker News Network and UK Hacker News Network
These Web sites provide the latest hacker news along with plenty of hacker and security programs to defend or attack other computers (http://www.hackernews.com and http://www.progenic.com/ukhackers).

Hackers.com
A hacker site that pledges to uphold the "old school" of hacking, which provides information to the curious but avoids destructive and malicious hacking tools, such as computer viruses or Trojan Horses (http://www.hackers.com).

Insecure.org
Lists plenty of security flaws and exploits in all your favorite operating systems including Windows, Solaris, and Linux (http://www.insecure.org).

LOpht Industries
A hacker group known for publicizing embarrassing security holes in major programs, i.e., practically anything pub-lished by Microsoft (http://www.l0pht.com—note that the second character in the domain is a zero, not the letter O).

New Order
Provides plenty of links to various hacker resources such as anonymous remailers, encryption software, ICQ exploits, Novell network hacking, and hacker e-zines (http://neworder.box.sk).

HACKER MAGAZINES
One of the best ways to keep up with the ever-changing underground culture of computer hackers is to read hacker magazines. Since you probably won't find a hacker magazine

at your favorite newsstand (with the exception of *2600* magazine), your best bet is to read some hacker magazines online. Hacker magazines tend to have an irregular publishing schedule, so don't be surprised if the latest issue is several months old.

2600

The home of the quarterly hacker magazine, *2600*. While its Web site doesn't offer any articles from the magazine, it does provide the latest hacker news along with an archive of defaced Web pages (http://www.2600.com).

Computer Underground Digest

A journal carrying news, research, and discussion of legal, social, and ethical issues concerning computer culture (http://sun.soci.niu.edu/~cudigest).

Crypt Newsletter

An online publication that pokes fun at the latest media hype surrounding computer viruses, hacker attacks, or encryption regulations. Covers computer crime, viruses, and the comical attempts of governments and corporations to control hackers for their own profit (http://sun.soci.niu.edu/~crypt).

Phrack

The online version of one of the oldest hacker magazines, in operation since 1985. *Phrack* focuses on networking, telephony, and phone phreaking and occasionally delves into other computer hacking topics as well (http://www.phrack.com).

Private Line

An unusual magazine specializing in the telephone system. If you want to know how the phone network or cellular telephones work, this is the magazine for you (http://www.privateline.com).

FINDING HACKER WEB SITES

Only a handful of hacker sites stay up for longer than a year. The majority of them appear with a flurry of activity and disappear when the founders lose interest and move on to other hobbies. Because hacker Web site life spans are so short, finding these sites can be difficult.

Hacker search engines

Fortunately, there are a variety of specialized search engines for finding hacker Web sites (see Figure 5-2). These hacker search engines can help you quickly find anything from the source code to the latest dreaded virus to the current version of an online harassment program that attacks America Online or ICQ users.

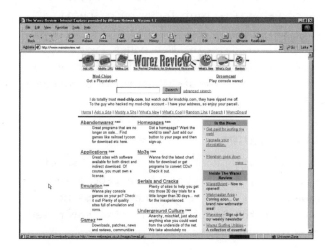

FIGURE 5-2:

Use a hacker search engine like Warez Review to find the hacking tool you need.

So if none of the hacker sites listed above have what you need, try one of the following specialized search engines instead: AntiSearch (http://www.antisearch.com), AstalaVista (http://astalavista.box.sk), Cyberarmy HakSearch (http://www.cyberarmy.com/search), Security Search (http://www.securitysearch.net), or Warez Review (http://www.warezreview.net).

Hacker Web site lists

Many hackers like to claim that their Web site is the best, most comprehensive source of hacker information on the Internet. Since so many Web sites make this claim, hackers have put together lists that arrange competing hacker sites according to the number of votes each one gets from users. So if you want to find the most popular hacker sites at the moment, browse through these lists and vote for your favorite hacker Web site: EliteTopList (http://www.elitetoplist.com), Fringe of the Web (http://www.webfringe.com), SecureRoot (http://www.secureroot.com), or Underground Sub-List (http://underground.sub-list.com).

Web rings

Instead of blindly groping around the Internet with a search engine, you might want to try using a Web ring instead. Web rings provide links to Web sites that focus on a specific topic. If you're interested in, say, computer virus writing, harassing America Online, or defacing Web pages, visit the Web Ring site (http://www.webring.org) and click on the Computers section and then the Computer Underground category for a list of additional hacker Web sites.

HACKER USENET NEWSGROUPS

Hackers often communicate with each other through Usenet newsgroups. Unlike ordinary newsgroups where people share information and answer questions, hacker newsgroups more often resemble shouting matches full of insults, sprinkled between ads for get-rich-quick schemes or pornography Web sites.

Still, if you don't mind wading through these types of messages cluttering hacker newsgroups, you can learn about the newest hacker Web sites and share source code and hacker programs with others on the newsgroup.

General hacking newsgroups

To start learning about hacking in general, try one of the general-purpose hacking newsgroups listed below. Unlike other types of newsgroups that focus on stamp collecting or photography, hacker newsgroups tend to stray from their topics. For example, the alt.binaries.hacking.beginner newsgroup, which says it is about helping new hackers find and use hacking programs, is often filled with discussions about virus programming and encryption, or, if you're lucky, vicious insult wars. Here are some more hacking newsgroups: alt.hacker, alt.hacking, alt.binaries.hacking.beginner, alt.binaries.hacking.websites, alt.2600.hackers, and comp.hackers.

Computer virus newsgroups

Computer virus writers often publish their latest creations in newsgroups (or post URLs where you can download their latest virus creations). If you want to find the latest live virus (or the source code to a virus), visit one of the following newsgroups: alt.comp.virus, alt.comp.virus.source, alt.comp.virus.source.code, or comp.virus.

Encryption newsgroups

Since hackers often skirt the legal boundaries of their nation's laws, they wisely hide their identity or messages using encryption, the same technology that government agencies use to protect national secrets. To learn the latest about using and writing encryption (which you'll learn more about in Chapter 19) to protect your sensitive data, visit one of the following newsgroups: alt.cypherpunks, alt.security, alt.sources.crypto, misc.security, sci.crypt, or sci.crypt.research.

Cracking newsgroups

Most games and applications are copy-protected to keep people from sharing them with their friends. Likewise, many shareware programs provide limited features until the user pays for a code or key to unlock the additional features.

Some hackers try to circumvent, or *crack*, copy-protected and "locked" shareware programs. Cracking methods include sharing serial numbers, unlocking codes, or using programs designed to unlock or copy copy-protected games. To read about these programs and techniques, visit any of the following newsgroups: alt.2600.crack, alt.2600.crackz, alt.binaries.cracked, or alt.cracks.

FINDING HACKERS ON IRC

You can chat with a hacker in real time in one of the many hacker chat rooms that pop up on nearly every Internet Relay Channel (IRC) network.

You need a special IRC program, such as mIRC (available at http://www.mirc.co.uk) to use IRC. Once you have an IRC program, you'll need to pick an IRC network to join. Some of the more popular networks are EFnet, DALnet, Undernet, and 2600 net (run by the hacker magazine *2600*).

Once you're connected to an IRC network server, you can create a new chat room or join an existing one. While the 2600 network is specifically designed for hackers, you may have to search the other networks for chat rooms containing hackers. To find a hacker chat room, look for rooms with names like #2600, #phreak, #carding, #cracks, #anarchy, or any other phrase that sounds hackerish.

Using IRC is a special skill in itself, and many hackers may get upset if you intrude on their chat rooms, so use care when exploring the different networks and chat rooms. With enough patience, you can eventually meet and make friends in the various chat rooms. Soon you too can become a regular and experienced IRC user so you can chat with hackers all over the world. To learn about how to use IRC, pick up Alex Charalabidis' *The Book of IRC,* published by No Starch Press.

HACKER CONVENTIONS

A hacker convention is a good place to meet people you may have only met in a chat room or through a newsgroup; it's also a good place for meeting new friends from both the hacker side of the computer underground as well as the law enforcement side, including FBI and Secret Service agents who may be attending the conference. Anyone can attend a hacker convention; you don't need credentials! Whether you're a hacker, a law enforcement agent, or just someone curious to see what life looks like in the computer hacking world, you might find something of interest at these top hacker conventions.

DefCon

Annual hacker convention (see Figure 5-3) held in Las Vegas, often attended by hackers, media, and government officials. One popular contest is "Spot the Fed," where attendees attempt to locate FBI agents keeping an eye on the conference (http://www.defcon.org).

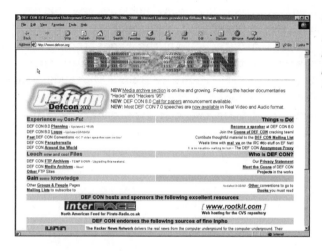

FIGURE 5-3:

DefCon is one of the most popular and most publicized of all the hacker conventions.

Beyond Hope

An annual convention run by *2600* magazine, focusing on all aspects of hacking including phone phreaking, virus writing, social engineering, and information warfare (http://www.hope.net).

SummerCon

One of the oldest hacker conventions, it focuses on hacking, phone phreaking, and computer security (http://www.summercon.org).

DON'T PANIC: HACKERS ARE PEOPLE, TOO

As you meet more and more hackers, whether through newsgroups, Web sites, or in person at a hacker convention, your perception of hackers may well change. Some hackers you meet might fit into the hacker stereotype, but others will vary dramatically from any preconceived notions you may have about them.

Of course, like any group of people, there will always be some that you would do well to avoid. Some of these malicious hackers may try to snare your credit card number, use your identity online, or just harass you by routing a 900 sex hotline to your home phone.

Rather than openly harass you, many hackers may just ignore you and label you a "newbie," a derogatory term for "newcomer," meant to intimidate you in the hopes that you'll go away and stop wasting their time. Don't let them frighten you away! You have the right to learn whatever you want, and even the most seasoned hacker was once a novice too. Just keep learning on your own and from others who are willing to help you, and soon you too can be as knowledge-able as the rest of them.

PART 2

GAMES PEOPLE PLAY

6

Computing on a Shoestring

FOR MANY PEOPLE, THE BIGGEST BARRIER TO LEARNING ABOUT COMPUTERS IS THE COST. Don't get seduced into thinking you have to spend thousands for the most advanced computer available: New computers plummet in value faster than new cars. To reduce expenses, do a little research and you could save hundreds of dollars on your next computer—and, with a little creativity, load it with software for nothing, or next to nothing.

GETTING A COMPUTER ON A BUDGET

If you absolutely must buy a new computer, don't pay the premium price for the latest one on the market. Instead, save yourself some money by buying a used, refurbished, or closeout computer that's say six months to one year old. You won't have the fastest processor or largest hard disk on the block, but you're likely to have a perfectly fine machine, and you won't notice the difference.

If your local computer store doesn't sell older models, try online auctions or resellers. The bizrate.com and shopper.com Web sites have extensive lists of online computer dealers.

When buying used or refurbished PCs, pay particular attention to warranty periods and bundled software. If you buy through a person-to-person auction site, like eBay, you probably won't get a warranty, but you may get lots of bundled software (though often without the manuals and CDs). When you buy from a reseller or online auction like Ubid, you'll probably get some sort of warranty but little if any software—often not even an operating system.

I have enough money to last me the rest of my life, unless I buy something.

—JACKIE MASON

Also, consider buying machines with processors other than Intel. Because Intel is the leader in the processor market, their prices are usually higher than those of compatible rivals such as Advanced Micro Devices (AMD). These competitors often offer lower prices and better performance.

Floor models and returns

Every computer store has floor models that customers can bang away at for a test-drive. If you must have the latest technology, consider buying a floor model. Most stores will be happy to cut the price a bit to make a sale.

Alternatively, consider buying a returned or "open box" machine. Many of the larger computer stores allow customers to return new computers within a specified period of time. Usually stores will have one or two returned models that are perfectly good but out of their original packaging or in an opened box, so the store will sell them at lower prices.

Online auctions

Online auctions are a great place to buy inexpensive computers and computer parts (see the list of online auction sites below). The computers, parts, and even "antique" computers sold on these sites come from individuals off-loading their old hardware or from liquidators and brand name distributors (such as Dell Computers and Egghead Software) who need to dump their surplus or old stock. And, if you hunt around long enough, you just may find that elusive part you need to keep your computer running, and get it at a bargain price.

Since online auctions offer so many different computers and accessories, make sure you know what you're buying before you dive in. With a little research and plenty of patience, you can buy new or used equipment or software at prices far below what you could ever find through mail-order or in a retail store. To find computer equipment through an online auction, visit one of the following Web sites: CNet Auctions (http://auctions.cnet.com), Ebay (http://www.ebay.com), EggHead Auctions (http://www.

egghead.com), Egghead.com/Onsale.com (http://www.onsale.com), Outpost Auctions (http://www.outpostauctions.com), or Ubid (http://www.ubid.com).

Factory outlets

Computers from manufacturer factory outlets often come with the same technical support as their newer computers, including a limited warranty. If you don't mind getting a slightly used computer, buying one from a factory outlet may be a great way to get a top-of-the-line machine without paying top-of-the-line prices.

CompaqWorks
Compaq sells its discontinued and refurbished desktop and laptop computers through its subsidiary called CompaqWorks. In addition to computers, you can also buy refurbished Compaq printers, monitors, and handheld computers (http://www.compaqworks.com; 888-215-8864).

Computer Factory Outlet
Specializes in selling refurbished IBM and Compaq laptops. If you don't mind a slightly slower and heavier laptop than the latest model, you might find a decent machine at a reasonable price here (http://www.cfo2u.com).

Dell Computers
Dell Computers is another mail-order computer giant that has its share of returned products, which it sells at a discount (http://www.dell.com/factoryoutlet; 877-471-DELL).

Outlet Zoo
Sells discontinued and returned computers, monitors, printers, and software (http://www.outletzoo.com).

PC Factory Outlet
Packard Bell, eMachines, and NEC sell their returned or discontinued models here (http://www.pcfactoryoutlet.com; 800-733-5858).

RefurbCity.com

Offers most major laptop brands, including IBM, Toshiba, Dell, and Compaq, at a discount (http://www.refurbcity.com; 800-278-4009).

Government auctions

Every year police departments around the country confiscate property from criminals. After taking the good stuff for themselves, the police hold an auction to get rid of what's left and to raise money.

At police auctions (usually held monthly, but that of course depends on where you live) you'll see everything from cars and yachts to houses, office furniture, and, of course, computers. (Call your local police department to see when they hold property auctions.)

Before the auction begins, try to inspect the equipment to make sure it's working. (This may not always be possible.) Auctioned computers come with no guarantees, so either assume they won't work and be prepared to strip them for parts, or just hope for the best.

Recycled computers

A few computer companies have popped up that buy old computers from corporations, refurbish them, and then resell them. Although you won't get the latest models when you buy recycled equipment, you can get a fairly decent used machine with a warranty to boot. Just make sure that the cost of the recycled computer really is less than a floor model or open box. Here are some good sites for recycled machines: Artel Resources (http://www.artelsources.com), Computer Express (http://www.compexpress.com), Comp-Recycle.com (http://www.comp-recycle.com), Computer Warehouse Outlet (http://www.cwoutlet.com), and Used-PCs.com (http://www.used-pcs.com).

Build it yourself

If you're handy, you can build your own computer. You may save some money—but not a lot. The fact is, there are so many computers on the market and the technology moves so fast, that you can probably get a decent assembled computer quite cheaply if you shop wisely. Still, you can't put a price on the experience you'll get by building your own machine — experience which may help to protect you from rip-off or inept repair people.

Look online or in any issue of *PC Magazine*, *PC World*, or *Computer Shopper* to find tons of dealers who sell computer parts, or find a local computer store (usually one without a fancy franchise name), and buy the parts you need. If you need help, pick up a do-it-yourself computer book with a title like *Build Your Own Pentium III Computer and Save a Bundle* (although the best way to learn is simply to watch someone else build one), or search online where you'll find lots of tutorials and reviews of various hardware (try http://www.pcguide.com, http://www.storagereview.com, or http://www.anandtech.com).

Computers are relatively easy to build since they consist of easily purchased and replaceable components that you simply snap or screw together. If you can build a toy house out of Lego building blocks, you should have little trouble putting together your own computer. It just takes a little more fiddling.

The biggest hassle with building your own computer is getting the right parts and getting them to work correctly together. Even new computers crash, so don't expect a computer you've built to be any different.

ALMOST-FREE SOFTWARE

Once you have your computer you'll need an operating system and software. The operating system (such as MS-DOS, Microsoft Windows, Linux, or OS/2) is the most crucial piece of software, and all of the rest of your software will run on top of it. But you'll want more than just an operating system.

Free software

If you've got your machine but you're without software, you might consider installing and running Linux on it. Linux is a PC-based version of the Unix operating system—and it's free. There are also lots of free Linux applications.

If you don't want to download or purchase a branded copy of Linux in a retail shop, visit any decent computer tradeshow and you'll probably find a Linux company handing out its version. Or order a copy of any Linux version (called a distribution) from Cheapbytes.com (www.cheapbytes.com) for about five dollars. Then, once you're online, you can download tons of Linux software for free.

Shareware and freeware

Shareware programs let you use a program for a trial period, usually 30 days or so, after which they ask you to pay for it if you continue using it. Best of all, shareware programs are often just as good (or even better) than their higher-priced, brand-name counterparts and often cost less. No matter what type of a program you need (virus scanner, word processor, paint program, and so on), you could well find a good shareware version.

Freeware programs are given away—you can legally use and own them without ever paying for them. Some freeware is software that has been abandoned by a company or an early version of a program used by a company to help market the commercial version. (The idea is that if you like the freeware version, you might want to upgrade to the commercial version later to get more features.) But some freeware is just a good piece of software that someone has decided to give away—which is why Linux and the free programs that run on Linux exist. You'll find great collections of freeware and shareware here: DaveCentral (http://www.davecentral.com), Download.com (http://download.cnet.com) Shareware.com (http://shareware.cnet.com), Jumbo (http://www.jumbo.com), and Tucows (http://www.tucows.com).

Pirating software

If you're running Windows instead of Linux, or if freeware doesn't satisfy you, you can always pirate what you need. When you pirate software you steal it. You can pirate software by borrowing a friend's original copy of a program to install on your computer (this may seem harmless, but it is still theft), downloading it online from an illegal software archive, or even by buying CD-ROMs of pirated software.

When "borrowing" a friend's copy, you'll probably find that you need a CD key or registration number to install it. If you're installing from an original CD, the CD key is usually printed on a sticker glued to the back of the CD case. If you don't have the CD key number or it's missing, you have two choices:

→ Visit a hacker Web site that lists valid serial numbers for various programs and pick the one you need (search for the product you're looking for together with the search term "serial," "crack," or "appz").

→ Use a special CD key number generator program (on a friend's computer if yours isn't working yet) to create a key number for your particular program and use the generated serial number to install your software (see Figure 6-1).

If you can't be bothered with borrowing a CD (or you can't find anyone to lend one to you), there's another simple solution to getting software—find and download your programs online. Many hacker Web sites post entire pirated programs, called warez or appz, that have been cracked to remove annoying copy-protection schemes. Just visit one of these Web sites and download all the software you want.

FIGURE 6-1:

Use a CD key number generating program to register your pirated software.

(Note: Most pirated software on Web sites are games, but if you hunt around you'll find all kinds of pirated programs.)

Needless to say, warez and appz sites with serial numbers, CD key number generators, or pirated software move around a lot. To find them, search for "serial numbers" (see Figure 6-2), "pirated software," "warez," "cracks," "serials," or "CD key generator."

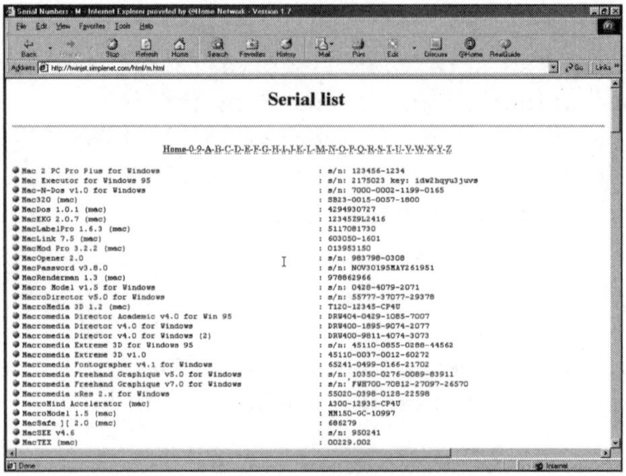

FIGURE 6-2:

Many Web sites contain lists of valid serial numbers for a variety of programs.

Just don't forget the risk involved in using warez. Sometimes the programs aren't complete so you could waste time downloading them only to find they don't work. Even worse, many hackers like to infect warez with viruses or Trojan Horses to "punish" people for trying to use software they haven't bought.

Cracking software

But don't let someone else do all of the work—why not crack some software yourself? Software cracking involves modifying a program to either turn a trial version into a fully functional one, or to shut off a shareware program's nag screen that keeps reminding you to register. Essentially, cracking allows you to trick a program into thinking it's registered.

To crack Windows software, you need several tools:

→ A disassembler to reveal the program's assembly language source code so you can see how it works.

→ A debugger to examine how a program runs so you can identify the part of the program that you want to change (such as the part requiring a registration number).

→ A hex editor to modify the executable version of a program.

→ A Windows registry viewer to modify any Windows registry entries necessary to make the cracked program run properly.

Remember, software cracking requires an intimate knowledge of assembly language, so it's not for the beginner. To learn how people crack software or how to become a software cracker yourself, search www.astalavista.com or www.cyberarmy.com for the programs and tutorials you'll need.

Buying software at an academic discount

College and university bookstores usually sell academic versions of nearly all major software. Software publishers sell their programs at a substantial discount to students, because they know that students can't afford (and won't spend) hundreds of dollars to buy a program that they could just pirate instead. A program that normally costs $495 might be sold by a university bookstore for $100.

Of course, the catch is that if you want to buy software from a university bookstore, you have to have a student ID. If you're young enough you can try buying it without an ID; otherwise, ask a younger friend to try. If the cashier hassles you or your friend for a student ID, claim that you left it back in the dorm. Or pretend that your son or daughter goes to the school and that you're buying it for them.

To make sure the cashier accepts your "I forgot my student ID" or "I'm buying this for my son" story, buy the software at the beginning of the semester, when hordes of students are busy buying their textbooks for upcoming classes. With lines of ten or more students behind you, it's unlikely that the university bookstore cashier will care whether you have a student ID or not. If they do hassle you, just get upset or indignant and make everyone behind you impatient and angry as well. Most cashiers will just try to get you out of the bookstore as quickly as possible so they can help the rest of the customers and live through the rest of their shift.

Upgrade offers

In an effort to grab as much market share as possible, nearly every software publisher offers two different prices: an ordinary retail price and a discounted upgrade price for people who own the previous version of the program or a similar rival program. Unless you have more money than sense, you need never pay full retail price for any software.

To qualify for the upgrade price, you may need proof that you own either a previous version or a rival program, or have an actual copy of a previous version or rival program on your hard disk. Microsoft typically sells special upgrade versions of their software that peeks at your hard disk for a previous version or rival program. If neither one exists, the upgrade version won't install itself.

Here's where you can get creative. If you're buying software directly from the software publisher, they'll ask that you mail or fax them proof that you own a previous version or a rival program, such as the front page of the manual. So if you want the upgrade version of Microsoft Excel, you'll need to prove that you own a rival spreadsheet, such as Lotus 1-2-3 or Quattro Pro.

The simplest way to handle this is to find a friend who owns the program you need (such as Lotus 1-2-3) and fax a photocopy of the manual's front page.

If you can't find anyone with the program you need, try to find an older version of the program either online or at your local computer store. By buying an older version (which you can always sell on eBay), you'll qualify for the less-expensive upgrade. The cost of the upgrade plus a boxed older version will nearly always be less than the full retail price for any program.

Or maybe better yet, just use the older version of the program—who needs the latest version anyway?

Try these sites for older versions of software: Ellen's Software (http://www.ellens.com), Oldsoftware.com (http://www.oldsoftware.com), Software & Stuff (http://www.software-andstuff.com), Bargain Software Catalog (http://www.computercost.com), and Ubid (http://www.ubid.com).

FREE MUSIC

Nearly all new computers come with a CD-ROM drive, a sound card, and speakers, which can turn any computer into a simple CD audio player. You can play your own audio CDs on your computer, but you may have more fun scouring the Internet for free music to play from your hard disk or a CD-R (CD recordable) drive.

One reason there are so many free music files on the Internet is the restrictive nature of the recording industry. In the old days, recording artists could only get massive public exposure by signing with a major record label. If they couldn't get a contract, they were rarely heard by the general public.

To get around this problem, a few renegade musicians offered samples of their music for free over the Internet. But in the early days of digital sound (prior to the arrival of MP3), a high-quality sound file of a single song could be as large as 30MB.

Then came MP3—Motion Pictures Expert Group Layer 3 compression technology. MP3 allows entire songs to be compressed into relatively small files (a few megabytes), while retaining the audio quality of the original recording. Fast Internet access (such as cable or DSL modems) has made downloading and sharing MP3 files fast and convenient. Many enterprising bands and musicians regularly release their songs in MP3 format for people to download, copy, and enjoy for free, hoping that if you like their songs, you'll buy their albums.

Of course, that's the legal, sanctioned use of MP3 technology. Many people use MP3 illegally to record songs off their favorite CDs, store them as MP3 files, and trade them with others over the Internet, violating copyright laws and cheating artists out of their royalties.

Once you have your favorite songs stored in MP3 format, you can use a recordable CD-ROM drive to create your own audio CDs. Just as cassette tape decks have allowed people to record, copy, and trade their favorite songs with one another on blank cassette tapes, the MP3 format has done the same thing on a global scale using the power of the Internet.

To take advantage of music stored in MP3 format, you need a player (so you can hear the music stored in MP3 format), a ripper (for saving your MP3 files on a CD), and one or more Web sites where you can download MP3 files.

MP3 players

Here's where to get some of the more popular MP3 players: MuzicMan (http://www.muzicman.com), Sonique (http://sonique.lycos.com), or Winamp (http://www.winamp.com) for Windows, MacAMP (http://www.macamp.net) for Macintosh, and MPG123 (http://www.mpg123.de) for UNIX.

MP3 rippers

These programs will let you save your MP3 files to CD so that you can play them back later: AudioCatalyst (http://www.xingtech.com/mp3/audiocatalyst) for Windows and Macintosh, CD Paranoia (http://www.xiph.org/paranoia) for UNIX, Play & Record (http://www.hycd.com) for Windows only, and SoundJam MP (http://www.soundjam.com) for Macintosh only.

MP3 search engines

Start with these sites when searching for MP3 files: MP3.com (http://www.mp3.com), MP3 Search (http://mp3.lycos.com), Music Seek (http://www.musicseek.net), or Yahoo! Digital (http://digital.broadcast.com).

An alternative to using an MP3 search engine is to run the free MP3 sharing program Napster (http://www.napster.com). Napster lets you connect to a centrally located server to exchange MP3 files with other Napster users.

Unfortunately, Napster can be stopped by shutting down its central server, which people in the recording industry are trying to do all the time. But no problem—if Napster isn't working for you you can use Gnutella (http://www.gnutella.wego.com). Gnutella is similar to Napster except that it doesn't use a central server. Instead, people create a private and temporary network linking all their computers together. Once connected to a Gnutella network, you can exchange any type of file, including MP3s, software, graphics, or images.

Since Gnutella networks can spontaneously appear and disappear, it's nearly impossible for anyone to shut them down. While law-abiding citizens may use Gnutella to exchange their favorite recipes or tips for winning at computer games, others have used Gnutella to exchange pornography or copyrighted materials such as MP3s or commercial software.

FREE INTERNET ACCESS

While you may use an Internet account at work or school, you can get a free one from a number of companies. While free Internet accounts may be harder to connect to and bombard you with advertisements, they still provide you with free Internet access.

Advertising-sponsored Internet accounts

Network television is free because advertisers pay the cost of producing the shows in return for marketing their products to a vast audience. Similarly, many Internet providers now provide free Internet accounts in exchange for displaying advertisements on your computer screen or tracking your online usage for marketing purposes. Many of these have limitations or various restrictions which change over time, so read their descriptions carefully.

To find the latest and greatest free Internet accounts, search for "freenet" or "free Internet," visit the Internet 4 Free Web site (http://www.internet4free.net), or try one of the following: BlueLight.com (http://www.bluelight.com), Winfire (http://www.winfire.com), Free Internet (http://www.freeinternet.com), Juno (http://www.juno.com), NetZero (http://www.netzero.net), or WorldSpy (http://welcomews.juno.com/worldspy).

Internet accounts that pay you to surf

The rabid competition among Internet providers and advertisers has spawned a new generation of Internet service providers that pay you for every second you use the Internet. Not only can you get a monthly check just to look at different advertisements and answer surveys, but if you refer your friends to these networks, you also get paid when they use the Internet. To try one, visit AllAdvantage.com (http://www.alladvantage.com), ePipo (http://www.epipo.com), GoToWorld.com (http://www.gotoworld.com), or Spedia (http://www.spedia.net). At least two other sites will pay you for your opinion, to listen to music, or to refer others to their Web site: RadiofreeCash (http://www.radiofreecash.com) and Epinions (http://www.epinions.com).

Cybercafes and public libraries

The latest trend among coffeehouses and other public places where artists, students, and bohemian types gather is the cybercafe—a cafe that provides free Internet access. Visit a cybercafe, buy a cup of coffee or sandwich, and you can spend 30 minutes to an hour using their computers to surf.

To find a list of cybercafes in your area, visit coffeehouses near universities or search for "cybercafe" or "cybercafe list."

Larger public libraries also offer free Internet access where you can browse the Web and read or send email from your own email account, such as Hotmail or Yahoo!.

FREE EMAIL

Free email accounts are perfect if you need to send email that can't be easily traced to you—like from work. So, if your boss scans your work email account, there won't be any embarrassing messages.

Many free email accounts offer special features including: encryption (to protect your email from prying eyes), a self-destruct capability (to wipe out your email after a specified period of time), support for multiple languages, and anonymity (to hide your true identity from the rest of the world).

To sign up for a free email account, visit your favorite search engine and search for the string "free email." For a quick overview of what different free email services have to offer, visit one of the following Web sites: Email Anywhere (http://www.emailanywhere.com), Flash Email (http://www.flashemail.com), Hotmail (http://www.hotmail.com), Lycos Mail (http://www.lycosemail.com), or Yahoo! Mail (http://mail.yahoo.com).

FREE FAX SERVICES

If you need to send a fax to someone you don't need a fax machine or even fax software. Various free services let you send a free fax anywhere in the world. Some (like Fax4Free) even capture faxes that others send to you and forward them to your email account as graphic files for later viewing. Try these: eFax (http://www.efax.com), Fax4Free (http://www2.fax4free.com), FreeFax (http://www.freefax.com.pk), or ZipFax (http://www.zipfax.com).

FREE WEB SITE HOSTING

Many online services or Internet providers give you several megabytes of storage space so you can put up your own Web site. Unfortunately, the amount of space available may be too small, or the Internet provider may censor what type of information you can post. For example, online services like

America Online tend to frown on anyone using their service to post anti—America Online comments on a Web site.

If the rules or storage space of your current Internet provider aren't satisfactory, try one of the many companies that offer free Web sites. These companies usually don't care what type of information you post—all they really care about is attracting people to their own Web site so they can sell ads. Search for "free web site" or "free web page" to find a company that offers free Web sites or try these: Geocities (http://geocities.yahoo.com), Homestead (http://www.homestead.com), The Globe (http://www.theglobe.com), Tripod (http://www.tripod.lycos.com), or WebProvider (http://www.webprovider.com).

COMPUTING ON A BUDGET

Although the cost of computers can widen the gap between the haves and the have-nots, this doesn't have to be the case. With a little creativity and a lot of persistence, everyone can access the Internet. Who knows? Using your access to the Internet, you might one day help change political policy, meet new friends, or just broaden your mind by exploring the whole world from the comfort of your home—all without going bankrupt buying lots of expensive computer equipment that you don't really need after all.

Stalking People

7

EVERY TIME YOU USE A CREDIT CARD, APPLY FOR A JOB, OR FILL OUT A SURVEY, YOU ARE GIVING AWAY YOUR PRIVACY. Even worse, your information will likely be stored on a computer where any government, company, or individual may be able to access it 24 hours a day, seven days a week. If you're worried that others can access your personal information without your knowledge or consent, your fears are completely justified.

Of course, information works both ways. Even though others may be able to retrieve your personal information, you can retrieve personal information about them as well. You can find an old roommate, track down a family member, even stalk someone you are obsessed with. With the help of the Internet and this chapter, you can find names, addresses, and phone numbers of others and minimize the spread of your own personal information to others.

If you think your private life is private, visit any of the Web sites listed in this chapter and search for your own name. You may be surprised to find out how much information is available about you on these Web sites—information available to anyone, anytime.

The only thing we have to fear on the planet is man.

—CARL JUNG

FINDING PHONE NUMBERS, STREET ADDRESSES, AND EMAIL ADDRESSES

People may join the ranks of the "missing" for many reasons. Some may appear missing to you because they change addresses and phone numbers so often that eventually you lose touch with them. Others may have deliberately erased their trail by adopting a false name and disguising their appearance. Still others seem to simply disappear.

Yet no matter how people wind up missing, they almost always leave behind some form of paper trail you can use to find them—phone book directory listings, tax records, even utility bills. Even when people deliberately "disappear" to avoid arrest, lawsuits, or other legal responsibilities, they usually leave behind at least a clue about where they've gone.

The first step to finding someone is to gather up as much personal data about your target as possible, details like his or her full name, Social Security number, date of birth, age, and last known address. Useful information sources include marriage, medical, and military records, property transfers, and vehicle registrations. The more you know about your target, the quicker your search will be.

People finders

Since you probably know at least the person's name, use a people-finding Web site (like the one shown in Figure 7-1) to search for a recent mailing address or home phone number. These Web sites get their information from publicly available sources like telephone books, and many are free.

You can also use the following people-finding sites to track down your target's relatives, friends, or former

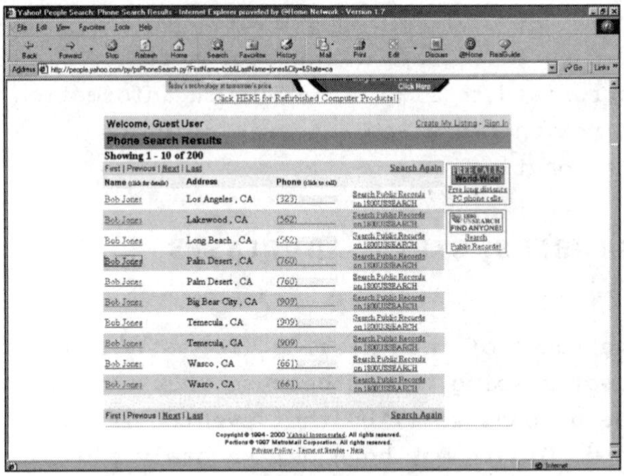

FIGURE 7-1:

The Yahoo! search engine can help you find the phone number and city of someone you know.

neighbors. Although the person you're trying to find may be erasing his or her paper trail, chances are good that ex-colleagues or neighbors are not.

555-1212.com
Provides Yellow Pages directory to search for businesses, White Pages directory to search for individuals, and reverse lookups to find someone based on their telephone number, email address, or street address (http://www.555-1212.com).

InfoSpace
Search businesses by name, category, or city, or search for individuals by name or city (http://www.infospace.com).

InternetOracle
Look for individuals based on name, city, and state using a variety of the most popular people-finding search engines such as Switchboard, WorldPages, and Four11 (http://www.searchgateway.com/find.htm).

Populus
Look for individuals by name, phonetic sound of their name, email address, city, state, colleges they attended, date of birth, and personal interests (http://www.populus.net).

Switchboard
Search for businesses and individuals by name, city, and state (http://www.switchboard.com).

Telephone Directories on the Web
Search for businesses and individuals using telephone directories published from all over the world, including North America, Europe, Asia, and Africa (http://www.teldir.com).

WhoWhere
Search for people by name to find their email address, phone number, or any Web pages that contain their name (http://www.whowhere.lycos.com).

Yahoo! People Search
Search for individuals by name, city, state, or email address (http://people.yahoo.com).

If you'd rather not dig through the Internet to look up somebody's name, you might find it more convenient to use a compact disc containing information scanned in from the White Pages of telephone directories from around the country instead. (Just remember that by the time a company scans in and saves names and addresses on a CD, packages the whole thing in a fancy box, and ships the package to a store, the data may well be out-of-date.)

To locate a CD containing a database of names, visit CD Light (http://www.zipinfo.com) or InfoUSA.com (http://www.phonedisc.com).

If all else fails, visit your local public library. Many libraries keep old phone directories and criss-cross directories (from city censuses) indexed by year. Old phone directories can help you verify the correct spelling, middle initial, and previous address of a person. City census directories often contain unlisted phone numbers, names of a spouse or children, occupation information, and mailing addresses.

If your local library doesn't store old census directories, check with the Chamber of Commerce or the Better Business Bureau in the city where you think your target may be living. You can also request information from the public libaries in the other cities by phone or letter if it is impractical to visit them yourself.

Reverse searches

Telephone numbers are another great way of tracing someone. If you have a phone number scribbled on an envelope or cocktail napkin but can't figure out who the number belongs to, use a reverse phone search. This searches through publicly available phone books to match a name and address to a given phone number.

Just be aware that reverse phone searches can only search through phone books, so if someone has an unlisted number, a reverse phone search may not turn up anything. Some reverse search engines can also work with someone's email or street address. To do a reverse search, try one of the following Web sites: 555-1212.com (http://www. 555-1212.com/look_up.cfm), AnyWho (http://www.anywho.com), InfoUSA.com (http://adp.infousa.com), InfoSpace (http://www.infospace.com/info/reverse.htm), or WhitePages.com (http://whitepages.com).

Track down someone using a Social Security number

The fastest way to track someone down in America is through a Social Security number. Because it is required by employers, the Internal Revenue Service, and banks, a Social Security number can be the quickest tracking device to pinpoint where someone lives and works.

Finding the Social Security number may be difficult unless you once employed or were married to that person. Then your search may not be too difficult. For example, if you're trying to track down a former spouse, try to find your former spouse's Social Security number on an old joint tax return. If you don't have a copy, you can order old copies of your joint tax returns from the IRS or your local State Tax Commission.

Joint applications for credit cards, loans, and bank accounts almost always list both partners' Social Security numbers, and you may ask the credit agency or bank for a copy of these old applications. Take a look at your divorce papers, because many states require both parties to list their Social Security numbers.

If you're trying to track down a former employee, you can find Social Security numbers from old employment applications or tax forms.

Once you have your target's Social Security number, a number of Web sites can help you track down that person for a small fee. Here are a few: Computrace (http://www.amerifind.com), Fast-Track (http://www.usatrace.com), USSearch (http://www.1800ussearch.com), and Find A Friend (http://findafriend.com).

The Social Security Administration's location service can also help you find a person if you have the person's Social Security number. Although they won't give out addresses, they will forward a letter for you, and you might get a reply. You might increase the chance of getting a reply by making up a phony letter offering a prize, inheritance, or similar incentive to trick your target into replying and revealing his or her current address.

To forward a letter through the Social Security Administration, write to:

Social Security Location Services
6401 Security Blvd.
Baltimore, MD 21235

Using a Social Security number is the fastest and most accurate way to track a person down. If the person is still alive, the Social Security number can lead you to a current mailing or work address. If that person is dead, the Social Security Administration will verify this information too.

Finding people in the military

The military maintains a vast database of everyone who has served in it. If you're looking for someone currently on active duty in the armed forces, the military should be able to help you track a person down no matter where in the world he or she might be stationed.

To find someone on active duty, call or write to the appropriate address below and include as many of the following personal details as possible:

Name
Service serial number
Last known address
Date of birth
Social Security number

You'll need to pay a fee for this search. Here's some contact information for the different branches of service:

Air Force: Directorate of Administrative Services
Department of the Air Force
Attn: Military Personnel Records Division
Randolph AFB, TX 78148
(210) 565-2660

Army Personnel World Wide Locator:
(703) 325-3732

Coast Guard (Enlisted Personnel) Commandant (PO)
U.S. Coast Guard
1300 East St. NW
Washington, DC 20591

Marine Corps
Commandant of the Marine Corps
Attn: MSRB-10
Washington, DC 20591
(703) 784-3942

Chief of Naval Personnel
Department of the Navy
Washington, DC 20270
(901) 874-3070

If you're searching for someone no longer on active duty (such as an old military buddy), try one of these Web sites: Department of Veterans Affairs (http://www.va.gov), Military City Web site (http://www.militarycity.com), or Military Search Database (http://www.militarysearch.com).

Searching public records

Public records are another good source of names and addresses. If you know the general vicinity in which the person last lived, check with the utility companies and services (garbage collection, cable television) in that area. Also check with that state's motor vehicles department and search its voter registrations. Marriage records can be especially helpful in discovering a woman's married name, because they contain the wife's maiden name and address along with witnesses' and parents' names. Look also for the marriage license application, which may include each partner's Social Security number.

Here are some more ideas:

→ Tax records can provide another clue to some-one's location. Every homeowner pays a property tax, which the government records. These records list the person's name, current address, and sometimes a forwarding address.

→ Licensing and certification boards in many states regulate certain professionals such as real estate and insurance agents, attorneys, and doctors. If your target needs a license to run a business, the state licensing agency can give you a business address and phone number.

→ Try the county or state fishing and hunting license department. License applications contain the applicant's full name, date of birth, and address.

→ Dog licenses, building permits, and boat, car, or airplane registrations are other sources. Check with the Federal Aviation Agency for both aircraft registration and pilot certification by contacting Aircraft Registration (post email to http://registry.faa.gov/arfeed.htm) or Pilot Certification (405-954-3205).

→ The FAA can provide you with a copy of someone's pilot's license, which includes an address. To get this information, you need a name and birthdate or Social Security number. To use this service, contact:

FAA Airman Certification Branch VN-460
P.O. Box 25082
Oklahoma City, OK 73125

→ Because almost everyone gets a traffic ticket at one time or another, check the county court records. Traffic tickets will not only list someone's name and address, but also date of birth and driver's license number.

→ If you're trying to find someone who once worked for the federal government, you can obtain records with a Freedom of Information Act request. This information won't give you that person's home address, but it will include present and past positions (and maybe locations) that person held in the federal government. For more information write to:

National Personnel Records Center
111 Winnebago Street
St. Louis, MO 63118

→ To check a person's driving record, credit history, voter registration information, criminal record, or birth and death certificates, visit one of the following Web sites and have your credit card ready to pay a fee: American Information Network (http://www.ameri.com), National Credit Information Network (http://www.wdia.com).

➔ If you're looking for someone who has committed a major crime, visit the Most Wanted Criminals Web site (http://www.mostwanted.org). Who knows? If you find a criminal before the police do, you could get yourself a reward (see Figure 7-2).

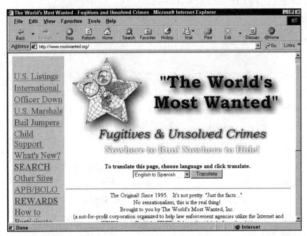

FIGURE 7-2:

You can check to see if a friend, loved one, or enemy's name appears on the Most Wanted Criminals Web site.

Searching driver's license and automobile registration records

If the person you're looking for owns a car, try searching state vehicle registration records. To search the vehicle registration records, you just need your target's full name and (in case of duplicate names) date of birth. The vehicle registration records can give you the last known address of the person you're looking for. If that person sold the vehicle, you can use these records to find the address of the buyer, who might be able to provide some information to help you further track down your wanted person.

You can also order the driver's license records from the state motor vehicle department. These records provide a wealth of information about a person including his or her current or last known address; height, weight, eye and hair color; previous names, if any; and the numbers and types of currently owned vehicles. If your target has moved,

driver's license records will also show the state where the
person surrendered his or her driver's license. Even if a
person uses phony names, you may recognize one of the
aliases.

For a list of every state's driver's license bureau,
visit the Foundation for American Communications (FACS) Web
site (http://www.facsnet.org). The FACS organization provides tips and resources to help journalists track down
information for their news stories.

Searching death records

If the above methods fail, try searching the death records
of the person's relatives. Death records often reveal the
names and addresses of a dead person's survivors and heirs.

Every state provides a bureau that tracks births,
deaths, and marriages. To find the state bureau near
you, visit the FACS Web site.

If state records don't provide you with what you need,
try the Social Security Administration's Master Death
Records. These records contain more than 43 million names
and the details of everyone who has died in the United
States since 1962, the year the system was automated. The
Master Death Records provide the following information
about each dead person:

Social Security number
First and last name
Date of birth
Date of death
Zip code where the death occurred
Zip code where the lump sum death payment was made

To access the Master Death File, contact the Social
Security Administration. For faster access, visit a large
city library, particularly a federal depository library,
which will likely have the Master Death File available on
a compact disc that you can access for free.

To use the Master Death File, follow these steps:

1. Search the Master Death File for the missing person's parents. If one of them has died, the search will reveal the zip code where they died.

2. Using this zip code, determine the town where the parent died and order a death certificate from the local county clerk or health department. The death certificate will identify the funeral home that performed the burial or cremation.

3. Contact the funeral home and examine their records to determine the names and possible addresses and phone numbers of the dead parent's next of kin.

Finding relatives

When you're looking for someone, always check the public records at the county courthouse or other state government building. If you're looking for a relative, this search can be quite easy because either you or other family members are likely to know specific information about a missing person such as full name, birth date, and birthplace.

To find a birth parent, start by examining the Birth Index Records—an index of all births in a particular state, indexed by name or date. The Birth Index is usually available as a public record, whereas most birth certificates are not.

If you know someone's birth date, scan the Birth Index for a list of all children born on that date. Then eliminate all children of the wrong gender. Finally, to narrow the search to a few names, eliminate all children born in cities other than the one you're looking for. Scan through this remaining list, and you should be able to find the names of that person's birth parents.

To track down brothers or sisters, start with school records. High schools hold regular reunions, and these reunion committees can often lead you directly to a brother or sister. Colleges also keep records of students and often solicit donations from alumni. If you know what college your target attended, you might be able to find his or her address. Even if the address is old, you can use it as a starting point.

If you're adopted and would like to find your birth parents, or if you gave up your child for adoption and would like to see what became of him or her, visit one of the following Web sites, which can help reunite parents and children: Adoption.com (http://www.adoption.com/reunion), Find-Me (http://www.findme-registry.com), International Soundex Reunion Registry (http://www.plumsite.com/isrr), Reunion Registry.com (http://www.reunionregistry.com), or WhereAbouts, Inc. (http://www.whereabouts.org).

Also try browsing your county civil court records for information about lawsuits, divorces, name changes, adoption, and other litigation. Divorce records can be particularly revealing because they contain property settlement agreements (listing vehicles, houses, boats, real estate, bank accounts, and so on) and child custody agreements (including detailed information about the children—their names, ages, and Social Security numbers).

Finding email addresses

With so many people flocking to the Internet, the odds are getting better the person you want to find could have an email address. To track down somebody's email address, you need his or her name and, if possible, location (such as city, state, or country). Start here:

Deaf World Web
Searches for someone's email address by name, city, and country (http://dww.deafworldweb.org/net/dir).

EmailChange
Searches for someone's email address by name or their last known email address (http://www.emailchange.com/emailchange).

MESA

Searches several search engines simultaneously to look for someone's email address by name (http://mesa.rrzn. uni-hannover.de).

NedSite

Search for someone's email address by name, phone or fax number, street address, college attended, ancestors, or military history (http://www.nedsite.nl/search/people.htm#top).

If you don't know the person's location, or if the above search engines can't trace an email address, try Deja News (http://www.deja.com/usenet, shown in Figure 7-3). Maybe your target has contributed messages to a newsgroup recently. If so, searching Deja News for his or her name will find the message, and the elusive email address.

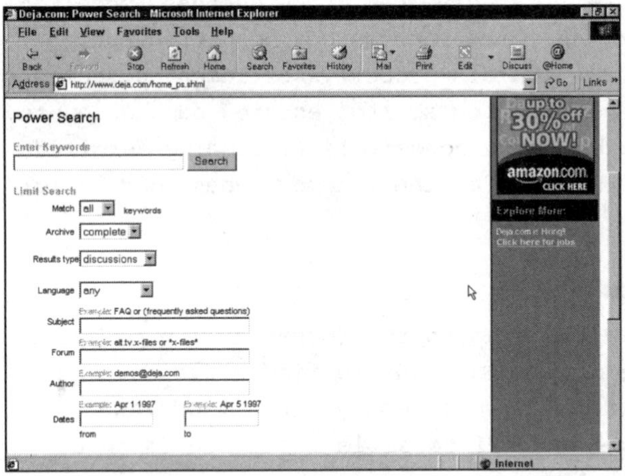

FIGURE 7-3:

The Deja News Web site can help you track down messages left by a particular email address.

PROTECTING YOURSELF

Now that you know how to track someone down, you also know how others can track you down, and you can take steps to protect your private information. If you don't want to find your name and home address splashed across the World Wide Web, try one or more of the following techniques:

→ Get an unlisted phone number. This prevents most of the people-tracking Web sites from finding your name, address, and phone number (it won't be in the telephone directory).

→ Use a fake or misspelled name. The phone company doesn't care what name you use, just as long as you pay your phone bill on time. A fake name will throw off the majority of these people-tracking Web sites, even if someone knows your actual phone number.

→ Avoid listing your street address. This way, even if someone finds your phone number in a phone directory, they won't be able to find out where you live.

→ Contact the people-finding Web site directly and request that your name be removed from their listing. Unfortunately, with so many people-finders popping up all the time, this might mean having to contact a dozen different Web sites — and then there's still no guarantee that a new people-finding Web site won't turn up with your information anyway.

If you don't want to make your email address available to anyone who might be searching for it, try one or more of the following techniques:

→ Use an anonymous remailer before posting any messages to a Usenet newsgroup. This method also helps keep your email address off mailing lists used by spammers.

→ Change email addresses frequently. If receiving email isn't that important to you, use multiple email accounts, and shut them down periodically.

→ If you really need to hide, avoid leaving a
paper trail of any sort. Don't sign up for
telephone service (or, if you must, use a fake
name); avoid using credit cards; pay cash for
everything; and avoid magazine subscriptions
that use your real name. Eliminating your paper
trail can be a lot of work, but it might be
worth it if you're hiding from someone dangerous (like the Internal Revenue Service).

8

Con Games
on the Internet

COMBINE LAZINESS WITH GULLIBILITY AND GREED, AND YOU HAVE THE PRIME INGREDIENTS FOR LOSING YOUR MONEY TO ONE OF THE MANY SCAMS CIRCULATING AROUND THE INTERNET. In addition to unparalleled opportunities for mass communication on a worldwide scale, the Internet has created global opportunities for cheating people as well. Of course, the Internet itself isn't to blame for con games. The Internet simply provides a new medium for con artists to lure new victims.

Con games always involve three elements:

→ Exploiting the victim's trust

→ Forcing the victim to pay money in advance

→ Promising fantastic amounts of money in return for little or no effort

Because nearly everyone would love to make a lot of money without doing anything to earn it (which may explain why so many people go into politics), all of us risk becoming potential con game victims. To keep yourself from falling prey to a con game, take some time to educate yourself on the different types of cons that have been fleecing people for years.

THE AREA CODE SCAM
Area code scams play off people's ignorance of the growing proliferation of different telephone area codes. The con artist starts by contacting you, either by leaving a message

There's a sucker born every minute.

—P.T. BARNUM

on your answering machine, by sending you email, or by paging you. The goal of the message is to get you to call a telephone number in another area code, either by claiming you won a fabulous prize in a contest or by claiming that one of your relatives has died, been arrested, or fallen ill.

The moment you call the phone number, you may be put on hold or put in touch with someone who claims to speak broken English. In any event, the person on the other end simply tries to keep you on the phone as long as possible because (surprise!) the area code phone number is really a "pay-per-call" (much like 900 numbers) where you (the caller) ring up astronomical charges, which can amount to as much as $25 per minute!

The most common area code used in the scam is the 809 area code, which is actually located in the Caribbean, so the scammer can avoid any American laws warning you of the charge, the rate involved, and a time period during which you may terminate the call without being charged. And, since you don't need to dial an international area code to reach the number (you simply dial 1-809 and the number), most people won't realize that they're making an international call.

Area code scams are extremely hard to prosecute. Since you actually did make the call, neither your local phone company nor your long distance carrier will likely help you or drop the charges since they are simply providing the billing for the foreign phone company.

To avoid this scam, be careful when returning unknown phone calls with a different area code. To help you locate other area codes located in the Caribbean, visit the LincMad Web site (http://www.lincmad.com/caribbean.html). To learn about all the different area codes located around the world, visit the AT&T Web site (http://www.att.com/traveler/tools/codes.html#a) or the North American Numbering Plan Administration Web site (http://www.nanpa.com/area_codes/index.html). To learn more about the 809 scam, visit your favorite search engine and look for the phrase "809 fraud" or "809 scam."

BEWARE OF NIGERIA

Many people in other countries hate Americans, which may seem natural because the only contact most overseas countries have with Americans is through the actions of American tourists (whom they don't like) and American politicians (whom we don't like).

Other countries also get their information about Americans through American television shows. So after watching shows like *Baywatch* or *Sex and the City*, most countries believe that Americans are not only rich and beautiful, but lousy actors as well.

But no matter how people in other countries perceive Americans, the fact remains that America is one of the wealthiest countries on the planet. Given the wide disparity between the average American's income and that of people in other countries, it's no surprise that other countries feel no guilt or shame in conning Americans out of their money at every available opportunity.

For some odd reason, not only have many of these scams originated in Nigeria, but the Nigerian government has often been involved to the point where many people believe that international scams make up the third largest industry in Nigeria.

The general view in Nigeria is that if you can cheat an American out of his money, it's the American's fault for being gullible in the first place.

Nigerian scams are often called "Advance Fee Fraud," "419 Fraud" (Four-One-Nine after the relevant section of the Criminal Code of Nigeria), or "The Fax Scam." The scam works as follows: The victim receives an unsolicited fax or letter from Nigeria containing a money-laundering proposal, a seemingly legitimate business proposal involving crude oil, or a proposal about a bequest left in a will.

The fax or letter usually asks the victim to facilitate transfer of a large sum of money to the victim's own bank and promises that the recipient will receive a share of the money if he (or she) will pay an "advance fee," "transfer tax," "performance bond," or government bribe of some sort. If the victim pays this fee, complications mysteriously occur that require the victim to send more money until the victim either quits, runs out of money, or both.

With the growing popularity of the Internet, Nigerian con artists have been very busy, so don't be surprised if you receive email from Nigeria asking for your help. The following is a sample letter sent from Nigeria offering the lure of fantastic wealth in exchange for little work on your part:

Dear Sir

I am working with the Federal Ministry of Health in Nigeria. It happens that five months ago my father who was the Chairman of the Task Force Committee created by the present Military Government to monitor the selling, distribution and revenue generation from crude oil sales before and after the gulf war crisis died in a motor accident on his way home from Lagos after attending a National conference. He was admitted in the hospital for eight (8) days before he finally died. While I was with him in the hospital, he disclosed all his confidential documents to me one of which is the business I want to introduce to you right now.

Before my father finally died in the hospital, he told me that he has $21.5M (twenty one million five hundred thousand U.S. Dollars) cash in a trunk box coded and deposited in a security company. He told me that the security company is not aware of its contents. That on producing a document which, he gave to me, that I will only pay for the demurrage after which the box will be released to me.

He further advised me that I should not collect the money without the assistance of a foreigner who will open a local account in favor of his company for onward transfer to his nominated overseas account where the money will be invested.

This is because as a civil servant I am not supposed to own such money. This will bring many questions in the bank if I go without a foreigner.

It is at this juncture that I decided to contact you for assistance but with the following conditions:

1. That this transaction is treated with Utmost confidence, cooperation and absolute secrecy which it demands.

2. That the money is being transferred to an account where the incidence of taxation would not take much toll.

3. That all financial matters for the success of this transfer will be tackled by both parties.

4. That a promissory letter signed and sealed by you stating the amount US $21.5M (twenty-one million five hundred thousand US Dollars) will be given to me by you on your account and that only 20% of the total money is for your assistance.

Please contact me on the above fax number for more details. Please quote (QS) in all your correspondence.

Yours faithfully,
DR. AN UZOAMAKA

To learn more about scams originating from Nigeria, visit one of the following Web sites: http://home.rica.net/alphae/419coal, http://www.superhighway.is/iis/nameste2.htm, or http://www.cslnet.ctstateu.edu/attygenl/nigeria.htm.

PYRAMID SCHEMES

The idea behind a pyramid scheme is to get two or more people to give you money. In exchange, you give them nothing but the hope that they can get rich too—as long as they can convince two or more people to give them money. The most common incarnation of a pyramid scheme is a chain letter.

A typical chain letter lists five addresses and urges you to send money ($1 or more) to each of the addresses. To add your name to the chain letter, you copy the chain letter, remove the top name from the list of addresses, and put your own name and address at the bottom of the list. Then mail five copies of the chain letter to other people and wait for fabulous riches to come pouring into your mailbox within a few weeks.

To avoid the stigma of the chain-letter label, many chain letters claim that you must sign a letter stating that you are offering the money as a gift or that you are buying the five addresses as a mailing list. In this way, the chain letter claims you will not be breaking any laws.

Multilevel marketing (MLM) business opportunities are similar to chain letters. Valid MLM businesses offer two ways to make money: by selling a product or by recruiting new distributors. Most people get rich within an MLM business by recruiting new distributors. Unfortunately, many scams masquerade as legitimate MLM businesses with the key difference that, as a phony MLM business, you can only make money by recruiting others, and the only product being sold is a nebulous "business opportunity."

Pyramid schemes often make a few people very wealthy, but at the expense of nearly everyone else at the bottom of the pyramid. Most pyramid schemes attempt to recruit new members through Usenet newsgroups or by spamming (see Chapter 17) multiple email accounts. As long as you realize that pyramid schemes need your money to make other people rich, you can learn to ignore pyramid scheme offers that come your way, no matter how tempting. (And if you want to con others out of money, there's no faster way than by starting your own chain letter with your name at the top.)

Beware of Mega$Nets

The prevalence of computers and the Internet has brought with it an electronic version of the chain-letter pyramid scheme known as Mega$Nets (see Figure 8-1). Unlike paper chain letters that require each person to be honest (and not put their own name at the top of the chain-letter list), Mega$Nets uses software to track a list of names and keep people from cheating. You often buy the Mega$Nets software for about $20 (although many people just give it away for free).

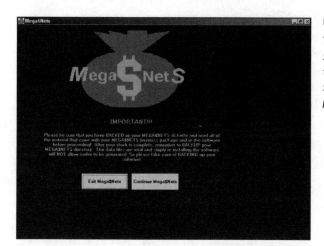

FIGURE 8-1:

The Mega$Nets program is simply a chain letter in the form of a freely distributable program.

Once you have the Mega$Nets software installed on your own computer, a list of five names and addresses appears. You're supposed to send each person $20 and, in return, each person sends you a six-character computer code. After you have paid for computer codes from all five people, the program adds your name to its list. From this point on, you can sell (or give away) copies of the Mega$Nets program to others, who will have to pay you $20 for your special computer code so they can put their names on the Mega$Nets list and so on.

The Mega$Nets program prevents people from cheating in two ways. First, people can't erase someone else's name, because Mega$Nets stores the names in an encrypted file. Second, the only way you can put your own name on the Mega$Nets list (so others will send you $20) is to first pay all five people on your list $20 for their codes.

To avoid the appearance of a chain letter (which it is), the Mega$Nets "business opportunity" claims that you are selling both the Mega$Nets program (for $20) and computer codes (for another $20) that only the Mega$Nets program can generate. Unlike valid MLM plans where people get a usable product (like vitamins or food supplements), the Mega$Nets plan simply sells everyone the Mega$Nets program itself, which you can only sell to other suckers who think they can make money by selling the Mega$Nets program too.

To view various Web sites created by people who got suckered into the Mega$Nets scam (as shown in Figure 8-2), visit your favorite search engine and look for the "mega$nets" string.

FIGURE 8-2:

Many deluded souls have put up Web sites in an effort to convince others to download the Mega$Nets software and join in on the online scam.

Cracking Mega$Nets

Mega$Nets can be cracked by using the Visual Basic program on the CD included with this book. This Visual Basic program, whimsically dubbed Mega$Hack (as shown in Figure 8-3), can edit the Mega$Nets encrypted data file so you can erase other people's names and add your name to the list without paying anyone $20 for their codes. By cheating, you can either convince others of the futility of relying on Mega$Nets to make money, or you can con others into paying you money because they think you legitimately joined Mega$Nets.

FIGURE 8-3:

With the Mega$Hack
program, you can
display the magical
secret codes embedded
in Mega$Nets.

WORK-AT-HOME BUSINESSES

Besides pyramid schemes, many people receive messages offering them fabulous moneymaking opportunities that can be done at home. Here are some typical scams.

Stuffing envelopes

The most common work-at-home business scam claims that you can earn hundreds of dollars stuffing envelopes in your spare time.

First of all, who in their right mind would want to spend their life stuffing envelopes for a living? If this logic still escapes you, and you actually send money for information on how you can earn money by stuffing envelopes, you need to seriously examine your dreams in life. If you do send money, you'll probably receive the following:

→ A letter stating that if you want to make money, just place your own ad in a magazine or newspaper offering to sell information on how others can make money by stuffing envelopes. In this case, stuffing envelopes is just a pretense to get you to send the company your money in the first place.

113

→ Information about contacting mail-order companies and offering to stuff their envelopes for them. Unfortunately, the money you can make stuffing envelopes is so trivial you'll soon find that stuffing envelopes pays less than making Third World wages. See? They tricked you into thinking that you could actually make money doing mindless work without getting a government job.

Make-it-yourself kits

Another work-at-home business scam offers to sell you a kit (like a greeting card kit) at some outrageous price. You're supposed to follow the kit's instructions to make custom greeting cards, Christmas wreaths, flyers, or other useless products that people are supposed to buy. The business may sound legitimate, but the kit is usually worthless, and the products that it claims you can sell will rarely earn you enough money to recoup the cost of your original investment.

Work as an independent contractor

If you don't want to stuff envelopes or make custom greeting cards, why not pay to work as an independent contractor (once again at a phenomenally inflated price)? This scam typically claims that a company is willing to pay people thousands of dollars a month to help the company build something, like toy dolls or baby shoes. All you have to do is manufacture these items and sell them to the company.

What usually happens is that the work is so boring that most people give up before they even have a chance to sell one product. For those stubborn enough to actually manufacture the products, the company may claim that the workmanship is of poor quality and thus refuse to pay you for your work. Either way, someone else now has your money.

Fraudulent sales

People have been fooled into buying shoddy or nonexistent products for years. The Internet just provides one more avenue for con artists to peddle their snake oil. Two popular types of fraudulent sales involve "miracle" health products and investments.

Miracle health products have been around for centuries, claiming to cure everything from cancer and impotence to AIDS and indigestion. Of course, once you buy one of these products, your malady doesn't get any better—and may actually get worse. In the meantime, you're stuck with a worthless product that may consist of nothing more than corn syrup and food coloring.

Investment swindles are nothing new either. The typical stock swindler dangles the promise of large profits and low risk, but only if you act right away (so the con artist can get your money sooner). Many stock swindlers are frequent visitors to investment forums or chat rooms on America Online or CompuServe and scout these areas for people willing to believe that the stock swindler possesses "ground-floor" opportunities, which entices people to hand money to complete strangers.

Like worthless miracle health products, investment scams may sell you stock certificates or bonds that have no value whatsoever. Typically these investments focus on gold mines, oil wells, real estate, ostrich farms, or other exotic investments that seem exciting and interesting but prove to be nonexistent or worthless.

The Ponzi scheme

One of the oldest and more common investment scams is a variation of a pyramid scheme known as the Ponzi scheme, named after post—World War I financier Charles Ponzi, who simply took money from new investors and used it to pay off early investors. Because the early investors received tremendous returns on their investments, they quickly spread the news that Charles Ponzi was an investment genius.

Naturally, as this news quickly spread, new investors rushed forward with wads of cash, hoping to get rich too. At this point, Charles Ponzi took the new investors' money and disappeared.

Ponzi schemes can usually be spotted by the promise of unbelievably high returns on your investment within an extremely short period of time. If anyone claims that they can double or triple your money with no risk in a week or two, be careful. You may be about to lose your money in a Ponzi scheme.

The infallible forecaster

Any time you receive a letter or email from a stranger who wishes to help you for no apparent reason, watch out. Many con games start by offering a victim something for nothing, which immediately plays off the victim's greed and willingness to cut corners (proving the adage "You can't cheat an honest man").

In this investment scam, a "broker" may contact you and offer you an investment prediction at no charge whatsoever. The purpose is simply to demonstrate the broker's skill in forecasting the market. The broker may tell you to watch a particular stock or commodity—and sure enough, the price goes up, just like the broker claimed.

Soon you may see another message from the same broker, offering still another prediction that a stock price or commodity is about to drop. Once again, the broker simply wants to convince you of his infallible forecasting abilities—and once again, the price does exactly what the broker predicted.

Finally you may receive a message offering a third prediction, but this time giving you a chance to invest. Because the broker's previous two predictions seemed accurate, most people are likely to jump at this chance for a "sure thing," often by giving the broker as much money as possible. At this point the broker takes the money and disappears.

What really happened was that in the first letter, the broker contacted 100 people. In half of those letters, the broker claimed a stock or commodity price would go up; in the other half, that the price would go down. No matter what the market does, at least 50 people will believe that the broker accurately predicted the market.

Out of these remaining 50 people, the broker repeats the process, telling 25 of these people that a price will go up and 25 people that the price will go down. Once more, at least 25 of these people will receive an accurate forecast.

So now the con artist has 25 people (out of the original 100) who believe that the broker can accurately predict the market. These remaining 25 people send the broker their money—and never hear from the broker again.

PACKET SNIFFERS, WEB SPOOFING, AND PHISHERS

Many con games have been around for years; others are brand new to the Internet. The prime con game on the Internet involves stealing your credit card number so the con artist can rack up charges without your knowledge. Con artists have three ways to steal your credit card number: packet sniffers, Web spoofing, and phishing.

Packet sniffers

When you type anything on the Internet (such as your name, phone number, or credit card number), the information doesn't go directly from your computer to the Web site you're viewing. Instead, the Internet breaks this information into "packets" of information and routes it from one computer to another, like a bucket brigade, until the information reaches the actual computer hosting the Web site you're viewing.

Packet sniffers search for credit card numbers by intercepting these packets of information. Typically, someone will plant a packet sniffer on the computer hosting a shopping Web site. That way a majority of packets that are intercepted will contain credit card numbers or other information that a thief might find useful.

Packet sniffers intercept information on the Internet in much the same way that a thief can intercept calls made with cordless or cellular phones. If you order merchandise over a cordless or cellular phone, a thief could intercept your call and steal your credit card number as you recite it over the phone for the order taker.

After the packet sniffer intercepts a credit card number, it copies it and sends the credit card number to its final destination. Consequently, you may not know your credit card number has been stolen until you find unusual charges on your next bill.

To protect yourself against packet sniffers, never type your credit card over the Internet. If you still wish to order merchandise online, Internet advocates suggest that you encrypt your credit card number before sending it through the Internet. Some will say this method isn't as safe as Internet merchants might lead you to believe.

To provide a secure way to send sensitive information (such as credit card numbers) over the Internet, Netscape (http://www.netscape.com) created something called the Secure Sockets Layer (SSL). However, SSL has created a challenge for others to crack its encryption methods, which means even SSL may ultimately not protect your credit card number over the Internet.

Web spoofing

Web spoofing is quite similar to packet sniffing; but instead of secretly installing a packet sniffer on a computer host, Web spoofing involves setting up a fake Web site that either looks like a legitimate online shopping Web site or masquerades as an existing, legitimate Web site (see Figure 8-4).

Fake Web sites often have URL addresses similar to the Web site they're spoofing, such as http://www.micrsoft.com (misspelling Microsoft), so victims will believe they're actually connected to the legitimate site. When you think you're sending your credit card number to a legitimate firm to order merchandise, you're actually handing the thieves your credit card number.

To protect yourself against Web spoofing, make sure you can always see the Web site address in your browser.

If you think you're accessing Microsoft's Web site (http://www.microsoft.com), but your browser claims that you're actually accessing a Web site address in another country, you might be a victim of Web spoofing.

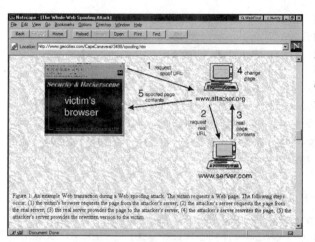

FIGURE 8-4:

Web spoofing tricks your computer into visiting a computer masquerading as a legitimate Web site.

Phishing

The boldest way to get someone's credit card number is just to ask for it. Naturally most people won't hand over their credit card numbers without a good reason, so con artists make up seemingly valid reasons.

Phishing involves contacting a victim by email or through a chat room. The con artist may claim that the billing records of the victim's Internet service provider or online service need updating, so would the victim be kind enough to type their credit card number to verify their account? (See Figure 8-5.) Phishing is especially

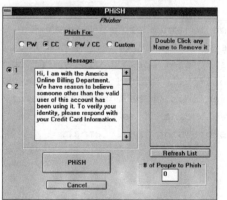

FIGURE 8-5:

A typical phishing feature found in an online harassment program.

popular in the chat rooms of online services like America Online or CompuServe. Many con artists use online harassment programs, as described in Chapter 10, to automate the process of phishing for credit card numbers.

Obviously, no legitimate business has any reason to ask for your credit card number through a chat room or by email. To protect yourself from these scams, make sure you never give out your credit card number to strangers through the Internet or any online service.

REROUTING YOUR INTERNET CONNECTION

Along with Web spoofing, sniffers, and phishers, another Internet-only scam involves rerouting your Internet connection. This scam begins by inviting you to view pornographic graphic files. The catch is that if you want to view these files, you need to download a "free" program.

Once you have downloaded this "free" program, it takes control of your modem, turns off your computer's speakers, cuts off your local Internet connect, and then secretly dials a number in the former Soviet republic of Moldavia.

The more time that people view the pornographic files, the longer they stay connected to this foreign Internet service provider, which may ring up toll charges of $2 to $3 a minute. The customers don't realize they have been scammed until they receive their phone bills.

Although the Federal Trade Commission (FTC) shut down the original scam shortly after it appeared, watch out for copycat scams. Anytime a Web site requires that you download "free" software before you can continue browsing their Web pages, watch out. If you have an external modem, watch the status lights to make sure your modem doesn't disconnect and then mysteriously reconnect all by itself. If you have an internal modem, your only defense is to be careful whenever a Web site lures you into downloading "free" software as a prelude to spending more time browsing the Internet.

ONLINE AUCTION FRAUDS

One of the more recent crazes on the Internet is online auctions where people can offer junk, antiques, or collector's items for sale to anyone who wants to bid on them. But be careful! Besides having to deal with fraudulent bids from people who have no money or intention of buying an item up for auction, consumers have to watch out for con artists selling their own fraudulent items.

The simplest con game is to offer an item for auction that doesn't even exist. For example, every Christmas there is always a must-have toy that normally costs $10 to purchase, but because of its scarcity in stores, it can cost up to several thousand dollars if purchased from a private seller. So many con artists will claim to offer such a product, you send them the money, and the con artist simply disappears.

Other online auction frauds include misrepresentation: For example, selling counterfeit collector's items such as autographed baseballs or sports jerseys. To protect yourself against online auction fraud, follow these guidelines:

→ Identify the seller and check the seller's rating. Online auction sites, such as eBay, allow buyers and sellers to leave comments about one another. By browsing through these comments, you can see if anyone else has had a bad experience with a particular seller.

→ Check to see if your online auction site offers insurance. eBay will reimburse buyers up to $200, less a $25 deductible.

→ Make sure you clearly understand what you're bidding on, its relative value, and all terms and conditions of the sale, such as the seller's return policies and who pays for shipping.

→ Consider using an escrow service, which will hold your money until your merchandise safely arrives.

→ Never buy items advertised through spam. Con artists use spam because they know that the more email offers they send out, the more likely they'll run across a gullible victim who will send them money. If someone's selling a legitimate item, they're more likely to go through an online auction site instead.

The Scambusters Web site (http://www.scambusters.org/ Scambusters31.html) offers additional sage advice:

→ Don't conduct business with an anonymous user. Get the person's real name, business name (if applicable), address, and phone number. Verify this information before buying. Never send money to a post office box.

→ Be more cautious if the seller uses a free email service, such as Hotmail, Yahoo!, etc. Of course, most people who use these services are honest. However, most problems occur when a free service is used. After all, with a free email service, it is very easy for the seller to keep his or her real identity and information hidden.

→ Always use a credit card to purchase online because if there's any dispute, you can have the credit card company remove the charges or help you fight for your product.

→ Save copies of any email and other documents involved in the transaction.

THE FALLACY OF INTERNET MALLS

You may receive email or junk mail urging you to start your own business by offering products or services through an Internet Mall. By selling your products through an Internet Mall (so the mall owner claims), you can realize the benefits of an actual shopping mall with the convenience of the Internet.

Although the cost to set up a "storefront" through an Internet Mall may not always be extravagant, the real con is that Internet Malls fail to provide the same benefits that a physical shopping mall offers. In a real shopping mall, people often browse neighboring stores. But in an Internet Mall, the cusomer has to click on a store to see it. So even though your store is "only a click away," the chances of a customer seeing it are quite slim.

Given the choice between setting up your own Web site or paying someone extra money to set up a storefront in an Internet Mall, you're better off just creating your own Web site. Not only will it be less expensive in the long run, but you'll be able to choose your own easy-to-remember domain name as well. In general, the only people who get rich off Internet Malls are the ones selling the concept to unsuspecting merchants.

URBAN LEGENDS

An urban legend is a story that everyone swears is really true but nobody seems able to find any proof that it ever actually happened. Common urban legend stories include free (but non-existent) promotional offers from major companies like Microsoft or Hewlett-Packard, horror stories about insect parts or other unsavory items found in meals served by popular fast-food restaurants, or terrifying killings or mutilations occurring in certain parts of the world. Urban legends are not only false and potentially libelous, but highly annoying. If you email someone one of these urban legends, it can be as unwelcome as unsolicited email (spam) from advertisers.

To learn more about the various urban legends both past and present, visit About.com (http://urbanlegends. about.com/science/urbanlegends), ScamBusters (http://www. scambusters.org/legends.html), or the Urban Legends Reference Page (http://www.snopes.com).

CREDIT CARD FRAUD

While many people worry about typing and sending credit card numbers over the Internet, the reality is that few credit card numbers are stolen off the Net. Not only would a potential thief need to tap into your Internet account at the exact moment you're sending your credit card number to a Web site, but he or she would have to break the encryption scheme that many Web sites use to protect your credit card numbers online.

If someone's going to steal your credit card number, they're more likely to get it by breaking into the computers of a large organization such as Amazon.com or CD Universe and stealing the credit card numbers stored there. Such companies may have the odd untrustworthy employee who has access to the company's list of customer credit card numbers, and can steal a number simply by copying it off the computer screen.

Credit card fraud is actually much more troublesome for merchants because merchants are responsible for verifying credit card orders. If a thief steals someone's credit card and orders thousands of dollars worth of merchandise, the merchant pays for the loss, not the owner of the stolen credit card.

So if you're a merchant, be extra careful when accepting credit card orders. To help protect your business, follow these guidelines:

→ Validate the full name, address, and phone number for every order. Be especially vigilant with orders that list different "bill to" and "ship to" addresses.

→ Watch out for any orders that come from free email services (hotmail.com, juno.com, usa.net, etc.). Free email accounts are easy to set up with phony identities, which means most credit card thieves will list a free email account when asked for an email address. When accepting an order from a free email account, request additional information before processing the order, such as asking for a non-free email address, the name and phone number of the bank that issued the credit card, the exact name on credit card, and the exact billing address. Most credit card thieves will avoid such requests for additional information and look for a less vigilant merchant to con.

➜ Be especially careful of extremely large orders that request next-day delivery. Thieves usually want their merchandise as quickly as possible before they can be discovered.

➜ Likewise, be careful when shipping products to an international address. Validate as much information as possible by email or preferably by phone.

For more information about protecting yourself from credit card frauds and other online thievery, visit the AntiFraud Web site at http://www.antifraud.com.

PROTECTING YOURSELF

To protect yourself, watch out for the following signs of a scam:

➜ Promises of receiving large quantities of money with little or no work.

➜ Requirements of large payments in advance before you have a chance to examine a product or business.

➜ Guarantees that you can never lose your money.

➜ Assurances that "This is not a scam!" along with specific laws cited to prove the legality of an offer. When was the last time you walked into K-Mart or McDonald's and the business owner had to convince you that you weren't going to be cheated?

→ Ads that have LOTS OF CAPITAL LETTERS and punctuation!!! or that shout "MIRACLE CURE!!!" or "Make BIG $$$$$ MONEY FAST!!!!!" should be viewed with healthy skepticism.

→ Hidden costs. Many scams offer free information, then quietly charge you an "entrance" or "administrative" fee.

→ Any investment ideas that appear unsolicited in your email account.

Just remember: You can't get something for nothing (unless you're the one running a con game on others).

To learn more about scams (whether to protect yourself or to get ideas on how to fleece others), visit your favorite search engine and look for the following strings: scam, fraud, pyramid scheme, ponzi, and packet sniffer.

Or contact one of the following agencies:

Cagey Consumer
Offers updated information about the latest promotions, offers, and con games (http://www.geocities.com/WallStreet/5395/consumer.html).

Council of Better Business Bureaus
Check out a business to see if it has any past history of fraud, deception, or consumer complaints filed against it (http://www.bbb.org).

Federal Trade Commission
Lists consumer protection rules and guidelines that all businesses must follow; also provides news on the latest scams (http://www.ftc.gov).

Fraud Bureau
A free service established to alert online consumers and investors of prior complaints relating to online vendors including sellers at online auctions and to provide consumers, investors and users with information and news

on how to safely surf, shop, and invest on the Net (http://www.fraudbureau.com).

International Web Police
The International Web Police provide law enforcement services for Internet users. Many International Web Police officers are also land-based law enforcement officers who can help resolve crime through the Internet (http://www.web-police.org).

National Fraud Information Center
Issues timely news on the latest scams and the status of ongoing and past investigations. Allows you to lodge your own complaint against a business and read information to help avoid scams (http://www.fraud.org).

ScamBusters
Provides information regarding all sorts of online threats ranging from live and hoax computer viruses to con games and credit card fraud. By visiting this Web site periodically, you can make sure you don't fall victim to the latest Internet con game (http://www.scambusters.org).

Scams on the Net
Provides multiple links to various scams circulating around the Internet. Search through here to make sure any offer you receive doesn't fall under the scam category that has tricked others (http://www.advocacy-net.com/scammks.htm).

ScamWatch
ScamWatch assists victims of Web fraud and scams. Their Web site allows anyone to post suspected scams for other Web users to read and post their comments and/or suggestions concerning these scams. If ScamWatch determines that a scam exists, they'll work to help resolve the problem (http://www.scamwatch.com).

Securities and Exchange Commission

The SEC regulates security markets and provides investing advice, information on publicly traded companies, warnings about investment scams, assistance to investors who believe they may have been conned, and links to other federal and state enforcement agencies. If you're one of those boomers flinging money into the stock market, check it out (http://www.sec.gov).

PART 3

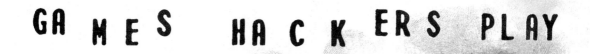

9

Phone Phreaking and Other Phun

PHONE PHREAKING IS ABOUT MANIPULATING THE TELEPHONE SYSTEM IN WAYS THAT THE TELEPHONE COMPANY ITSELF DOESN'T TRULY UNDERSTAND OR BELIEVE IS POSSIBLE. On the noblest level, phone phreaking is about exploring, experimenting, and learning as much as you can about the telephone system out of sheer curiosity. On a more malicious level, it can mean making free phone calls at somebody else's expense, denying phone service to valid customers, or wrecking telephone company equipment.

Unlike computer hacking, which can often be practiced in isolation on a single personal computer, phone phreaking requires more extensive preparation that includes software, hardware, and social engineering expertise. One moment you may be reprogramming the phone company's computers, another you may be soldering wires together to alter a pay phone, and still another you may be chatting with a telephone employee to get the passwords for a different part of the phone system. Like computer hacking, phone phreaking is an intellectual game where players try to learn as much as they can about the system (usually) without breaking any laws to do so.

Technological progress is like an ax in the hands of a pathological criminal.

—ALBERT EINSTEIN

A SHORT HISTORY OF PHONE PHREAKING

In the early days of the phone system, you picked up a telephone and talked to an operator who put your call through. As more people got phone lines, the phone company began to replace its operators with special switching equipment. When you dialed a number, your telephone sent a signal to the switching equipment, which routed your call to its destination. Such switching systems could handle more calls more efficiently than human operators. But they also opened the door to phone phreaking. Trying to trick a human operator into letting you make a free phone call to Brazil was nearly impossible, but tricking a mindless machine into letting you make free phone calls only required sending signals identical to the phone company's. If you knew the right signals, the switching systems would blindly obey your orders.

Perhaps the most famous phone phreak was a man nick-named Captain Crunch because of his accidental discovery of a unique use for a toy whistle found in a box of Cap'n Crunch cereal. He found that blowing this toy whistle into his phone's mouthpiece emitted a 2600 Hz tone, which was the exact frequency used to instruct the telephone com-pany's switching systems.

Other people soon discovered this secret, and some even developed the ability to whistle a perfect 2600 Hz tone. For those unable to obtain the original Cap'n Crunch toy whistle, entrepreneurs started selling devices, known as blue boxes, that simply emitted the 2600 Hz tone. With the introduction of personal computers such as the Apple II, phone phreaks started writing computer programs that could emit the proper 2600 Hz tone from their computer's speaker.

Blue boxes worked as long as the telephone company relied on their old electromechanical switching systems. But eventually these were replaced with newer electronic switching systems (known as ESS), which rendered blue boxes (and the infamous 2600 Hz tone) useless for manipulating the telephone system (although blue boxes may still work on older phone systems outside the United States).

Of course, the introduction of ESS brought a whole new set of problems. With the older electromechanical switching systems, a technician had to physically manipulate switches and wires to modify the switching system. With ESS, techni-cians could alter the switching system remotely over the phone lines.

Naturally, if a technician could perform this feat of magic over the telephone, phone phreakers could do the same—if they only knew the proper codes and procedures to use. Obviously the telephone company wanted to keep this information secret, and the phone phreakers wanted to let everyone know how the telephone system works (which is partly what the ongoing struggle between the telephone company and phone phreakers is all about).

To learn more about phone phreaking, visit one of the following phone phreaking Web sites: Hack Canada (http://www.hackcanada.com), Phone Losers of America (http://www.phonelosers.org), Phone Rangers (http://www.phonerangers.org), SWAT Magazine (http://www.swateam.org), or United Phone Losers (http://www.phonelosers.net). Or try the alt.phreaking and alt.2600.phreakz newsgroups for messages about phreaking.

POSSIBLY TRUE STORIES ABOUT PHONE PHREAKING

If you have a telephone, anyone in the world, including the legions of phone phreakers just goofing around with the telephone system, can call you. Steve Wozniak reportedly once called the Vatican and pretended to be Henry Kissinger. Other phone phreakers have attempted to call the Kremlin through the White House hot line and have rerouted a prominent TV evangelist's business number to a 900-number sex hot line. Because a large part of phone phreaking lore involves performing progressively more outrageous acts and then boasting about them, the following phone phreaking stories may or may not be true. Nevertheless they will give you an idea of what phone phreakers can achieve given the right information. The three stories are "urban myths" circulating around the Internet and are reprinted here verbatim.

The toilet paper crisis in Los Angeles

> One thing that was really easy to do was pop into the AutoVerify trunks by accessing the trunks with that "class mark." You couldn't just dial an 800

number that terminates into Washington DC; you also had to pop over to a trunk class marked for "auto-verification."

This is used when a phone user has to reach some-one and the line is busy. The normal procedure goes like this: The operator selects a special trunk, class marked for this service, and dials either the last five digits of the phone number, or a special TTC code like 052, followed by the whole seven-digit number. After that, the operator hears scrambled conversation on the line. The par-ties talking hear nothing, not even a click.

Next, the operator "flashes forward" by causing the equipment to send a burst of 2600 Hz, which makes a three-way connection and places a beep tone on the line so that both parties originally on the line can hear the initial click (flash, in this case) followed by a high-pitched beep. At this point, the parties can hear you, and you can hear them. Usually, the operator announces that it's an emer-gency, and the line should be released. This is called an "emergency interrupt" and is a service normally reserved for emergencies. It's available today for a $2 fee ($1 in certain areas).

Earlier, I had mapped every 800 number that termi-nated in Washington DC by scanning the entire 800-424 prefix, which then indicated Washington DC.

That scan found an impressive quantity of juicy numbers that allowed free access to Congressional phone lines, special White House access numbers, and so on.

While scanning the 800-424, I got this dude whose bad attitude caught my attention. I determined to find out who it was. I called back and said, "This is White Plains tandem office for AT&T, which sub-scriber have we reached?"

This person said, "This is the White House CIA crisis hot line!"

"Oh!" I said, "We're having problem with crossed lines. Now that I know who this is, I can fix it. Thank you for your time—good-bye!"

I had a very special 800 number.

Eventually my friends and I had one of our info-exchanging binges, and I mentioned this incident to them. One friend wanted to dial it immediately, but I persuaded him to wait. I wanted to pop up on the line, using AutoVerify to hear the conversation.

Our first problem was to extract what exchange this number terminated in, because AutoVerify didn't know about 800 numbers.

At that time, all 800 numbers had a one-to-one relation between prefix and area code. For instance, 800-424 = 202-xxx, where xxx was the three-digit exchange determined by the last four digits. In this case, 800-424-9337 mapped to 202-227-9337. The 227 (which could be wrong) was a special White House prefix used for faxes, telexes, and, in this case, the CIA crisis line.

Next we got into the class marked trunk (which had a different sounding chirp when seized) and MF'ed KP-054-227-9337-ST into this special class marked trunk. Immediately we heard the connection tone and put it up on the speaker so we would know when a call came in.

Several hours later, a call did come in. It did appear to have CIA-related talk, and the code name "Olympus" was used to summon the president. I had been in another part of the building and rushed into the room just in time to hear the tail end of the conversation.

We had the code word that would summon Nixon to the phone. Almost immediately, another friend started to dial the number. I stopped him and recommended that he stack at least four tandems before looping the call to the White House.

Sure enough, the man at the other end said "9337."

My other friend said, "Olympus, please!"

The man at the other end said, "One moment sir!" About a minute later, a man that sounded remarkably like Nixon said, "What's going on?"

My friend said, "We have a crisis here in Los Angeles!"

Nixon said, "What's the nature of the crisis?"

My friend said in a serious tone of voice, "We're out of toilet paper, sir!"

Nixon said, "WHO IS THIS?"

My friend then hung up. We never did learn what happened to that tape, but I think this was one of the funniest pranks — and I don't think that Woz would even come close to this one. I think he was jealous for a long time.

To the best of my recollection, this was about four months before Nixon resigned because of the Watergate crisis.

The Santa Barbara nuclear hoax

General Telephone, once the sole phone service for Santa Barbara, used older equipment. Some calls into certain exchanges got routed through inter-region exchanges. A lot of these used the older 2600 Hz—pulse method of signaling.

One of my phone-phreak friends got the bright idea of dialing out on two lines at once to see what happens. Normally, one line would be busy, and the other one would get through. But sometimes, this would jam the lines on both sides of the trunk but still indicate the trunk was free. In telephone talk, this creates a "glare" condition, where one side glares at the other. Calls coming in would just terminate into emptiness, and the trunk would appear to be free to the trunk selector.

Eventually calls came in that terminated to our phone(s). One of my pranky friends said the following to a caller: "What number are you calling? This is a special operator!" The other person said they were calling Santa Barbara and gave us the number. My friend asked, "What area is that in?" then said, "We've had a nuclear accident in that area, please hang up so we can keep the lines open for emergencies only."

Pretty soon, others called—some reporters and other official types. When calls really started to pour in, we broke the connection.

That next day, the Los Angeles Times carried a short news article headlined "Nuclear hoax in Santa Barbara." The text explained how authorities were freaked out and how puzzled they were. The phone company commented, "We don't really know how this happened, but it cleared right up!" Five years later, Santa Barbara replaced that old faulty equipment with newer electronic systems.

The President's secret

Recently, a telephone fanatic in the Northwest made an interesting discovery. He was exploring the 804 area code (Virginia) and found that the 840 exchange did something strange. In all of the cases except one, he would get a recording as if the exchange didn't exist. However, if he dialed 804-840 followed by four rather predictable numbers, he got a ring!

After one or two rings, somebody picked up. Being experienced at this kind of thing, he could tell that the call didn't "supe," that is, no charges were being incurred for calling this number. (Calls that get you to an error message or a special operator generally don't supervise.) A female voice with a hint of a southern accent said, "Operator, can I help you?"

"Yes," he said, "What number have I reached?"

"What number did you dial, sir?"

He made up a number that was similar.

"I'm sorry. That is not the number you reached." Click.

He was fascinated. What in the world was this? He knew he was going to call back, but before he did, he tried some more experiments. He tried the 840 exchange in several other area codes. In some, it came up as a valid exchange. In others, exactly the same thing happened—the same last four digits, the same southern belle.

He later noticed that the areas where the number worked were located in a beeline from Washington, DC, to Pittsburgh, Pennsylvania. He called back from a pay phone.

"Operator, can I help you?"

"Yes, this is the phone company. I'm testing this line and we don't seem to have an identification on your circuit. What office is this, please?"

"What number are you trying to reach?"

"I'm not trying to reach any number. I'm trying to identify this circuit."

"I'm sorry, I can't help you."

"Ma'am, if I don't get an ID on this line, I'll have to disconnect it. We show no record of it here."

"Hold on a moment, sir."

After about a minute, she came back. *"Sir, I can have someone speak to you. Would you give me your number, please?"*

He had anticipated this and had the pay phone number ready. After he gave it, she said, *"Mr. XXX will get right back to you."*

"Thanks." He hung up the phone. It rang. INSTANTLY! *"Oh my God,"* he thought, *"They weren't asking for my number — they were confirming it!"*

"Hello," he said, trying to sound authoritative.

"This is Mr. XXX. Did you just make an inquiry to my office concerning a phone number?"

"Yes. I need an identi- . . ."

"What you need is advice. Don't ever call that number again. Forget you ever knew it."

At this point my friend got so nervous he just hung up. He expected to hear the phone ring again, but it didn't.

Over the next few days, he racked his brains trying to figure out what the number was. He knew it was something big — so big that the number was programmed into every central office in the country. He knew this because if he tried to dial any other number in that exchange, he'd get a local error message, as if the exchange didn't exist.

It finally came to him. He had an uncle who worked in a federal agency. If, as he suspected, this was government related, his uncle could probably find out what it was. He asked the next day and his uncle promised to look into it.

When they met again, his uncle was livid. He was trembling. "Where did you get that number?" he shouted. "Do you know I almost got fired for asking about it? They kept wanting to know where I got it!"

Our friend couldn't contain his excitement. "What is it?" he pleaded. "What's the number?"

"IT'S THE PRESIDENT'S BOMB SHELTER!"

He never called the number after that. He knew that he could probably cause quite a bit of excitement by calling the number and saying something like, "The weather's not good in Washington. We're coming over for a visit." But my friend was smart. He knew that there were some things that were better unsaid and undone.

GETTING STARTED

To start phone phreaking, you need access to a telephone other than your personal phone. Phreaking from your own phone will not only cost you in phone charges, but also provide the telephone company with a convenient way to track you by tracing your phone line. To be a true phone phreak, you need access to the telephone system and a way not to get billed.

"SHOULDER SURFING" CALLING CARD NUMBERS

The crudest level of phreaking is known as shoulder surfing, which is simply looking over another person's shoulder who is typing in a calling card number at a public pay phone.

The prime locations for shoulder surfing are airports, because travelers are more likely to use calling cards rather than spare change to make a call. Given the hectic nature of a typical large airport, few people will notice someone peering over their shoulder while they punch in their calling card number, or listening in as they give it to an operator.

Once you have another person's calling card number, you can charge as many calls as you can to it until the victim receives the next billing statement and notices your mysterious phone calls. As soon as the victim notifies the phone company, they will usually cancel that calling card number, and you'll have to steal a new calling card number. Since it is theft, true phone phreakers look down on calling card number stealing as an activity unworthy of anyone but common thieves and juvenile delinquents.

TELEPHONE COLOR BOXES

The simplest method to access the telephone system anonymously is through a pay phone, and one of the earliest ways phone phreaks learned to manipulate the telephone system was through telephone "color boxes." These boxes emit special tones or physically alter the wiring on the phone line, allowing anyone to make free phone calls, reroute phone lines, or otherwise raise havoc with the phone system.

Although the Internet abounds with different instructions and plans for building various telephone color boxes, just remember that many of them no longer work with today's phone system—although they might work in other countries or in rural areas. To satisfy your curiosity, though, here are some descriptions of various color boxes that others have made and used in the past. But first, a warning from a phone phreaker regarding the legality of building and using such boxes:

> You have received this information courtesy of neXus. We do not claim to be hackers, phreaks, pirates, traitors, etc. We only believe that an alternative to making certain info/ideas illegal as a means to keep people from doing bad things - is make information free, and educate people how to handle free information responsibly. Please think and act responsibly. Don't get cockey, don't get pushy. There is always gonna be someone out there that can kick your ass. Remember that.

Aqua box

The surest way to catch a phone phreak is to trace his phone calls. One technique the FBI uses is called a Lock-in-Trace, which allows the FBI to tap into a phone line much like a three-way call connection. Because every phone connection is held open by electricity, the Lock-in-Trace device simply cuts into a phone line and generates the same voltage as when the phone line is being used. The moment you hang up, the Lock-in-Trace device maintains the voltage of the phone line as if the phone were still in use, thus allowing the FBI (or anyone else) to continue tracing the origin of a particular phone call.

The aqua box simply lowers the voltage level on a phone line, preventing the Lock-in-Trace device from maintaining the necessary voltage to keep the line open (and possibly even shorting out the Lock-in-Trace device itself). It should block any attempt by the FBI (or anyone else) to trace your phone call.

Beige box

A beige box mimics a lineman's handset, which means that you can do anything a telephone company lineman can. Just open up any of the telephone company's protective metal boxes (usually found on a street corner), attach your beige box to an existing phone line (preferably not your own, which would defeat the whole purpose of the beige box), and you can make free long-distance calls at your neighbor's expense or eavesdrop on their calls.

Black box

Before you receive a phone call, the voltage in your phone line is zero. The moment someone calls you and the phone starts ringing, the voltage jumps to 48V. As soon as you pick up the phone, it drops to 10V, and the phone company starts billing the calling party.

A black box keeps the voltage on your phone line at a steady 36 volts so that it never drops low enough to signal the phone company to start billing—incoming callers never get billed for talking to you.

Cheese box

A cheese box tricks the phone company into thinking that your ordinary phone is actually a pay phone that can make outgoing calls but can't accept incoming calls. Cheese boxes were supposedly invented by bookies as a way of making calls to people while making it impossible for others (such as the police) to call them.

Crimson box

A crimson box is a device that lets you put someone on hold so that they can't hear you but you can still hear them. Great for listening to what telemarketers say to their co-workers when they think you're not listening.

Lunch box

The lunch box connects to an ordinary phone and turns that phone into a transmitter. That way you can use a receiver and eavesdrop on other people's phone calls while listening from a safe distance away.

Red box

Each time you drop a coin into a pay phone, the pay phone sends a tone over the line. When you toss in enough coins, the telephone company opens up the line so you can place a call. The red box simply generates the same tones that the pay phone generates when it receives a coin. By playing the tones from a red box into the mouthpiece of a pay phone, you can fool the phone company into thinking that you dropped coins into the pay phone, thus allowing you to make a free phone call.

Many of the above color boxes were developed to work with the older phone systems, which means they may not work with your phone systems. Of course, if you happen to live somewhere remote that hasn't updated its phone system, or if you're living in a country that still uses obsolete telephone equipment, you might experience better results. Since phone phreaking is about experimenting, you could try these telephone color boxes at your own risk and see what happens.

COLOR BOX PROGRAMS

To make a telephone color box, you often needed to solder or connect different wires together. But with the popularity of personal computers, people soon wrote programs to mimic the different telephone color boxes (see Figure 9-1). By running a telephone color box program on a laptop computer, you can experiment with the phone system from any pay phone in the world.

Of course, personal computers aren't the only tools available to phone phreaks. If you visit the Hack Canada (http://www.hackcanada.com) Web site, not only can you learn about hacking the Canadian phone system, but you can also download the source code to telephone color box programs (dubbed RedPalm) that run on a PalmPilot handheld computer.

By using the RedPalm program, you can make your PalmPilot emit tones that mimic the sounds made when you put real money into a Canadian payphone. The tones make the pay phone respond as if you had dropped in a nickel, dime, or quarter, letting you make phone calls for free.

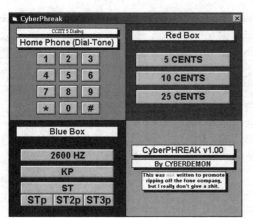

FIGURE 9-1:

With the right program, any computer can be turned into a telephone color box.

In addition to using a personal computer or PalmPilot to run telephone boxing programs, a group of hackers calling themselves TeamKNOx has released a program called PhreakBoy, which mimics red and blue telephone boxes and includes C source code. The PhreakBoy program even runs on Nintendo GameBoy systems.

WAR DIALERS AND PRANK PROGRAMS

Besides writing programs to mimic telephone calling boxes, phone phreakers have also created special programs called war dialers or demon dialers. War dialers are an old, but still effective, method for breaking into another computer (see Figure 9-2).

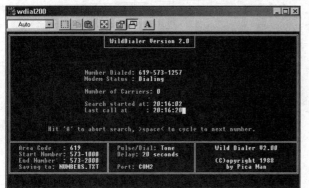

FIGURE 9-2:

A war dialing program relentlessly dials phone numbers, looking for answering modems that reveal a possible entrance into a computer.

War dialers work by hunting for telephone lines connected to a modem and a computer, which means that every person, corporation, and organization are potential targets. Because most people don't advertise their modem numbers, war dialers dial a range of phone numbers and keep track of any of the dialed numbers that respond with the familiar whine of a computer modem. A hacker can then use this list and dial each number individually to determine what type of computer he has reached and how he might be able to break in to it.

For example, many businesses have special phone lines that allow traveling employees to control their desktop computers with their laptop computers and special remote-control software, such as pcAnywhere, RapidRemote, or CarbonCopy. If a hacker finds this special phone number and uses a copy of the same remote-control software, guess what? With the right password, the hacker can take over the desktop computer too and then erase or copy all of its files.

Since war dialers can dial a number over and over again, they can also be used to harass people. Some of the more unusual harassment programs include a pager program that repeatedly dials a victim's pager number and randomly types in a phone number. Other phone harassment programs dial a single number over and over again at random intervals or play a computer-generated voice to insult a caller the moment he or she picks up the phone (see Figure 9-3).

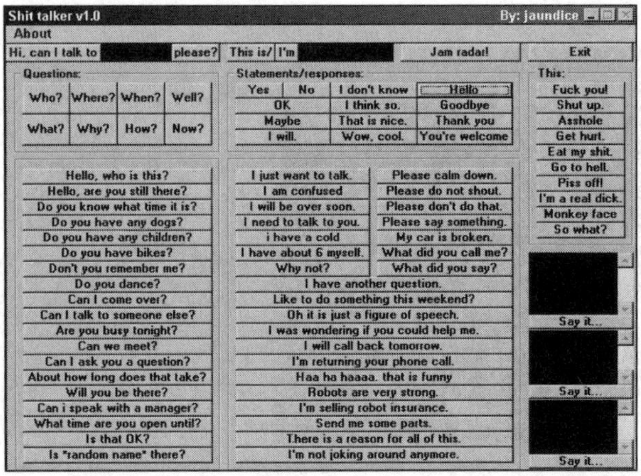

FIGURE 9-3:

With the right program, you can harass others over the phone using your personal computer.

(Just remember that with caller ID, available in most parts of the country, a victim can track your phone number, so it's not a good idea to call from any phone number that can be traced back to you.)

VOICE MAILBOX HACKING

Voice mail is the corporate alternative to answering machines. Rather than give each employee a separate answering machine, voice mail provides multiple mailboxes on a single machine. Because a voice mail system is nothing more than a programmable computer, phone phreaks quickly found a way to set up their own private voice mailboxes buried within a legitimate voice mailbox system.

The first step in hacking a voice mail system is finding the system's phone number — something a war dialer can do for you. (Many voice mailboxes even have toll-free numbers, so don't forget to scan those numbers too.) If you have legitimate access to a voice mail system, you could practice hacking into it so you have a better idea of what to expect when you work on somebody else's.

When you call a voice mail system, you might have to press a special key, such as * or #. Then a recording will usually ask for a valid mailbox number, typically three or four digits. After choosing a mailbox number, you'll need a password to access the mailbox, play back messages, or record your own messages.

People will usually choose a password that's easy to remember (and easy to guess). Some people base their password on their mailbox number, so try typing the mailbox number itself or backward (if the mailbox number is 2108, try 8012 as the password). Other people might use a password that consists of a repeated number (such as 3333) or a simple series (6789).

Once you manage to guess a password, you'll have free access to the voice mailbox, which means you can play back or erase any stored messages. Of course, if you start erasing somebody's messages, they'll notice fairly quickly and get the system administrator to change the password to lock you out again.

Most voice mail systems always have several empty mailboxes, either leftovers from previous employees or extra capacity for anticipated newcomers. Voice mailbox hackers simply hunt around a voice mailbox system until they find an unused mailbox that they can claim for themselves.

After they've claimed a voice mailbox, hackers can send and retrieve messages from their buddies all over the world. Many companies are providing mailboxes for hackers without even knowing it while other companies ignore or tolerate this minor transgression. As long as the hackers don't mess up the voice mail system for legitimate users, it's often cheaper just to pretend they don't exist on the system at all.

CELLULAR PHONE FRAUD AND TV SATELLITE DESCRAMBLING

With the introduction of cellular phones, a whole new realm has opened up for phreaks. Unlike a beige box, which requires a physical connection to make a free call on an existing phone line, cellular phone theft requires only a radio scanner.

Even when your cellular phone isn't in use, it must constantly transmit its electronic serial number (ESN) and mobile identification number (MIN) so the cellular network knows where to send an incoming call. With a radio scanner and additional data-capture equipment, a thief can capture and store the ESN and MIN of a legitimate cellular phone. Later, the thief can program the stolen ESN and MIN into another cellular phone. All calls made from this "cloned" cellular phone now get billed to the victim's cellular phone.

(The cellular phone equivalent of shoulder surfing calling card numbers is to sign up for cellular phone service using a fraudulent name. Then just use the service until the cellular phone company cuts you off for nonpayment.)

To prevent cellular phone "cloning," phone companies now use encryption. When a user makes a call with these newer cellular phones, the cellular network asks for a special code. Legitimate cellular phones will be able to supply the proper authentication code; cloned cellular phones will not.

Cable and satellite TV companies face a similar problem: Cable and satellite TV broadcasts often get intercepted by people using special receivers and descramblers. By browsing the Internet, you can even find companies that sell plans, instructions, and actual kits for building your own cable or satellite TV descrambler (for educational or legitimate purposes only, of course!).

To buy cable or TV satellite descrambler equipment, kits, or instructions, visit one of the following Web sites: http://www.acelectronics.com, http://www.cable-tv-descramblers.net, or http://www.covertelectronics.net.

The corporations continue to develop more sophisticated methods for protecting their broadcasts, and the video pirates always come up with new methods for cracking the protection schemes. Video pirates often claim that if the broadcasting companies lowered their prices, fewer people would steal their services. Broadcasting corporations make the counter-claim that the cost of fighting the pirates keeps prices artificially high.

The question is, if video pirates and cellular phone cloners disappeared overnight, would corporations lower their prices? If you think so, then perhaps video pirates and cellular phone thieves deserve to be caught. But if you think that corporations would keep their prices the same whether they had to absorb the cost of fighting thieves or not, then video pirates and cellular phone thieves might be considered modern-day Robin Hoods after all.

Be careful if you steal service from the telephone or cable TV companies. Stealing service for yourself is enough to earn you a free trip to the police station, but if you get greedy and try to resell the service to other people, you're really asking for trouble.

Of course, if your government restricts the flow of information, stealing from the telephone and cable TV companies may be the only way to communicate with others and receive news from the rest of the world. Ultimately, you have to decide if you're breaking the law out of greed or rebellion against unfair government laws. And take the consequences.

10

Harassing Others Online

NEARLY EVERYONE HAS HEARD HORROR STORIES ABOUT THE INTERNET. Pornography abounds, mentally deranged perverts stalk innocent victims while posing as women or children, hackers lie in wait to steal your credit card numbers. Sounds scary, right? But there's no need to be a victim. Once you learn how people stalk, harass, and attack others online, you'll know how to protect yourself against such threats.

CYBERSTALKING

The Internet is full of people, just like the real world. And you can do many of the same things online that you do in your "bricks-and-mortar" world: make friends, share information, even fall in love. But you can also be conned online. Or be used by someone you thought you could trust. Even worse, the Internet allows anyone to contact you at any time, spawning a new breed of online harassment known as *cyberstalking*.

Cyberstalking is like physical stalking except it's done over the Internet, usually through harassing or threatening email messages. Once a cyberstalker has a little bit of information about you (such as your email address or real name), he can find other personal information fairly easily through online directories and white pages (see Chapter 7).

What the cyberstalker wants

Most cyberstalkers are men, and most victims are women or children. Cyberstalkers may already know their victims or they may simply target someone they meet in a chat room. No matter what the relationship between the cyberstalker and his victim, the goal is usually to repeatedly harass, intimidate, or annoy the victim. Many cyberstalkers enjoy the "power" they hold over a victim who can never tell when or what the cyberstalker may do next. The more pain and distress a cyberstalker can cause you, the happier he feels.

Some cyberstalkers are less malicious, but still intimidating and annoying. For example, some cyberstalkers "fall in love" with and ceaselessly harass their victim with inquiries, gradually escalating into angry threats if the victim refuses to respond in a certain way. These cyberstalkers may claim they really love their victims, but the end result is the same—intimidation, fear, and harassment.

Eventually, some cyberstalkers move from the Internet to the real world. No longer is their threat merely "virtual." In the real world, cyberstalkers pose very real physical dangers. Once a cyberstalker has learned some personal information about his victim, he can make crank phone calls, send harassing letters in the mail, run up excessive charges on the victim's credit card, or (most dangerous of all) confront the victim in person.

Protecting yourself against cyberstalking

Since most cyberstalkers are men, their most obvious and frequent targets are women. To avoid attracting attention to yourself, make up a gender-neutral name. Calling yourself The Wizard of Words is a lot less noticeable than calling yourself SexyPussyCat (or even simply Jane). Besides targeting women, cyberstalkers also target novices (because they're easier to harass since they usually aren't aware of the different ways they can protect themselves).

Once a cyberstalker has singled out a victim, he often tries to learn some personal information about the target such as age, place of employment, phone number, and so on. One of the easiest ways a cyberstalker can find personal information about someone is by visiting that person's Web site. Many people happily post information about themselves on a Web site that they would never dare give out through a

154

chat room. But a Web site is every bit as public and accessible as a chat room. So if you're going to create a Web site, be careful of what you post.

Because you may not even be aware that you're being stalked, it's best to just avoid giving out any personal information at all. Also consider using a free email service (such as Hotmail or Yahoo) so you can lose a cyberstalker by abandoning your free email account.

Since cyberstalkers thrive on the pain and anguish they cause a victim, one of the best weapons against a cyberstalker is silence. By ignoring any comments a cyberstalker sends, you deprive him of the satisfaction of controlling you, and he'll likely move on to find a more cooperative victim.

If, despite being ignored, a cyberstalker continues to harass you, you should save all evidence in case he becomes a real stalker. You'll have a much stronger case in court if you ever need to take legal action.

If you keep your personal information to yourself, avoid flirting or antagonizing others online, and ignore any threatening people you may meet in chat rooms, you can minimize the chances that a cyberstalker will want to go after you. For more information about protecting yourself against cyberstalking, visit the Los Angeles County District Attorney Web site at http://www.lovemenot.org, CyberGuards at http://www.cyberguards.com/CyberStalking.html, or the WHOA (Women Halting Online Abuse) site at http://www.haltabuse.org/harass.html.

In fact, WHOA got its start after Jayne Hitchcock became a 3-year victim of cyberstalking. In 1996, Hitchcock wrote a complaint to other writers on the Usenet newsgroup misc.writing about the Woodside Literary Agency, which ran a scam asking writers to send them a $50 to $250 reading fee—at which point the agency would never contact the writers again.

After Hitchcock wrote about the predatory practices of the Woodside Literary Agency, she became the target of an email bomb that flooded her email account. She then started to find her name, address, and phone number posted on various Usenet newsgroups insulting the newsgroup members, and inviting people to call her any time to discuss their sexual fantasies.

Hitchcock believes the email bomb attack and the phony newsgroup postings were the work of Ursula Sprachman and James Leonard, the two owners of the Woodside Literary Agency. Federal prosecutors soon arrested the pair and charged them with conspiracy to commit mail fraud. In addition, Hitchcock is suing the pair for 10 million dollars in one of the first recorded cyberstalking harassment lawsuits.

THE INTERNET AND PEDOPHILIA

Popular online services such as America Online prohibit their members from using obscenity or transferring pornography through their services. In theory, this sounds perfect for families with children. In practice, these rules are enforced as often as politicians take pay cuts. And it's precisely because services like AOL seem safe for unsupervised children that they have attracted so many pedophiles and have become online stalking grounds.

How pedophiles stalk children

If you're horrified at the thought of a pedophile contacting your child online, one solution is to pull out your modem and stop using Internet services. Doing so will guarantee that no pedophile will find your child online, but it will also deny your child the many useful resources offered by service providers like AOL. You do have other options, though.

For example, America Online offers a parental control feature that allows you to selectively block portions of the service from your child. However, unless you know what portions to block, this feature won't be of much use.

Chat rooms, where members can type messages to one another in real time, are one of AOL's most popular features for both legitimate use and as a hunting ground for pedophiles. Because talk in chat rooms happens instantaneously, without supervision, as soon as one kid in Boston types a message, children in Seattle, Houston, and Chicago can read that message and respond to it. But chat rooms are like costume parties—people often mask their identities, including age and sex, which means that the kid from Boston might really be a middle-aged man.

Typically, a pedophile will enter a chat room geared toward children, such as a homework-help chat room. After watching the conversations and perhaps typing a few messages of his own, he looks for a victim. At this point, the pedophile has no idea whether a particular nickname belongs to a real child or another adult pretending to be a child.

To find a suitable target, the pedophile directs a few innocent remarks toward several other chat room members. The responses can help identify which nicknames belong to adults and which belong to children (misspellings and simple language are the most common giveaways). After focusing on nicknames that seem to belong to actual children, the pedophile is ready for the next step.

Private messaging leads to a private meeting

Chat rooms let you communicate with public and private messages. Public messages appear on the screen for everyone in the chat room to read. Private messages can only be read by the person who sent it and the person who receives it.

Once a pedophile has identified nicknames belonging to real children, he sends a private message to one or more of his chosen targets. Usually these private messages ask more personal questions, such as the child's age, favorite foods, or hobbies. During this stage, the pedophile tries to gain the child's trust and friendship.

Eventually, the child may have to leave the chat room, so the pedophile arranges a time when they can meet in a chat room again. Because many children think they have found a new friend, they often readily agree. As the pedophile gains the trust of the child, he'll start asking more personal questions to determine where the child lives, what his or her parents do for a living, and when they might be out of the house.

After several weeks or months, the pedophile may suggest meeting in person, even if it means that the pedophile has to fly to another city to meet his victim. Because the child may still be unaware of his new "friend's" true intentions, he or she may give out personal information such as a home address or phone number.

Because pedophiles don't want to meet their potential victim's parents, they'll play off a child's desire for secrecy. When arranging a place and a time to meet, they tell the child, "Don't tell your parents where you're going." Depending on the child's relationship with his or her parents, the child may balk and tell his parents anyway, or he may go along with the pedophile's suggestions as a way to rebel against his parents. After all, the idea of a secret meeting with a new friend can be exciting.

Of course, pedophiles rarely meet most of their intended targets. Either the child stops using chat rooms, gets bored with his new "friend," or becomes suspicious and breaks off the relationship. But pedophiles can be patient, and whether it takes one or one hundred tries, they're willing to continue stalking chat rooms for children— because they know that eventually they'll find one child gullible enough to believe their sweet promises.

Protecting your kids from online pedophiles

The best way to protect your child from pedophiles online is to supervise their online activities and turn on safety features such as America Online's parental controls to block access to chat rooms, as shown in Figure 10-1 (AOL keyword: Parental Control).

To help friends find one another online, AOL offers a special feature called a Buddy List. You list your friends in your Buddy List and the moment any of your friends dial into AOL when you're connected, your Buddy List notifies you.

Of course, online stalkers can also use this feature. Once a pedophile has visited a few chat rooms, he can put all the names of his chosen victims in his own Buddy List. That way if your child connects to AOL at the same time the pedophile is online, the pedophile's Buddy List immediately notifies him so he can send a message to your child. By using a Buddy List, a pedophile can stalk fresh victims in

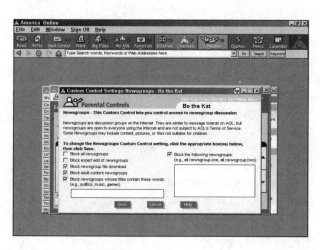

chat rooms while lying in wait for previously targeted victims as well.

To further protect your child from pedophiles, turn off the Buddy List feature to prevent your child's nickname from being put on anyone's Buddy List. Although this effectively prevents your child's friends from using the Buddy List to contact each other, it also prevents any pedophiles from knowing when your child is connected to AOL. (Just make sure that if you turn off the Buddy List feature, your child doesn't turn it back on again.)

Protecting your kids from instant messaging pedophiles

Pedophiles love AOL because of the many children who use that service, but don't think that avoiding AOL can keep your kids safe from pedophiles. Pedophiles also stalk instant messaging services like ICQ, PowWow, and AOL's Instant Messager.

Unlike AOL, instant messaging services provide far fewer controls for screening potential threats. To use AOL, you need to sign up with a credit card. But to sign up with ICQ or any of the other instant messaging services, you don't need to supply any personal information, making it easy to hide behind this additional layer of anonymity when stalking a victim online.

So how can you protect your children from pedophiles who use an instant messaging service? If you don't want to ban the use of instant messaging altogether, the best protection is to watch your child's computer use at all times. If this isn't possible, you can also use a monitoring program like Kid Control (http://www.kidcontrol.com), which records your child's computer activity so you can review it later, or a blocker like Enuff (http://www.akrontech.com), which limits the times kids can use the computer.

Parental control programs can reduce the risk of pedophiles stalking your children through an instant messaging service, but your best bet is to teach your child the following basic rules:

→ Never give out your real name, location, or phone number.

→ Never meet anyone in person who you've met online.

→ Never give out your email address. If a child needs to share email addresses, set up a free email account with a service such as Hotmail. This can make it more difficult for anyone to trace an email address to a physical location.

→ Never believe that people online are really who they say they are. Once a child understands that people often masquerade under different identities, they may be less apt to believe anything someone tells them online.

TRADING PORNOGRAPHY ON AMERICA ONLINE

AOL's rules state that you cannot transmit obscene or pornographic material through its services. Theoretically, this makes AOL safe for children and families to use. Realistically, expecting AOL to enforce its rules is hopeless. Figure 10-2 shows a typical list of chat rooms available on AOL 24 hours a day, 7 days a week.

AOL offers plenty of chat rooms where people can participate in *cybersex* (typing dirty messages to one another)

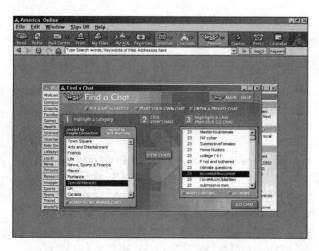

FIGURE 10-2:

America Online offers sexually oriented chat rooms.

or swapping pornographic files showing naked men, women, and children doing practically everything with anything. Despite AOL's public image as a family-oriented online service, it's used just as often to trade pornography as it is to trade computer tips or hobby information.

People commonly trade pornography over AOL by visiting a chat room and asking if anyone would like to swap GIF (graphic) files. Once two members agree to trade, they simply email the pornographic file to the other AOL member.

FINDING DIRTY PICTURES ON COMPUSERVE

Although many horror stories about online stalking and pedophiles center around AOL, they can happen anywhere—whether you use AOL, CompuServe, Prodigy, the Microsoft Network, or just a plain Internet account. The problem isn't the Internet or the online service, but the fact that the Internet can help anyone communicate with anyone else.

Although finding pornographic files on AOL is pretty simple if you're willing to take the time to visit a few chat rooms and send private messages to others, you might be surprised to learn that CompuServe openly allows the trading of pictures showing naked men and women.

By visiting the Adult Forum main menu (GO ADULT), you can view CompuServe's adult-oriented forums, which allow anyone to post, trade, and copy cartoons and photographs of naked men and women in various poses. Ostensibly, these forums provide an opportunity for models, photographers, and artists to showcase their work. As a result, you won't find hard-core pornography here, although you'll still find full frontal nudity.

Before you can access these areas, you'll have to fill out an Adult Content Agreement to confirm your age (no one's checking) and list a password. Like AOL, CompuServe also offers a parental control feature (GO CONTROLS) that lets you block access to adult-oriented forums; but because most parents don't even know these forums exist (or how to use CompuServe's parental control software), don't be surprised if you find your children eagerly visiting these forums.

HARASSING AN ONLINE SERVICE

America Online, CompuServe, and Prodigy have all made their share of blunders over the years. Besides America Online's history of censoring email, CompuServe once pulled the plug on entire Internet newsgroups because the German government considered them obscene. In their earlier incarnation, Prodigy once censored email as rigorously as America Online, causing widespread dissatisfaction among its members.

Given the constant, clumsy, and often unnecessary actions of online services trying to protect their services from pornography, obscenity, or just plain naughty words, it's no surprise that many people retaliate against them. Here are a few examples.

Generating fake online accounts

One of the most popular ways to harass an online service is to create a bogus account using a fake credit card number. Because online services want members to sign up as soon as possible, the moment you type in a valid credit card number, you can start using the entire online service right away.

The legal way to get a free account on an online service is to sign up with one credit card, cancel your account when your free trial period is over (typically one month or a fixed amount of usage, such as 50 hours), then sign back on to the same service with a different credit card, getting an additional free trial period. This method works as long as you can come up with different credit card numbers.

Because most hackers don't have multiple credit cards, they do the next best thing and create their own credit card numbers instead. Credit card companies, such as VISA or American Express, create their credit card numbers using a mathematical formula. You'll note that credit card numbers are rarely similar, and you'll never find two people with credit card numbers that differ by only one number because of the possibility of erroneously charging one person for another person's purchases.

Rather than try to guess the mathematical formula used to create valid credit card numbers, hackers just use special credit card—generating programs like Credit Master, Credit Card Commando, and Credit Wizard, as shown in Figure 10-3. These programs create credit card numbers using the same mathematical formula used by your own credit card company.

When you sign on to an online service with a credit card number created by a card generating program, the online service just checks to make sure the number is valid

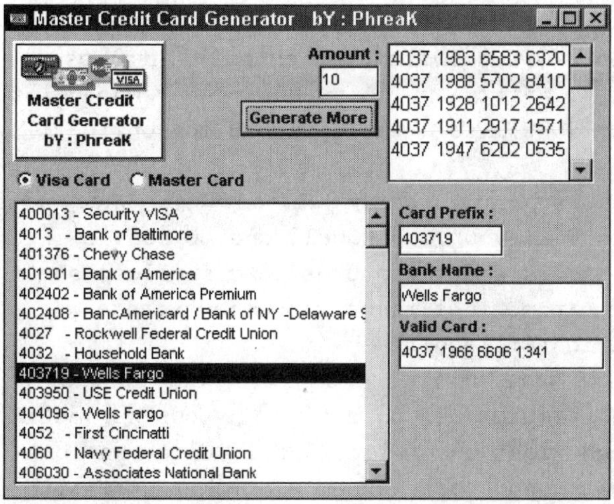

FIGURE 10-3:

A credit card-generating program can help you create a temporary account on an online service using a fake credit card number.

according to the credit card's mathematical formula. If the number is valid, the service lets you create an account. The service won't verify that the credit card number is valid for a day or two, so until the service catches on to your fake credit card number, you'll have free rein to download files, visit chat rooms, or do whatever else you want. And, if you use a fake name, address, and phone number, the service will never catch you—unless they take the time to trace your phone call.

The moment the online service finds out that you're using a fake credit card number, they can ask the phone company to trace your call from their dial-up connection phone number to your home. As long as you use fake credit card numbers sparingly, the service probably won't take the time to track you down.

CREATING HAVOC WITH ONLINE HARASSMENT PROGRAMS

Using an account created by a fake credit card number allows you to access the online service for free with little risk of getting caught. As a result, many people who create fake accounts also use special harassment programs such as AOHell for additional amusement.

AOHell

The first, and most famous, online harassment program is called AOHell (http://www.aolwatch.org/chronic2.htm) as shown in Figure 10-4. Written by an ex-AOL member who calls himself Da Chronic, AOHell sets the standard for online harassment programs.

AOHell runs in conjunction with AOL software. Once you're connected to AOL, you load AOHell and up pops a floating window that lists its features in a simple push-button interface—features that range from the extremely useful to the downright illegal.

Many of AOHell's more devious features focus around chat rooms. If a particular person grates on your nerves in a chat room, you can fight back with AOHell. Click one button and AOHell draws a gun pointing at a stick figure with

FIGURE 10-4:

The splash screen from AOHell.

the name of the person publicly displayed for all in the chat room to see. Click another button and AOHell scrolls an ASCII drawing of a raised middle finger.

If displaying insulting images is too tame for you, AOHell offers a special Punter feature, which floods a victim's computer with so much nonsensical data that either the computer crashes or the victim leaves the chat room in annoyance.

Sometimes people escape harassment by forming a private chat room. To get around this tactic, AOHell has a special chat room buster for forcing your way into private chat rooms. Once inside, you can harass members with a mass-mailer that sends email messages to every chat room participant. This trick can be particularly sneaky if you email someone a virus or Trojan Horse.

If someone starts harassing you in a chat room, you can let AOHell take care of the problem automatically with its auto-answering bot. This feature automatically sends back a message to anyone who types in certain key words (such as four-letter words).

AOHell also offers a fake "forward message to" feature, specifically designed to let you send email to America Online administrators, falsely claiming that another person is violating America Online's rules. The goal is to harass America Online's administrators and have them waste their time tracking down non-existent problems so they won't have time to investigate real ones.

Although AOL users are repeatedly warned that they should never give out passwords or credit card numbers to anyone online, some people still don't realize the danger. AOHell offers a password/credit card fisher that takes advantage of them. Just enter a chat room, click the Fisher button, and AOHell sends an official looking message to the person of your choice, claiming that America Online's billing department needs that person's password or credit card number (Figure 10-5).

FIGURE 10-5:

The AOHell program offers a Phishing feature for conning people out of their credit card numbers or AOL password.

Obviously, this AOHell feature can be exploited for illegal use; but now that you know it exists, it should remind you never to give out passwords online, and to give out other important information such as credit card numbers only when you are sure you are dealing with a reputable business.

Although AOHell was one of the first and most popular online harassment programs, copycat programs have popped up to harass AOL and similar online services such as CompuServe. Some examples are Icy Hot, CompuDaze, Apocalypse Now, CompuDemon, AOTurkey, LameProd, CISHack, Freon (see Figure 10-6), and America Flatline. Most of these programs offer similar features, although some require a password to use them (which you can find on various hacker Web sites).

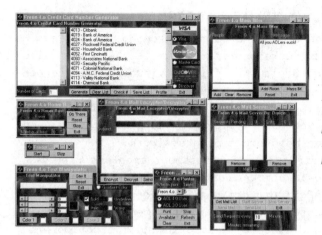

FIGURE 10-6:

Freon provides a variety of features for creating fake accounts, busting into chat rooms, encrypting your email, kicking other people offline, and flooding multiple people with email.

FINDING CREDIT CARD GENERATORS AND ONLINE HARASSMENT PROGRAMS

Credit card generators and online harassment programs can be found on many hacker Web sites. But these hacker Web sites tend to disappear with alarming regularity. Most manage to last for a few months before America Online (or another online service) threatens the Web site with legal action to force it to shut down.

The easiest way to find an online harassment program is to visit the Web Ring Web site (http://www.webring.org), click on the Computer Underground category under the Computers heading, and click on any Web ring that uses the term AOL in its name such as AOL Sux. You should see a list of hacker Web sites that distribute various online harassment programs you can download.

Or visit one of the many anti—online service newsgroups:

alt.aol	alt.online-service.compuserve
alt.aol-sucks	alt.online-service.prodigy
alt.compuserve-sucks	alt.online-services.compuserve
alt.msn-sucks	alt.hackers.aol
alt.msn.sucks	

167

WRITING YOUR OWN ONLINE HARASSMENT PROGRAM

Rather than use an online harassment program written by someone else, many hackers prefer to write their own using Microsoft's Visual Basic. Not only is Visual Basic inexpensive, but it allows anyone (including hackers) with little programming experience to write a Windows program quickly and easily. Once you have a copy of Visual Basic, you need to know how online harassment programs work.

Most of the first online harassment programs used two special Visual Basic commands called AppActivate and SendKeys. The AppActivate command loads and runs another program. In the case of an online harassment program, the AppActivate command is used to load the communication program for America Online, CompuServe, or Prodigy.

The SendKeys command mimics a person typing at the keyboard. For example, the SendKeys command can type a phrase, press CTRL-X, or choose menu commands from any program defined by the AppActivate command.

The combination of the AppActivate and the SendKeys commands lets you write a Visual Basic program that can type keystrokes into another program as if you were typing them yourself.

At the simplest level, an online harassment program is nothing more than a fast, automated typist that lets you raise havoc on the online service of your choice. If you were a fast typist, you could harass an online service just by typing insults or commands yourself; but because most people can't type at the speed of light, they let an online harassment program do the typing instead. That way they can quickly pop in and out of various forums or chat rooms on the online service, cause havoc, and disappear just as quickly as they arrived.

Unfortunately, the SendKeys and AppActivate commands are often slow and unreliable for anything more complicated than typing text automatically. For faster response, more reliability, and more powerful features, the latest versions of online harassment programs directly access the *Windows Application Programming Interface* (WAPI) commands.

Accessing the WAPI commands allows programs to directly access the internal workings of the Windows operating system, giving you control over any program running under Windows, such as the America Online communications program. A handful of hackers have taught themselves how to access WAPI commands directly through Visual Basic and have saved their work in special library files (with names like JAGUAR32.BAS or MASTER32.BAS) so that others can access WAPI commands without having to learn the specific details of the different WAPI commands.

No matter what technique an online harassment program uses, online harassment programs use the same programming techniques that legitimate online service add-on programs use (add-on programs automate features such as deleting email quickly or responding in a chat room with a prewritten response). Because they want to keep the add-on programs working, online services can never defend themselves against an online harassment program.

If you want to create your own online harassment program, you can either write one from scratch or modify an existing one. If you want to modify a program, you can get the VB source code for an older online harassment program such as AOHell from any hacker Web site. Keep in mind, though, that online harassment programs only work with specific versions of communications programs, such as AOL 4.0 or AOL 5.0.

But if you want to peek at the source code to a newer online harassment program, you may have to decompile it. To decompile a Visual Basic program, you need a program called the VB Decompiler, which is available on many hacker Web sites. This program dissects any program created by Visual Basic (version 3.0 or earlier) and generates the source code for you to examine. By using the VB Decompiler, you can decompile your favorite online service harassment programs to see how they work. Once you have generated the Visual Basic source code, you can copy or modify the source code and create your own online harassment program.

IRC HACKING

Rather than harass a specific online service such as CompuServe or America Online, many people prefer causing trouble through *Internet Relay Chat* (IRC) channels. IRC, one of the oldest forms of Internet chat, lets you type and view messages in real time.

To chat over IRC, you need three items:

→ An IRC client program (which allows you to com-municate with others)

→ Access to an IRC server (which allows you to physically connect to an IRC network)

→ An IRC channel

IRC actually consists of several different networks with obscure names such as EFnet, DALnet, and StarLink. To use IRC, load an IRC client program on your computer (you'll find some of the more popular ones on the CD) and then connect to a server. Windows IRC clients include mIRC (http://www.mirc.co.uk), Pirch (http://www.pirchat.com), and Visual IRC (http://www.visualirc.com). Macintosh clients are Ircle (http://www.ircle.com) and ShadowIRC (http://www.shadowirc.com).

After connecting to a network server, choose a specific channel within that network where each channel focuses on a specific topic, such as C++ programming or tropical fish breeding. (For a complete guide to setting up and using IRC, pick up *The Book of IRC* by Alex Charalabidis, pub-lished by No Starch Press.)

Scripts

Once you have an IRC client, you can automate it with scripts. Many hackers write scripts to attack others while others write and use scripts to protect themselves against attack. You'll find lots of such scripts at these Web sites:

Free-Scripts.com   http://www.free-scripts.net

Hackers.com   http://www.hackers.com

Hawkee.com	http://hawkee.com
mIRCScripts.com	http://mircscripts.com
mIRC-Scripts	http://www.mirc-scripts.net
mIRC4U	http://mirc4u.com
mIRCNet	http://www.mirc.net
Scripting Crypt	http://www.scriptingcrypt.com
Xcalibre	http://www.xcalibre.com

Flooding

One popular form of IRC harassment is *flooding*, or
sending excessive data to crash a victim's computer by over-
loading its memory. An attacker can use flooding to kick
someone out of a channel. If an attacker manages to kick
everyone out of a particular channel, he or she can control
the channel and prevent others from getting back in.

   If you find yourself the target of a flooding attack,
the easiest solution is to identify the flooder's nickname
and then put him or her on your *ignore list* (a list of people your computer will not accept messages from). For
further protection, you can find script files that automatically defend against flooding.

Bots

A *bot* (short for robot) is a program that can run by itself
without any intervention from its creator. Many IRC people
use bots to automate simple tasks like greeting everyone
who joins a particular channel. Others use them as offensive weapons. For example, an attacker can create multiple
bots and cause a flooding attack by having each bot send
data to some unsuspecting victim. An attacker could also
create a bot that types insulting messages under your
favorite nickname, thereby wrecking your online reputation.

Cloaking

An IRC attacker is said to *cloak* behind your nickname when
he or she takes over your nickname while you are logged on.
Anything a cloaker does appears to come from the nickname

they've cloaked. For example, a cloaker who takes over your nickname can type insulting messages using your identity. An attacker can also use cloaking to fool others into thinking that you're actually the attacker. Then, while other people start berating you for causing trouble, the real attacker fiendishly romps about to make you look foolish or threatening.

To defend against cloaking, be sure that your nickname doesn't suddenly start typing messages you didn't write. If it does, start typing your own messages to tell others that an attacker is cloaking your nickname. Then change your nickname right away. Once an attacker is no longer cloaked behind a valid nickname, others will be able to easily spot him.

Nukes

A nuke breaks a victim's connection with the IRC server, throwing him or her off an IRC server completely. There are two types of nukes: operating system nukes and port nukes.

Operating system nukes

An *operating system nuke* exploits flaws in a particular operating system to crash or freeze it. For computers running Microsoft Windows, the most common operating system nuke is an *out-of-band attack* (OOB) where a hacker deliberately sends "out-of-band/urgent" data that Windows can't handle, causing it to crash. To exploit this flaw in Windows, hackers have written a variety of programs with names like IceNuke, Teardrop, SPING, or Divine Intervention (see Figure 10-7).

Operating system nukes can crash or freeze your computer unless you've installed a patch for your particular operating system. Unfortunately, hackers discover new operating system flaws every day, which means that the operating system patch you install today may not protect you against any exploits discovered tomorrow.

To keep up with the latest security holes in different operating systems, visit AntiCode (http://www.antionline.com/cgi-bin/anticode/anticode.pl), Insecure.org (http://www.insecure.org), or Packet Storm (http://packetstorm.securify.com).

FIGURE 10-7:

Divine Intervention is a popular IRC attacking tool that can flood, nuke, or mail bomb a victim.

Port nukes

Port nukes, often sporting colorful names such as Death 'n Destruction, BitchSlap, or Winnuke, are less dangerous than operating system nukes but still troublesome: They attack the port a victim uses to access the Internet. By sending bogus or random data to that specific port, a nuker can foul up the victim's Internet connection. After getting hit by a port nuke, you may have to redial or switch to a different Internet account.

ICQ HACKING

ICQ (http://web.icq.com) is a program that allows anyone connected to the Internet to instantly send a message to anyone else registered and using ICQ. Unlike IRC, ICQ doesn't require users to visit the same chat room at the same time to chat with one another. To use it, download and run ICQ, register your nickname, and ICQ assigns you a *UIN* (Universal Internet Number). Now people can contact you through your nickname or your UIN the moment you log on to the Internet.

While instant messaging may seem useful and fun, ICQ's real power comes from writing your own programs that hook into the ICQ program. To help make ICQ the Internet standard for instant messaging, Mirabilis has released a special ICQ Applications Programming Interface (API) so developers can write programs that support ICQ, such as games, videoconferencing or Internet telephone service.

Of course, any time you provide developers with tools, some people will create legitimate add-ons and others will create an entirely unexpected family of hacking tools. With ICQ's growing popularity, it was only a matter of time before people started releasing programs specifically designed for hacking ICQ. Figure 10-8 shows a few of the features available in a program called Infra Red's ICQ

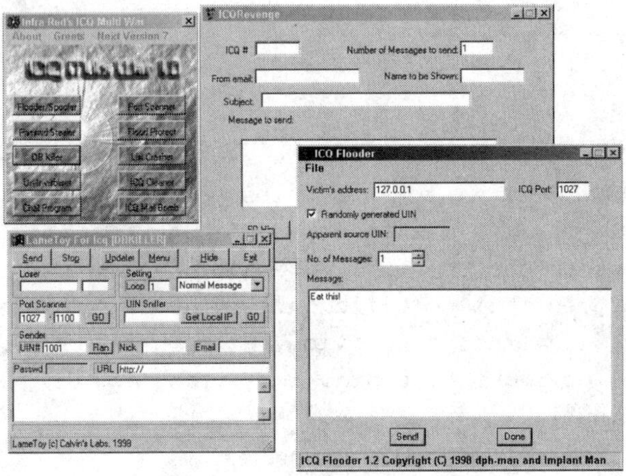

FIGURE 10-8:

ICQ hacking programs offer a variety of features for harassing other ICQ users.

Multi War. Using ICQ hacking tools, you can harass someone with insulting messages, mask your own identity so nobody can track you down, or steal another person's password so you can hijack their account.

Message flooding

Since ICQ is designed to send and receive messages, some of the more popular ICQ hacking programs are *message flooders*, which let you bombard another ICQ user with one or more messages. But for every offensive weapon, there is a defensive tool. With names like ICQBombsquad, ICQSWAT, and Deflooder, these defensive programs can automatically delete unread messages so you don't have to delete them manually and waste your time. That way, if you get flooded with annoying messages, a program like ICQSWAT can eliminate unwanted messages instantly, making message flooding a minor irritation instead of a major annoyance and inconvenience.

If you know the nickname or UIN of the person flooding you with multiple messages, you can turn on ICQ's Ignore feature. Any nickname or UIN stored in your Ignore list will be blocked from contacting you.

Spoofing

Flooding someone with harassing or threatening messages is pointless if you identify yourself with your ICQ nickname or UIN—you might as well mail threatening letters with your return address printed neatly on the envelope. To get around this problem, many ICQ hacking programs include a special *spoofing* feature that lets you bombard a victim with a flood of harassing messages and have each message look like it came from a different ICQ user. If you use spoofs, your victim won't know who to ignore and you'll be able to harass your victim over and over again.

But, of course, hackers have created programs to defend against spoofing. If you're being stalked online and you don't know the stalker's nickname or UIN, you can use general-purpose ICQ protection programs like Warforge ICQ Protect, ICQ Watch, or ICQ Hacking Utility Protector. These programs guard against all types of message flooding, whether they come from spoofed or actual UINs.

Defeating authorization lists and tracking invisible people

ICQ's Authorization feature lets you choose who will be notified the moment you log on to the Internet. When turned off, anyone can track you the moment you log on to the Internet; when turned on, you are visible only to those people to whom you have specifically granted permission.

You can defeat this Authorization feature with *ICQ Auto Authorize*. To track someone you're unauthorized to track, just add the nickname or UIN of that person and run the ICQ Auto Authorize program when the ICQ program tells you that you need permission from your chosen person. Now you'll be able to track this person even if she has her Authorization feature turned on.

ICQ also offers an Invisible feature, which prevents people from knowing when you're online. If you're Invisible, ICQ can still notify you when others have logged on, but they won't know when you're logged on. Unless, of course, they have a hacker program that can unmask any ICQ user using the Invisible feature.

Stealing passwords

If you can physically access a victim's computer, you can run a program, such as ICQr Information (see Figure 10-9) to read the ICQ database file with their personal information (like a list of their favorite contacts, email address, street address, and most importantly, their ICQ password). Armed with their ICQ password and identification number, you can spoof their identity. To get a copy of ICQr Information, visit its Web site at http://icqrinfo. headstrong.de.

PROS AND CONS OF HARASSING OTHERS ONLINE

If an online service, such as America Online, catches you harassing its members, their reaction can be as simple as cutting off your real (or fake) online service account, or as drastic as having you arrested for credit card fraud, illegal computer use, and whatever other crimes you commit.

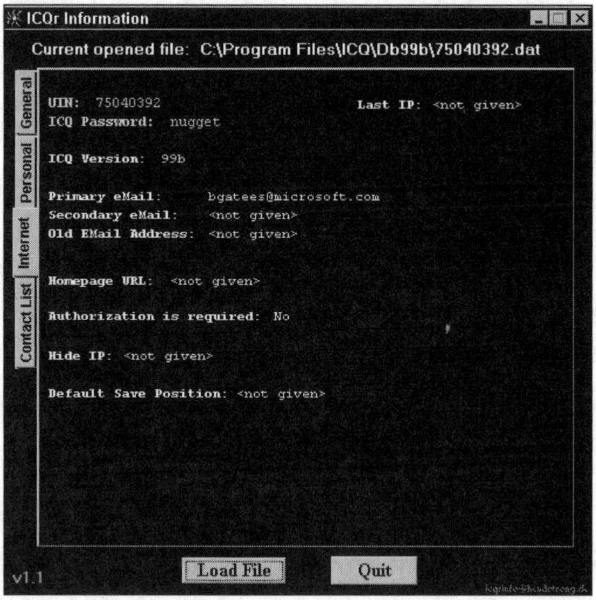

FIGURE 10-9:

With the ICQr Information hacking program, you can read a person's private information including their password.

But don't think that harassing others online is just for bad guys trying to spoil other people's fun. Many self-proclaimed online vigilantes, such as CyberAngels (http://www.cyberangels.org), Condemned.org (http://www.condemned.org), PedoWatch (http://www.pedowatch.org/leinfo), and AntiChildPorn.org (http://www.antichildporn.org) haunt online services, Web sites, and IRC channels specifically to track online stalkers such as pedophiles. The moment they find a pedophile trying to recruit a child in a public chat room, an online vigilante may use an online harassment program to send a warning to the offender, set off a mail bomb to flood the offender's email box, or just boot the offender off the online service as punishment.

Online vigilantes may also use hacker tricks to fool the pedophile into providing personal information about himself so law enforcement officials can identify and track that person down later. One online vigilante has even set up a Gnutella Wall of Shame (http://www.zeropaid.com/busted) that lists the IP addresses of people caught trying to download child pornography images.

An online harassment program, like any tool, can be used for either good or ill effect. Abuse it and you can make the lives of legitimate online service members miserable. But use it to defend children against pedophiles, and you may be considered a hero.

11

Break ing and Entering

ANYTHING YOU TYPE ON A COMPUTER CAN COME BACK TO HAUNT YOU.
No matter how well you've hidden your data or how many
times you may have encrypted it, there's always a chance
that someone somewhere will be able to find and read what
you have written.

So if you really want to get information about other
people or learn how to protect yourself from others trying
to get into your computer, keep reading. The secrets inside
your computer can be pried open easier than you think.

DEFEATING PASSWORDS

Although passwords restrict access to a computer, they're
the weakest link in any security system. The most secure
passwords are lengthy, consisting of random characters.
But most people tend to choose simple, easy-to-remember
passwords and use the same password for several different
systems (for example, their work computer, America Online
account, and Windows screensaver). If you discover a person's password, you'll often have the key to their other
accounts as well.

You have several methods of attack any time a computer
requires a password, and you don't know what it is:

➔ Disable or circumvent the program that
requires the password

➔ Steal a valid password

➔ Use a dictionary attack that methodically
tries common passwords

*The key to the
treasure is the
treasure.*

—JOHN BARTH

Disabling or circumventing a password

Often you will need a password to access someone's computer system. There are two common ways that computer systems are password-protected:

→ Use the operating system screensaver

→ Use a separate security program

Defeating the Windows 95/98 screensaver

The simplest way to defeat a Windows 95/98 password-protected screensaver is to turn off the computer and turn it back on (pressing CTRL-ALT-DEL won't work). When the computer comes back on, you should have complete access to the computer. Then you can right-click on the desktop, choose Properties, click on the Screen Saver tab when the Display Properties dialog box appears, and uncheck the Password-protected check box.

For the really devious, try assigning a new password instead of disabling password-protection. To do so, keep the Password-protected check box checked and click on the Change button. Then type in a new password for the screen-saver. Now anyone who tries to access this computer will be locked out unless he or she can guess the new password you registered.

Another way to break into a password-protected computer is to avoid loading security or opening menu programs that may run on start-up and lock you out of the computer. To avoid loading these programs, reboot the computer and press one of the following keys as soon as you see the "Starting Windows 95/98" message on the screen:

F8   Pressing F8 displays the Windows 95/98 start-up menu, which lets you choose whether to load Windows 95/98 without any start-up programs or go straight to MS-DOS.

SHIFT-F5   Pressing SHIFT-F5 bypasses any start-up programs and displays the MS-DOS prompt.

| **SHIFT-F8** | Pressing SHIFT-F8 allows you to step line by line through the start-up procedure so you can selectively choose which programs you want to load. |

Defeating third-party screensavers and security programs

Not everyone relies on the Windows screensaver for password protection, but you should be able to beat third-party screensavers the same way: Turn the computer off and on again, then use one of the above methods of holding down the F5, F8, or SHIFT keys (for Windows 3.1) or F8, SHIFT-F5, or SHIFT-F8 (for Windows 95/98) to keep the screensaver or security program from loading.

You probably won't be able to circumvent the better security programs by rebooting the computer. To get around these sophisticated programs, boot from a floppy disk to load MS-DOS, and then use MS-DOS commands to copy, move, or delete files on the hard disk at your leisure. If a third-party security program still blocks your access even after rebooting, you may have to resort to stealing the password to the security program.

Stealing a password

The easiest way to steal a password is by shoulder surfing—peeking over someone's shoulder as they type in a password. If that doesn't work, poke around the person's desk. Most people find passwords hard to remember so they often write them down and store them where they can easily find them, like next to their monitor or inside their desk drawer.

Still can't find that pesky password? Try one of these:

➜ A keystroke logger

➜ A desktop monitoring program

➜ A password recovery program

NOTE All of these programs require that you have access to the victim's computer so you can install or run the programs without the user's knowledge.

Using a keystroke recorder or logger

Keystroke recorders or "loggers" are programs that record everything a person types and either sends their typing to a monitoring computer or saves it to a file (see Figure 11-1). Since they simply record typing, it doesn't matter whether passwords are encrypted. When the user is away, you can remove the keystroke logging program from their machine and retrieve its logging file containing the password and anything else they typed.

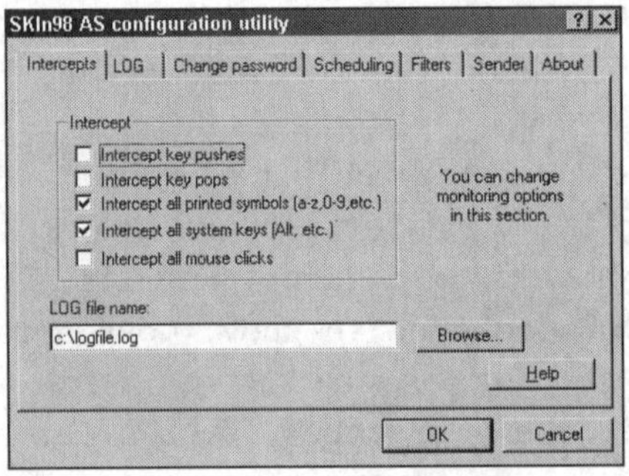

FIGURE 11-1:

A keystroke logger can record everything you type.

While many loggers were originally written for legitimate purposes, people have found creative ways to use them. (The program WinWhatWhere was originally written as a time and billing tool.) Remember, though, if you use one on someone's computer without permission you could be breaking Federal eavesdropping laws, punishable by up to five years in prison and $250,000 in fines.

Keystroke logging programs tend to be fairly small, so they're easy to hide on a victim's computer. Hackers have written and posted some simple keystroke logging programs with names like Playback, KeyTrap, or Phantom, but many companies have released shareware versions of keystroke loggers too, which you can find at sites like Download.com or Rocketdownload.com. Some of the more popular shareware and commercial keystroke logging programs include KeyKey (http://mikkoaj.hypermart.net), Keystroke Recorder (http://www.campsoftware.com/camp), and Stealth Keyboard

Interceptor (http://www.geocities.com/SiliconValley/Hills/8839/index.html).

Some keylogging programs, such as SureShot Ghost Keylogger (http://home.swipnet.se/~w-94075/keylogger) and Stealth Activity Recorder and Reporter (http://www.iopus.com/), can secretly email you the recorded keystrokes. Parents or employers may legitimately use a keystroke logger to see what their children or employees are doing. Hackers, though, may use keystroke loggers for less than legitimate puroposes, such as capturing valuable information such as passwords without having to physically access the targeted computer.

D.I.R.T.

Many hackers also use keystroke logging to capture credit card numbers, passwords, and encrypted data through remote access Trojan Horses like Back Orifice (see Chapter 16). Turning the tables on the hackers, law enforcement officials use a similar program called D.I.R.T. (Data Interception and Remote Transmission), available from Codex Data Systems (http://www.thecodex.com).

D.I.R.T. can secretly record keystrokes and email the captured keystrokes to another computer. That way law enforcement officials can capture evidence as the suspect types it in. If someone is secretly recording and reading your captured keystrokes, even the best encryption won't protect you. The Peeping Tom who is looking into your computer will already have the password you used to encrypt your data, as well as every keystroke you typed before encrypting your file.

Spying with a desktop monitoring program

Desktop monitoring programs (see Figure 11-2) are slightly more sophisticated than keystroke loggers. Like a computer surveillance camera, they secretly record the programs a person uses, how long the person uses each program, the Web sites viewed, and every keystroke. Many monitoring programs can store days of recordings, and some can be set to record at designated times only, when certain applications are run, or when a user logs on to the Internet.

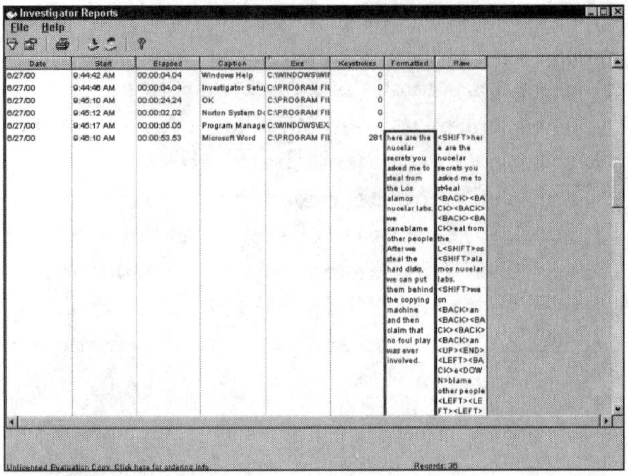

FIGURE 11-2:

Investigator monitors a user's computer activity.

Like keystroke loggers, many desktop monitoring programs were designed for legitimate use. Many people use them to protect their computer from abuse or to monitor their children's computer (see Figure 11-3). Desktop monitoring programs are also perfect for less-than-legitimate uses, such as spying on another person's computer. If you do, be sure to use the stealth mode so the user won't know that the program is tracking their actions. Then, when the person leaves, go back to the target computer to retrieve the captured data.

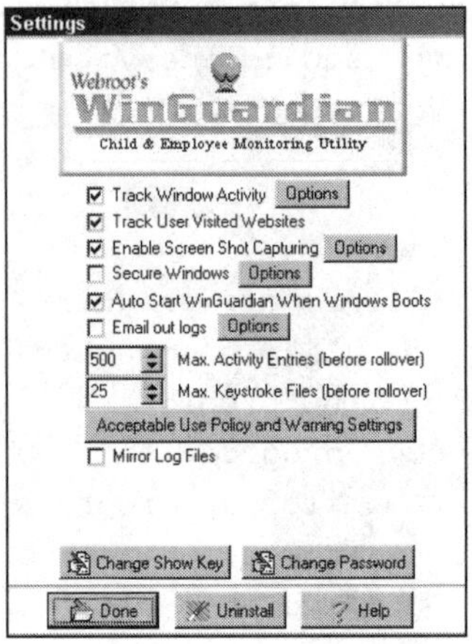

FIGURE 11-3:

A desktop monitoring program can track every program and keystroke used on a specific computer.

Like loggers, you can find several shareware versions of desktop monitoring programs at sites like Download.com. For specific programs, try these sites: AppsTraka (http://appstraka.hypermart.net), Desktop Surveillance (http://www.omniquad.com), WinWhatWhere Investigator (http://www.winwhatwhere.com), Security Officer (http://www.compelson.com), or WinGuardian (http://www.webroot.com).

Remotely viewing another computer's desktop

Desktop monitoring programs are useful if you have regular access to the computer you want to watch. But if you don't, you can use a remote desktop monitoring program instead. Just install a program such as QPeek (http://www.qpeek.com), NetBus (http://www.netbus.org), I-SeeU (http://www.faxtastic.com), or PC Spy (http://www.softdd.com) on the computer you want to monitor. Then anything someone types, views, or manipulates on that computer will appear live on your computer's screen.

Using a password recovery program

Because typing a password over and over again to access a program can be a nuisance, many programs let you store passwords directly in the program, hidden behind a string of asterisks (see Figure 11-4). Because people often forget these passwords and then can't access their programs or files, password recovery programs have been developed to retrieve these lost or forgotten passwords. You can, of course, also use these programs to retrieve other people's passwords.

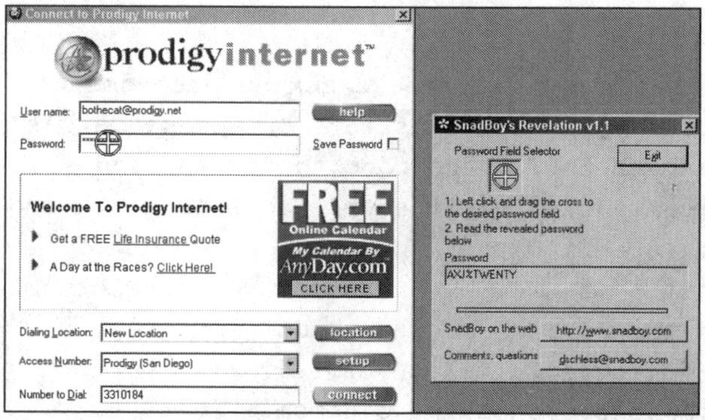

FIGURE 11-4:

The Revelation password recovery program can reveal the password needed to access a user's Internet account.

There are many shareware versions of password recovery programs. Look for 007 Password Recovery (http://www.iopus. com), Password Recovery Toolkit (http://www.lostpassword. com), or Revelation (http://www.snadboy.com).

Besides blocking access to a program, passwords can also block access to files like WordPerfect documents or Microsoft Excel spreadsheets (see Figure 11-5). To retrieve or crack password-protected files, get a special password-cracking program from one of these companies: Access Data (http://www.accessdata.com), Alpine Snow (http://www. alpinesnow.com), Crak Software (http://www.crak.com), ElCom (http://www.elcomsoft.com), Password Crackers Inc. (http://www.pwcrack.com), or Passware (http://www. lostpassword.com).

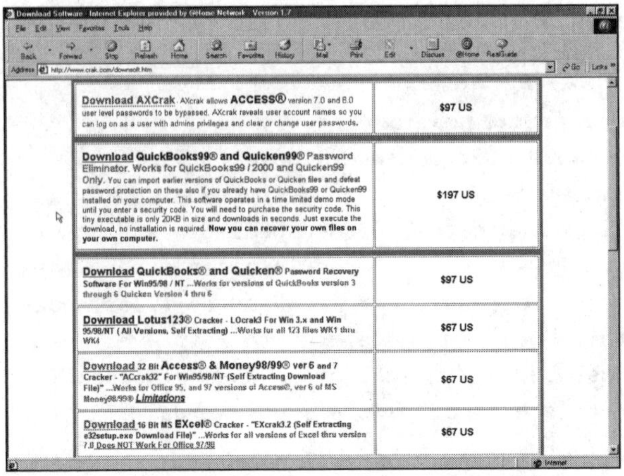

FIGURE 11-5:

A variety of password-cracking programs are readily available for purchase over the Internet.

You can also find plenty of free cracking programs on hacker Web sites or through Crak Software or Access Data's Web sites. Many provide the source code too so you can see how they work. Surprisingly, their source code is short and relatively simple, revealing the incredible weakness of the encryption algorithms used by Microsoft Word or Lotus 1-2-3. By studying the source code, you can learn how to crack open password-protected files yourself or even how to write your own password-cracking program.

If you need to retrieve passwords from a computer running Windows NT, grab a copy of the L0phtCrack program from the L0pht Heavy Industries Web site (http://www.l0pht.com). Windows NT encrypts user passwords—the L0phtCrack program simply studies these encrypted passwords and attempts to decrypt them.

Dictionary attacks on passwords

Most people choose easy-to-remember passwords, so hackers have created special dictionary files (sometimes called word lists) that contain common passwords such as actors' names, names of popular cartoon characters, popular rock bands, Star Trek jargon, common male and female names, technology-related words, and common words found in most dictionaries.

Password-cracking programs take each word from a dictionary file and type it into the program as a password until it finds one that works or runs out of words. If the password works, you have access to the program you want. Of course, if it runs out of words in its dictionary file, you can try other dictionary files until you find a valid password or run out of dictionary files. If a password is an ordinary word, it's only a matter of time before a dictionary attack will uncover it. To foil a dictionary attack, sprinkle some random characters (such as symbols and numbers) in your passwords or use a special password-generating program such as PassGen (http://www.noodlesoft.co.uk) or Quicky Password Generator (http://www.quickysoftware.com), which can create truly random passwords of varying lengths.

You can create your own password lists for use in a dictionary file with a dictionary-making program; these programs create random word combinations, words consisting of all uppercase or lowercase, words with random symbols mixed in, and so on (see Figure 11-6). (Dictionary attacks are most useful when you don't have to worry about being spotted, as when you're breaking into a remote computer through a phone line or the Internet.)

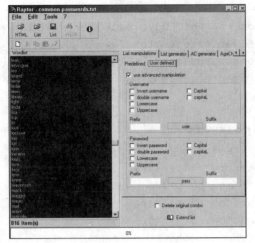

FIGURE 11-6:

You can create your own dictionary files or manipulate existing ones to make additional password lists.

To find dictionary files, use a Web search engine to search for "dictionary file" or "word lists." You can find a number of shareware and password crackers at Download.com, with names like Ultra Zip Password Cracker, CracPak, and Password List Recovery.

Using a dictionary attack to defeat UNIX passwords

UNIX operating systems are designed to handle multiple users on a single computer. To isolate users from one another, each user has an account defined by an ID or user name and a password.

Conveniently (for both hackers and system administrators), most UNIX systems store the list of account names and passwords in the /etc/passwd file. To provide a small degree of security, UNIX encrypts each person's password using an encryption algorithm (also called a hash function), usually using the Data Encryption Standard (DES).

To gain access to UNIX computers, hackers copy the /etc/passwd file to their own computer so they can run a dictionary attack that tries common passwords from a list of words encrypted with DES. If it finds a match between an encrypted word on its list and an ecrypted password in the file, then it knows it has found a legitimate password. At this point, the hacker can use that password to gain access to that unlucky person's account.

To increase the chances of finding a valid password, UNIX password-cracking tools like John the Ripper or CrackerJack not only try commonly used passwords, but also variations of those common passwords (typing them backwards or adding a 1 or 9 to the end or beginning). While this slows down the overall cracking process, it does make sure the dictionary attack isn't fooled by a simple variation on a common password.

PART 4

DESTRUCTIVE THREATS ON THE INTERNET

12

Internet Hacking

ON SEPTEMBER 1998, HACKING MADE THE FRONT PAGE OF THE *NEW YORK TIMES* WEB SITE WHEN A GROUP, CALLING THEMSELVES HFG, REPLACED THE ORIGINAL *NEW YORK TIMES* HOME PAGE WITH THE HFG LOGO, WHERE EACH LETTER OF THE LOGO TEASINGLY SHOWED A DIFFERENT NAKED WOMAN. Although this Web site hack made international headlines, it wasn't the first hack of a major organization's Web site.

On August 1996, hackers defaced the Web site of the Department of Justice, which was quickly followed up on September 1996 by a Web site hack of the CIA. While government Web sites are always the most popular targets, hackers strike just as often against each other as they do against governments and corporations. On April 1999, hackers defaced the the Hacker News Network Web site (http://www. hackernews.com) and then in July of 1999 hacked into the Web site of DefCon, one of the original hacker conventions held annually in Las Vegas.

The reason crime doesn't pay is that when it does, it is called by a more respectable name.

—JUSTICE TOM CLARK

HACTIVISM: POLITICALLY-MOTIVATED WEB SITE HACKS

For many hackers, defacing a Web site is just an electronic form of graffiti that allows them to reach a larger audience in a shorter period of time. While many hackers attack Web sites for the sheer challenge of breaking the security of another computer, others alter Web sites to express political opinions—known as *hacktivism*, an activity that even has its own mailing list (http://hacktivism.tao.ca).

Although hackers may be skilled at breaking into a Web site, a quick glance at some past Web site hacks shows that they often waste the opportunity to convey an intelligent message by cluttering the defaced Web pages with hacker slang (substituting numbers for letters such as d00dz [dudes] or lam3r [lamer]; adding greetings to friends; or posting pornographic pictures and sexual references). However, a handful of hactivists have taken the time to leave a coherent message.

Hackers vs. Indonesia

On November 12, 1996, the Indonesian Army killed 250 Timorese in what is now known as the Santa Cruz massacre. Since that infamous date, Portuguese hackers have repeatedly attacked the Indonesian government by defacing Indonesian Web sites and leaving behind political messages.

The first Web site hack (see Figure 12-1) occurred when hackers broke into the Indonesian Department of Foreign Affairs Web site (http://www.dfa-deplu.go.id) and left behind this message:

> *We hope to call attention to the necessity of self-determination and independence of the people of Timor, oppressed and violated for decades by the government of Indonesia. We hope you give your full attention to this historical step towards freedom, we ask that you help us fight the tyranny of Indonesia occupying Timor.*

FIGURE 12-1:

One of the earliest Indonesian Web site hacks.

Over the next two years, the hackers struck with six more attacks to protest the continuing Indonesian oppression of East Timor (see Figure 12-2). The latest attack on January 1998 was particularly notable since the hackers struck several Web sites at once, including the Indonesian General Education Ministry (http://www.dikmenum.go.id), the Jakarta Municipal Government (http://www.dki.go.id), the Supreme Audit Board (http://www.bepeka.go.id), and the Indonesian National Police site (http://www.polri.mil.id).

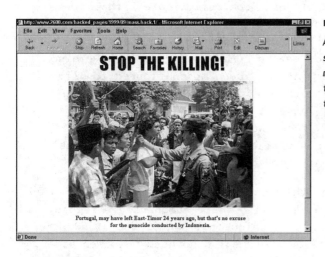

FIGURE 12-2:

A later Indonesian Web site hack showing a more graphic image of the violence marring the area.

To better understand why Portuguese hackers have targeted Indonesia and the relationship between Indonesia and East Timor, visit the East Timor International Support Center (http://www.easttimor.com) where you will find news about East Timor that you may never hear about from your national newspapers or magazines.

Hackers vs. China

China has become a favorite target for human rights hacktivists. On December 1998, hackers defaced the Chinese Tianjin Network of Information Science & Technology. Besides defacing Web pages, the hackers claimed to have reconfigured its firewalls so Chinese citizens could access the rest of the Internet. Part of the defaced Web pages contained the following message:

A few days ago a story ran about a man, Lin Hai, who was arrested in China and faces LIFE in a Chinese prison. What did he do, kill another man? Rape? Steal? Treason? No, he is accused of sending e-mails to a dissident publication ran in the USA, some of which criticize the present Chinese leadership. Life in prison. The Chinese government is scared to death of the Internet and the ease anyone can access information, and the ease its people, like Lin Hai, can communicate with the outside world and how they can now express what they think. . . . So in addition to this site being defaced, several Chinese firewalls have also been breached and have been misconfigured to allow anyone passing through it FREE ACCESS to any site they wish. I leave it up to the Chinese to find which and fix them, but in the meantime, I hope some of China's citizens enjoy the freedom to see what they want, and say what they want to say.

Oddly enough, the Chinese government had even created a special Web site detailing their human rights record (http://www.humanrights-china.org). On October 1998, the same day the Chinese government announced this Web site, hackers defaced it to display the following message:

I simply can not believe the total bullshit propaganda on this Web site. China's people have no rights at all, never mind Human Rights. I really can't believe our government deals with them. They censor, murder, torture, maim, and do everything we take for granite left the earth with the middle ages.

Two months after the Chinese government patched up this Web site, hackers struck it again to protest China's execution of two citizens accused of electronically stealing money from a bank.

Hackers vs. the United States

The United States is not immune from similar hacktivist attacks. Perhaps the least publicized of all the major Web site hacks occurred on May 1999 when someone hacked into the official White House Web site. Although this attack got almost no news coverage, the defaced Web pages remained up long enough to display the following message:

> Why did we hack this domain? Simple, we fucking could. Maybe this will teach the world a fucking lesson. Stop all the war. Consintrate [sic] on your own problems. http://www.freespeech.org/WH/ Welcome.html was damaged, but we not telling how we got in. Fear the end of the world is upon us, in a few short months it will all be over. Y2K is coming.

During the NATO bombing of Yugoslavia, both pro- and anti-NATO hackers posted their messages on various Web sites to protest or support the war (see Figures 12-3 and 12-4). Strangely enough, most of the defaced Web sites had little to do with the Yugoslavia bombings and seemed to have been targeted more because of their weak security rather than any political involvement.

FIGURE 12-3:

The American Windsurfer Magazine's Web site hacked by a Russian to protest NATO's bombing campaign.

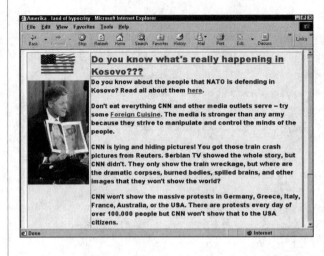

FIGURE 12-4:

A hacker defaced these Web pages to protest the censorship of the American media covering the war in Kosovo.

Hackers vs. racists

Besides targeting national governments, hackers have also gone after specific organizations. In May 1997, hackers broke into the WhitePower organization Web site and left this message:

> *Hey all you rascist SkinhEAD fewls listen up! You guys may think your on top, but guess what your wrong. Your ignorance has now been shamed by our knowledge. We are tierd of you fucking over other race's because of their ethic background and color. This time your the ones getting fucked, and look who's on top BaBY! We are "hackers", and we dominate your organization. We've gotten the greenlight to wipe you goons out.*

Early in January 1999, hackers broke into the Web site of The Alabama White Knights of the Ku Klux Klan (http://www.kukluxklan.net) and not only defaced their Web pages, but also erased files and accounts. The hacked version of the Klan's Web site displayed the following:

> *Your Webpage And All Accounts Associated With It Have Been Compromised, And Deleted, For Crimes Against The Human Race, by S C R E A M of the OLM (OnLine Mafia) and H.A.R.P (Hackers Against Racist Parties).*

SCANNING FOR TARGETS

To hack a Web site, you need to break into the computer
where the Web pages are stored. One of the most common Web
site hacking tools is a scanner (sometimes called a *port* or
network scanner). Scanning works much like wardialing,
which dials multiple phone numbers to find the ones connected to a computer. Scanning floods the Internet with
data packets to see which computers respond. In the same
way that an answering modem tone tells a wardialer that it
has reached a computer with a modem, a return message from
a computer tells a scanner which computers are open and
available for attack (see Figure 12-5).

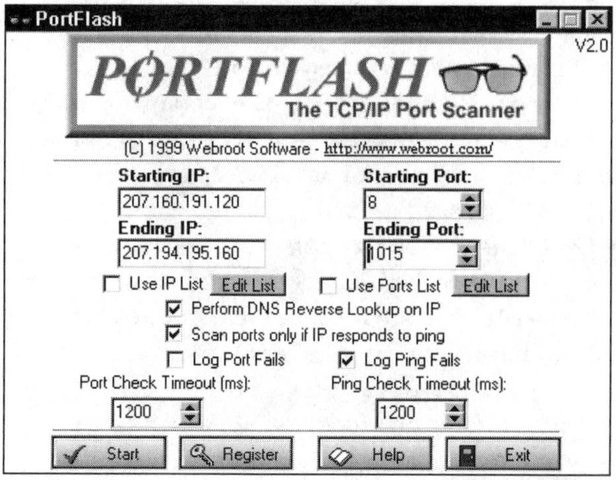

FIGURE 12-5:

*A port scanner can
search a range of IP
addresses for a com-
puter to attack.*

When a computer sends data to another computer, it
usually sends a SYN (synchronize) packet with the data.
If the target computer receives this packet, it returns
a SYN/ACK (synchronize/acknowledgement) packet. When it
receives the SYN/ACK packet, the original computer sends a
return ACK (acknowledgement) packet to the target computer
to complete the connection. Port scanners and probes use
this basic sequence of events to find open ports and to
probe them for additional information.

A scanner can reveal computers vulnerable to attack, the services (such as FTP, Telnet, finger, and so on) each provides, and the computer's operating system or server software. Some popular scanners are NetScan (http://www.nwpsw.com), SATAN (http://www.cs.ruu.nl/cert%2Duu/satan.html), AGNetTools (http://www.aggroup.com), and Nmap (http://www.insecure.org/nmap). You can find additional ones at Yippee (http://www.yippee.net) or TUCOWS (http://www.tucows.com).

Ping sweeping

Ping sweeping checks for computers by sending a small data packet to a remote computer at a specific IP address. The computer responds by returning the data, telling the ping sweeper that it is up and running. If the scanner running the ping sweep doesn't receive a return ping, there is either no computer at that IP address or the computer normally connected to that IP address is temporarily offline.

An ordinary ping uses a protocol called *Internet Control Message Protocol* (ICMP), which defines the way two computers transfer messages to one another. ICMP pings are harmless and not necessarily considered an attack, although some firewalls may block ICMP pings to certain ports to guard against ping flooding (one of the earliest and most primitive denial of service attacks, also called the "Ping of Death," where the attacking computer simply sends more pings than the receiving computer can handle).

If an ICMP ping can't get through to a computer that you know should be up and running, you can try using a port scanner, such as Nmap (see Figure 12-6) to send an ACK message (ping) to the target computer. ACK pings sometimes fool firewalls since they trick the target computer into thinking it's receiving an acknowledgement message from a legitimate connection that it has already established with another computer.

Pinging a range of IP addresses can be slow and time-consuming since your computer needs to send a ping then wait for a reply. To speed up this process, some scanners send a flood of pings without waiting for replies; each acknowledged ping reveals a computer that is a potential target.

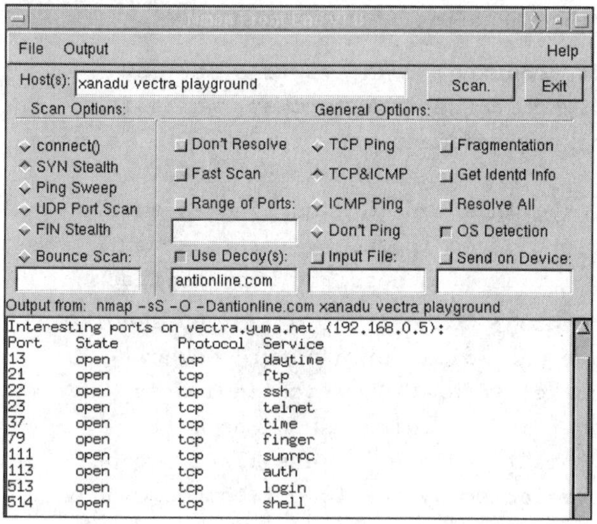

FIGURE 12-6:

Nmap can probe the Internet for vulnerable computers.

Port scanning

Once you have a target's IP address (either through ping sweeping or by looking up a domain name on the Network Solutions Web site at http://www.networksolutions.com/cgi-bin/whois/whois), the next step is to zero in on ports that may be open for attack.

Ports make different services available to other computers, and are the back door that hackers use to access their targets. Table 12-1 lists the more common ports, but keep in mind that a computer may have several hundred open ports.

TABLE 12-1: PORTS COMMONLY AVAILABLE ON EVERY COMPUTER ON THE INTERNET

Service	Port
File Transfer Protocol (FTP)	21
Telnet	23
Simple Mail Transfer Protocol (SMTP)	25
Gopher	70
Finger	79
Hypertext Transfer Protocol (HTTP)	80
Post Office Protocol, version 3 (POP3)	110

Some common port scanning techniques include:

→ **TCP connect scanning**: Connects to a port by sending a synchronize (SYN) packet, waits for a return acknowledgement packet (SYN/ACK), and then sends another acknowledgement packet to connect (ACK). This type of scanning is easily recognized and often logged by target computers to alert them of a possible hacker attack.

→ **TCP SYN scanning**: Connects to a port by sending a SYN packet and waits for a return acknowledgement packet (SYN/ACK), which indicates that the port is listening. Known as *half-scanning*, this technique is less likely to be logged and detected by the target than ordinary TCP connect scanning.

→ **TCP FIN scanning**: Connects to a port by sending a "No more data from sender" (FIN) packet to a port. A closed port responds with a Reset (RST) message while an open port simply ignores the FIN packet, thereby revealing its existence.

→ **Fragmentation scanning**: Breaks up the initial SYN packet into smaller pieces to mask your actions from a packet filter or firewall. Used in conjunction with other scanning techniques such as TCP connect, TCP SYN, or TCP FIN scanning.

→ **FTP bounce attack**: Requests a file from an FTP server. Because the request contains the IP address and port number of a target computer, an FTP bounce attack masks the source of the attack, and can bypass any firewalls or other security measures aimed at keeping outsiders (but not other computers on the same network) from accessing the target computer. A successful file transfer indicates an open port.

→ **UDP (User Datagram Protocol) scanning**: Uses the UDP instead of TCP. When a port receives a probe, its closed ports send an ICMP_PORT_ UNREACH error. Ports that don't send back an ICMP_PORT_UNREACH error are open.

Fingerprinting the target computer's operating system

Finding a computer and an open port can get you into a computer, but finding an open port is not enough. You must find out which operating system the computer uses so you can know which commands to use and how to take advantage of any known vulnerabilities in the software that could save you from having to guess the computer's password.

Most Web servers use a variation of Unix (such as Linux, Digital UNIX, or Solaris), but many run a version of Microsoft Windows. A handful of Web servers may even use OS/2 or the MacOS.

Probing the operating system

Operating system probing works by sending data to different ports. Since an operating system responds differently based on the data it receives at a specific port, this type of attack can identify the operating system used by the computer. By knowing how specific operating systems respond to different unexpected probes, hackers can deduce the type of operating system used on a target computer. Some common probing techniques include:

→ **FIN probing:** Sends a FIN ("No more data from sender") packet to a port and waits for a response. Windows responds to FIN packets with RST (Reset) messages, so if a RST message returns from your FIN probe, you know the computer is running Windows.

→ **FIN/SYN probing:** Sends a FIN/SYN packet to a port and waits for a response. Linux systems respond with a FIN/SYN/ACK packet.

→ **TCP initial window checking:** Checks the window size on packets returned from the target computer. The window size from the AIX operating system is 0x3F25 and the window size from OpenBSD or FreeBSD is 0x402E.

→ **ICMP message quoting:** Sends data to a closed port and waits to receive an error message. All computers should send back the initial IP header of the data with an additional eight bytes tacked on. Solaris and Linux systems, however, return more than eight bytes.

By using a program like QueSO or Nmap, hackers can scan a target computer and narrow down (or pinpoint) the operating system name and possibly even the version number as well.

Such probing can be difficult to block since hacker probing and legitimate connections between other computers can often be indistinguishable. As a result, hacker probes can often go unnoticed by firewalls or system administrators since they appear completely innocent and harmless.

OBTAINING A PASSWORD

To access a Web server, you'll need the password to a valid account, such as the system administrator's account. To get a password you can guess one (manually or with a dictionary attack), or steal a password file and decrypt it. Both approaches are discussed in Chapter 11.

SOFTWARE LOOPHOLES AND FLAWS

Rather than trying to get a password, many hackers take the alternative (but not always reliable) route of trying to exploit a flaw in the operating system or application server, thus bypassing the target computer's security. Exploits (called *'sploits* among the hacker community) that use software flaws are especially popular with novice hackers, called *script kiddies*, because they can use them to sneak into a system without knowing much about the system they're breaking into. In fact, script kiddies are often more dangerous than more technically skilled hackers because a script kiddie may damage or delete files through sheer clumsiness, while a more technically sophisticated hacker would know how to avoid causing accidental damage (although he would know how to do even more serious damage if he wanted).

Microsoft Internet Information Server (IIS)

Since so many people use Microsoft Windows, it's no surprise that a large number of Web sites run Windows NT and
its built-in Web server, Internet Information Server (IIS).
Given its popularity, it's also no surprise that Windows
NT/2000 is a favorite hacker target.

IIS buffer overflow hack

One of the first IIS flaws, dubbed the IIS buffer overflow
hack, was discovered by a professional security group
called eEye (http://www.eeye.com). They discovered that by
giving a server more input data than it can handle, such as
a long file name (consisting of 3,000 characters or more),
you could crash it.

Just crashing the server might be enough for some people, but the eEye group found a further exploit. If a hacker
floods a target computer with data along with a program
designed to listen for a connection and run the Windows command shell, he or she can gain complete control of the
server when the server runs the program (which it will do
before it crashes). When the server crashes, this rogue program (the eEye group used a modified version of a program
called Netcat, available from http://www.10pht.com/~weld/
netcat), listens for a connection. The moment it detects a
connection from another computer (presumably the hacker's
computer), it turns control of the Windows command shell to
this computer. At this point, the hacker has complete control of the entire server and can create or delete accounts,
format the hard drive, or modify and replace files such as
Web pages.

Microsoft has fixed this flaw in their Windows NT
Service Pack 6, but you can be sure that some complacent Web
site administrators have not installed this service pack
(there are so many of them and they take forever to install),
leaving their Windows NT servers wide open for an attack.

The shell() function

Another problem with Microsoft's Internet Information
Server occurs when administrators install the default configuration for Microsoft Data Access Components (MDAC) and

Remote Data Services (RDS), which are used to display information from database files. These components make Microsoft's Visual Basic for Applications (VBA) programming language available for running commands, and one of VBA's available commands is the shell() function—a function that allows a user access to the Windows command shell. Once a hacker can access the Windows command shell, he or she can modify files at will.

With the growing popularity of Windows NT/2000 and IIS, the number of available exploits seems to grow with each day. To keep up with the rapidly expanding list of such exploits, visit the Windows IT Security site at http://www.ntsecurity.net.

Red Hat Linux Piranha server

Although everyone loves to poke fun at the insecurity of Windows systems, other operating systems aren't always immune to these problems either. When Red Hat Software shipped their Linux Virtual Server (LVS) software (nicknamed "Piranha"), they inadvertently left in an undocumented back-door account with the user name set to "piranha" and a password set to "q," giving anyone who knew of this exploit access to servers running on Red Hat's LVS.

This exploit occurred because programmers often create backdoor accounts and passwords to test their software so they can bypass the login process and quickly access and test other portions of the program. When the company shipped the finished program, the programmers should have removed any backdoor accounts and passwords. If the backdoor account is not eliminated and a hacker manages to access the account, he or she can run any type of command on the server. Although Red Hat Software issued a patch to close this exploit in their software, you can be sure that many system administrators haven't downloaded or installed this patch yet.

The piranha problem highlights the double-edged nature of open source software such as Linux. While revealing the source code can help strengthen its security by allowing others to study the program, it also allows hackers the chance to find flaws they might not otherwise have been able to discover and exploit.

Allaire ColdFusion scripts

One of the more popular server programs for Windows NT and the Solaris operating system is Allaire's ColdFusion, because it's easy to use and offers a powerful scripting language for customizing a Web site. Unfortunately, Allaire shipped ColdFusion with sample scripts (openfile.cfm, displayopenedfile.cfm, and exprcalc.cfm in the \cfdics\ expeval folder) for users to study and modify for use on their own Web sites.

These sample scripts were meant to be run on a local machine. But when installed on a Web server they can be run remotely, allowing anyone to view and upload any file onto the server. Running these scripts remotely can help a hacker bypass any security measures and simply upload new Web pages to replace the existing ones stored on the server.

The next time you visit a Web site (usually run by a corporation), look for the telltale .cfm file extension in your browser's URL address bar, such as a file called "index.cfm" rather than "index.html". The .CFM file extension indicates that the Web site is running ColdFusion.

Finding more software exploits

Since hackers are discovering new flaws and exploits every day, Web site administrators spend much of their time just keeping up with the latest information. To read about the latest security exploits for Windows, visit Microsoft's Security Advisor site (http://www.microsoft.com/security) and download patches or read bulletins describing just how insecure your Windows network may really be. For another good source of Windows NT security exploits, visit the NTSecurity.net site (http://www.ntshop.net).

To stay up-to-date with the latest security breaches in non-Microsoft products such as Linux, ColdFusion, Solaris, FreeBSD, and Digital UNIX, visit Insecure.org (http://www.insecure.org), Security Focus (http://www.securityfocus.com), AntiCode (http://www.anticode.com), Packet Storm (http://packetstorm.securify.com), Security Watch (http://www.securitywatch.com), Linux Security (http://www.linuxsecurity.com), or 10pht Heavy Industries (http://www.lopht.com).

Since nearly every type of Web server software has flaws, many hackers have developed special tools that automatically scan a Web site for all known flaws, such as WebCheck, developed by a hacker group dubbed Illegal Crew (http://www.illegalcrew.org). Not only can a program like WebCheck methodically probe a Web site for known vulnerabilities, but it can also reveal the exact type and version number of the software used by a targeted Web site. As shown in Figure 12-7, WebCheck has found that the ABC News Web site (http://www.abcnews.com) uses Microsoft Internet Information Server (IIS) version 4.0.

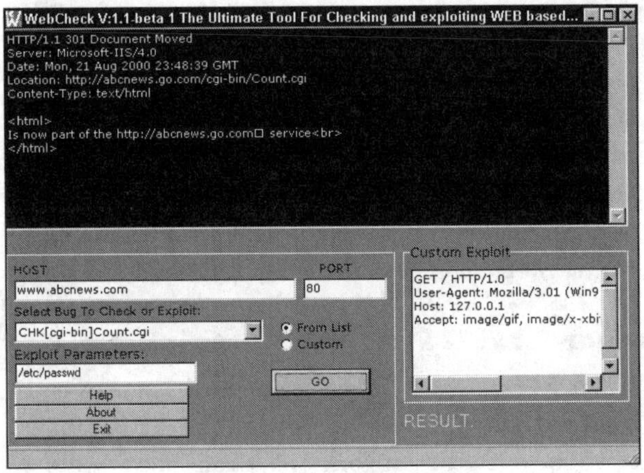

FIGURE 12-7:

WebCheck can determine what type of server software is used and whether a Web site is vulnerable to a known exploit.

PROTECTING A WEB SITE

If your Web site is hosted by an ISP, your site's security depends on their system administrator. Luckily, Web hosting companies and local ISPs tend to be staffed by experts who are more savvy than the average system administrator running a corporate or government Web site. But if you have any doubts, ask the system administrator about the company's security policies.

If you have your own network, your security is in your own hands. The following sections will give you an overview of some good security measures. To learn more about available software, resources, and information for protecting

a network from hackers, visit Firewall.com (http://www.
firewall.com), the Dutch Security Information Network
(http://www.hiverworld.com), or the Computer Intrusion
Detection System site (http://www.networkintrusion.co.uk).

Use difficult passwords

Passwords should ideally consist of a random mix of at
least six characters. For added protection, change your
passwords periodically, and give each account a completely
different password. Unix systems can use *shadowed* passwords, which are encrypted passwords stored in a special
file. Although passwords alone can't stop hackers, a good
one can at least slow them down.

Avoid using default configurations

One of the easiest ways to protect against hackers is to
shut down hidden backdoors or exploits by avoiding default
configurations. Many backdoors rely on default settings and
are blocked once these have been changed. Skilled hackers
can maneuver around this simple obstacle, but the majority
of less-skilled hackers may simply search for an easier
computer to attack.

Use a firewall

The most common Web site defense is a firewall. (See
www.firewall.com for more about firewall books, confer-
ences, and software.) At the simplest level, a firewall
blocks access to certain ports. For example, if a server
has no reason to use Telnet, finger, or FTP, a firewall
automatically blocks anyone from trying to access the
server through Telnet, finger, or FTP commands.

Besides blocking data, firewalls can also perform
packet filtering, a process by which they screen data based
on certain criteria. For example, if data comes from a network connection and claims to be from a trusted computer, a
firewall allows the data to pass. But if the data is coming
from a dial-up connection, yet claims to be from a trusted
computer that has no reason to connect to the target

computer through a dial-up, the firewall assumes that the IP address has been spoofed (faked) and blocks access.

A firewall can also detect suspicious probes, such as a hacker scanning for open ports. If a firewall detects suspicious activity, it can log the events and alert the system administrator that a hacker may be trying to break in. The administrator can then decide whether to track the hacker's activities to make sure he or she doesn't do anything harmful, or simply block the attack.

Detect changes in files

File integrity checkers, another tool used to defend against hackers, periodically examine files and calculate a *checksum* (a number that uniquely identifies a file based on its contents). If a checksum has changed (thus indicating that the file has been changed), the file integrity program alerts the system administrator that a hacker may be on the loose.

Some popular file integrity checkers include Veracity (http://www.veracity.com), Intact (http://www.pedestalsoftware.com), SmartWatch (http://www.wetstonetech.com), and Tripwire (http://www.tripwire.com), which is also available as an open source program at http://www.tripwire.org.

Restoring changed files

Once a file integrity checker detects a change in one or more files, the files need to be repaired. To automate this process, LockStep (http://www.lockstep.com) offers a unique program dubbed WebAgain.

WebAgain won't stop hackers or even detect their presence; instead, it periodically scans your Web pages to see if the file dates or contents have been altered. The moment it detects a change, it assumes that the pages have been changed without your permission, so it copies a backup version of the Web page over the defaced Web page, essentially defeating the hacker's defacing attack.

By storing WebAgain on a computer inaccessible from the Internet or your company network, you can ensure that hackers can't disable WebAgain and alter your Web page backups. So while your Web site may still be vulnerable to attack, at least any defacing attacks will be quickly detected and removed.

Use a honey pot

A *honey pot* (also called a *goat file*) is a collection of phony data or files used to lure a hacker. Cliff Stoll, the author of *The Cuckoo's Egg*, used a honey pot consisting of fake missile defense and nuclear warhead data to trap a German hacker who was trying to find secret files about the American "Star Wars" missile defense program so he could sell the data to the KGB.

A honey pot can serve three purposes:

1. To lure the hacker away from real data he or she might possibly destroy.

2. To alert the system administrators of a hacker's presence the moment someone starts accessing the phony files.

3. To keep the hacker occupied long enough to help the authorities trace his or her physical location.

Since it's impossible to tell what type of data might lure a hacker, some honey pots do nothing more than fake the data normally found on a server. This gives the hacker the illusion that he's just broken into a computer when he really hasn't. One unique honey pot program is NetBuster (http://surf.to/netbuster—see Figure 12-8), which mimics the NetBus Trojan Horse (see Chapter 16 for more information about remote access Trojan Horse programs).

NetBuster will detect and remove the NetBus Trojan and then wait for the hacker to return. The next time the hacker tries to access your computer through the NetBus Trojan, NetBuster notifies you and guards against any actions he may take. For example, if the hacker tries to delete your files, NetBuster displays a phony message telling him that he successfully deleted your files when he really hasn't. For the ultimate sting, you can even use

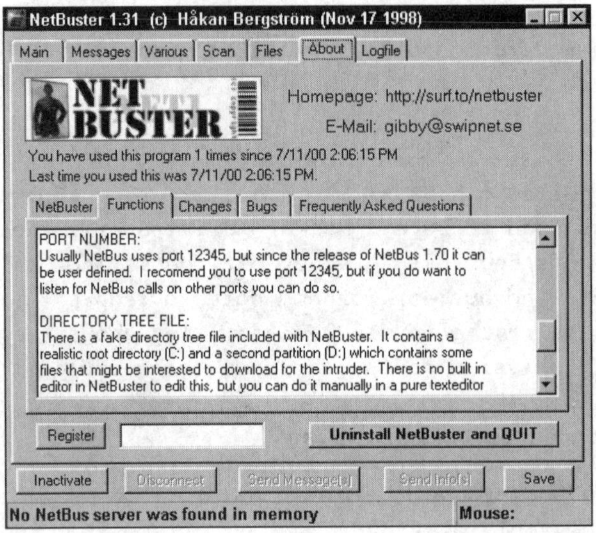

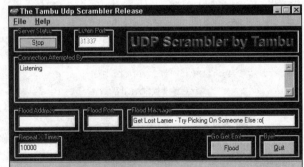

FIGURE 12-8:

NetBuster can mimic NetBus so you can track a hacker's attempt to break into your computer.

NetBuster to send an insulting message or picture back to the hacker to let him know that he's the one who has been fooled instead of you.

A more proactive honey pot trap is the Tambu UDP Scrambler (http://www.xploiter.com/tambu—see Figure 12-9). Not only will this program watch a specific port for a UDP packet (used by hackers to probe a computer), but once it detects a suspicious probe, it can flood the attack with a flurry of messages, clogging up the attacker's machine and forcing him to disconnect.

FIGURE 12-9:

The Tambu UDP Scrambler can turn the tables on a hacker by making him the victim instead.

Other examples of honey pot programs include CyberCop Sting (http://www.pgp.com), Mantrap (http://www.recourse. com), and Specter (http://www.specter.ch). All can store a hacker's keystrokes and activities for evidence to help trace them, which can be especially useful if the hacker is a co-worker or other trusted person normally allowed on a particular network.

To prevent detection, honey pot programs can mimic different types of operating systems. Unless a hacker is very skilled (or very suspicious), he may not realize he's actually been caught in a honey pot program and isolated from his real target.

Think like a hacker

One of the most effective ways to secure a network is to think like a hacker and try to break into the network. Many corporations hire special consultants, dubbed Tiger Teams, to use hacker tools to test the security of their network defenses. (In fact, many computer security consultants are ex-hackers themselves.)

Companies that can't afford to hire a Tiger Team (or a freelance hacker), can run a vulnerability scanner. These programs combine the features of an ordinary scanner with a database listing all known weaknesses that hackers commonly exploit. Vulnerability scanners list weaknesses that they find in a network and then offer suggestions for closing these possible openings. Some popular vulnerability scanners include Kane Security Analyst (http://www.intrusion. com), CyberCop (http://www.pgp.com), NetRecon (http://www. axent.com), Swarm (http://www.hiverworld.com), Internet Security Scanner (http://www.iss.net), SAINT (http://www. wwdsi.com/saint), and Retina (http://www.eeye.com).

Although no computer can be made 100 percent hacker-proof (short of turning it off altogether), you can always make your computer just a little tougher to crack. So unless a hacker has a specific reason to target your computer, he or she is more likely to wander off and search for an easier target.

13

Viruses I: History and Symptoms

COMPUTER VIRUSES CAN CAUSE A WIDE RANGE OF TROUBLE FOR ANY COMPUTER, FROM DISPLAYING NONSENSICAL MESSAGES ON SCREEN, TO MAKING THE KEYBOARD WORK ERRATICALLY, TO DELETING FILES OR ENTIRE HARD DISKS. People especially fear the unpredictability of computer viruses. Because few people have actually encountered a computer virus, many people cringe at its mere mention. Sure, computer viruses may be dangerous, but if you know what makes them work, they can actually be interesting and educational as well.

WHAT IS A COMPUTER VIRUS?

Computer viruses fall into two categories: wild or zoo specimens. Common viruses that spread quickly and easily are referred to as "in the wild," which means they're the viruses most likely to attack your computer. A zoo specimen will almost never be found in the wild because it is buggy or poorly designed, which means it doesn't spread and infect computers consistently, if at all.

A computer virus is nothing more than a program that:

→ Was written by a person using a programming language, such as assembly language, C/C++, BASIC, or Pascal.

→ Can make copies of itself.

A virus can't spontaneously appear on your hard disk like mold on week-old bread. Instead, you must deliberately (but unknowingly) copy and run the computer virus on your

The National Computer Security Association reports that the number of North American businesses infected by computer viruses tripled in the past year despite increased use of antivirus products.

Survey results indicate that email is one of the main culprits in spreading the viruses. Macro viruses in common word processing documents and spreadsheets were the biggest problem.

—INVESTOR'S BUSINESS DAILY

own computer. And, because computer viruses are computer programs, guess what? Many have fatal flaws (known in the programming industry as "bugs") that keep them from successfully copying themselves too rapidly.

If computer viruses are nothing more than programs that can copy themselves, why do viruses have such a bad reputation? Because many people write malicious viruses whose sole purpose is to screw up somebody else's computer (e.g., disable programs or delete data). If everyone wrote word processors that deliberately screwed up your computer, word processors would get a bad name, too.

To fully understand why viruses are so feared, you need to understand the distinctions between computer viruses and other threats, the history of computer viruses, and how the parts of a typical computer virus actually work.

Malware

Malware (short for *Malicious Software*) is a general term that describes three basic types of programs: viruses, worms, and Trojan Horses. The main distinction between the three program types is the way they spread.

A virus can only spread by infecting another object such as a program file, a document (such as a Microsoft Word file), or the boot sector of a floppy disk. If a virus fails to infect a file, document, or floppy disk, it cannot spread.

Unlike a virus, a worm is self-propagating. Worms copy themselves from one computer to another, often without the user's knowledge. Like a virus, a single worm can duplicate itself many times over.

A Trojan Horse program masquerades as another program to trick a person into running it. Once activated, the Trojan Horse distracts the user by displaying a game or message on the screen while it secretly takes some other action such as destroying files or installing programs without the user's knowledge. Unlike a virus or a worm, a Trojan Horse does not make copies of itself automatically.

Viruses, worms, and Trojan Horses are not inherently destructive, but their surreptitious nature makes them tempting vehicles for spreading trouble. In fact, malware programs often cause damage just by existing. For example, the 1988 Internet worm did nothing but multiply itself from one computer to another, but in the process it gobbled up memory and computing resources until the host computer ground to a halt.

A HISTORICAL PERSPECTIVE

The first known computer virus was created in 1986 when two brothers from Pakistan discovered that the boot sector of a floppy disk could contain instructions other than those for loading an operating system. Their program, later dubbed the Brain virus, provided instructions for infecting a computer and spreading the virus to a floppy disk.

Once other people understood how the Brain virus worked, the idea of creating computer viruses spread faster than the Brain virus itself. In this early stage, virus writing required technical knowledge of how computers stored data in memory and retrieved information from floppy disks.

For speed and efficiency, early viruses were written in assembly language, which requires a deep knowledge of both programming and computer hardware. This meant that only the most technically savvy programmers were able to create viruses or modify them. A few hardy souls did try to write viruses in the higher-level languages of C, Turbo Pascal, and even BASIC, but these viruses were largely inefficient.

Meanwhile, antivirus companies were doing their best to make writing a succesful virus even harder. Every time a virus writer created a new virus, antivirus companies quickly updated their antivirus programs. Many viruses barely had time to spread before antivirus companies updated their antivirus programs to catch these new creations, rendering the latest viruses practically harmless right from the start.

To combat the increasingly successful efforts of the antivirus community to neutralize the virus threat, virus writers tried a variety of tactics. Some wrote *retaliating viruses* that would spread by only infecting antivirus programs. When you ran an antivirus program infected by one of these retaliating viruses, your antivirus program would fail to detect the infection and, even worse, in the process of scanning your hard disk, the antivirus program would actually spread the virus while telling you that your computer was virus-free.

Virus writers also concocted viruses that could remain undetected. These so-called *stealth viruses* used arcane tricks to bury themselves in memory or on a disk in an attempt to prevent antivirus programs from locating them.

By far, the most successful attack on antivirus programs has come from *polymorphic viruses*, which alter their appearance to fool antivirus programs. Because an antivirus program can only identify known viruses, it has a much harder time detecting and removing viruses that constantly change their appearance.

Michelangelo

In 1992, the Michelangelo virus became the first virus to spread across the world when the Aldus Corporation and Leading Edge Computers discovered that they had inadvertently shipped thousands of infected floppy disks and computers. Antivirus companies such as McAfee Associates claimed that up to fifteen million computers could suffer damage from the Michelangelo virus, unless the computers were equipped with an antivirus program. Although the actual numbers of infected computers proved far lower, 1992 will be remembered as the year when computer viruses first made big news.

Virus writing spreads

To help spread their viruses, virus writers started bulletin board systems (BBSs were an early precursor to Web sites) where people could share virus source code. But despite widespread availability of virus source code, virus writing was restricted to the small minority of competent programmers willing to tackle assembly language programming.

Then a programmer in Bulgaria, calling himself the Dark Avenger, introduced the Dark Avenger Mutation Engine. The Dark Avenger Mutation Engine (DAME) provided a module that assembly language programmers could attach to their own virus creations to turn any virus into a polymorphic virus without any additional programming.

At the same time, another programmer, calling himself Nowhere Man, created the Virus Creation Laboratory (see Figure 13-1). The Virus Creation Laboratory (VCL) tried a different tack for making virus writing easier and faster. The VCL offered pull-down menus for choosing various features to include in your virus. After you chose your virus features, the VCL would automatically create your virus.

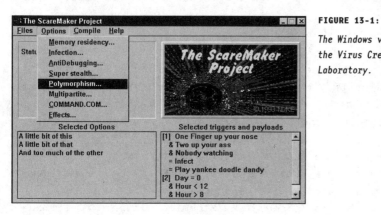

FIGURE 13-1:

The Windows version of the Virus Creation Laboratory.

But both the DAME and VCL eventually failed because antivirus companies soon learned how to identify any virus created by either virus creation toolkit, thereby neutralizing the effect of all these new viruses.

Macro viruses

In 1996, another virus-writing breakthrough occurred with the introduction of the Concept virus, the first breed of macro viruses. Unlike previous viruses that infected individual files or boot sectors, macro viruses infected Microsoft Word documents. Not only did these new viruses provide a new way for viruses to infect a computer, but they also simplified virus writing.

Instead of forcing virus writers to learn assembly language and the technical details of the machine, macro viruses used a simplified version of the BASIC programming language called WordBasic and later Visual Basic for Applications (VBA). Not only could nearly anyone learn to write and modify a macro virus written in VBA, but each macro virus infection provided potential virus writers with the actual virus source code as well—the macros themselves. (Viruses, like other programs, consist of two parts: the source code and the executable file. If your computer only has the executable file, you can't modify or study the virus unless you can disassemble the virus executable file.)

Melissa and the Love Bug

Not surprisingly, macro viruses quickly became the fastest growing virus threat as new variants appeared with frightful regularity. Then in 1999 the Melissa virus appeared.

Unlike other viruses, Melissa didn't passively wait for someone to send an infected file to another computer. Instead, it borrowed characteristics from worms and actively spread by mailing copies of itself to the first fifty email addresses found in the user's Microsoft Outlook or Outlook Express address book. The Melissa virus quickly spread throughout the world and, like Michelangelo before it, made international headlines. Then the Love Bug worm appeared, written in another BASIC language variant called VBScript (Visual Basic Script), a language that is easy to learn, understand, and modify. Anyone who receives the Love Bug worm also receives its complete VBScript source code and can create a new variant of the Love Bug worm right away.

The Love Bug worm lured its victims with clever email subject lines. The first version of the Love Bug worm printed "I LOVE YOU" while later versions displayed the words "fwd: Joke," "Mothers Day Order Confirmation," or a virus alert purportedly issued by Symantec, the publisher of the Norton Antivirus program. After the unsuspecting user opens the message, the Love Bug worm spreads itself by using Microsoft Outlook or Outlook Express address books. But where the Melissa virus needed to infect a Word document before it could spread, the Love Bug worm acts independent of any files, mailing itself to every email address stored in an Outlook address book.

What the future may bring

As viruses and worms become easier to write and even easier to modify, expect to see more copycat macro viruses and worms in the future. Within days of the original Love Bug worm's release, programmers had created 29 new variations. Although most changes were as trivial as changing the subject line message, this proved to be enough to allow the worm to slip past many of the email filters that ISPs had hastily erected.

As the Love Bug worm spread, the major antivirus companies released updates to their programs, but much damage had already been done. The lesson here is that you can't always rely on antivirus programs and updates to protect you from viruses. Since updates are often a knee-jerk reaction to viruses, a brand-new virus, worm, or Trojan Horse can often slip past antivirus programs and wreak havoc until the antivirus companies study the new threat and issue updates to their programs. Antivirus programs are only effective if you get the latest update before the new virus or worm finds you.

No matter what email filters or antivirus defenses your computer may use, they can never provide 100 percent protection against the most dangerous threats of all—the newest viruses and worms. Both antivirus programs and email filters identify only known threats and do not detect future viruses or worms. Thus every computer on the Internet will always be vulnerable to an attack at any time.

Even worse, future viruses and worms may activate themselves without requiring any user action, such as opening an email attachment. According to security specialist Michal Zalewski, a group of programmers has created a working prototype of a worm that can spread without any user involvement. Although the project has been halted, expect the next major threat to appear as a fully autonomous worm capable of spreading without relying on a user's actions.

Malware "Milestones"

1986	Brain virus: First computer virus released in Pakistan.
1986	PC-Write Trojan: First Trojan Horse disguised as a major shareware program, the PC-Write word processor.
1988	MacMag virus: First Macintosh virus released.
1988	Scores virus: First major Macintosh virus outbreak.
1988	Internet worm: First worm to cause widespread havoc on the Internet, shutting down computers all over the country and making worldwide headlines.
1989	AIDS Trojan: First Trojan Horse that held the user's data hostage by encrypting the hard disk and demanding that the user pay for an encryption key that would prevent the Trojan Horse from deleting data.
1990	First Virus Exchange Bulletin Board System (VX BBS) appears in Bulgaria where callers could trade live viruses and virus source code.
1990	*The Little Black Book of Computer Viruses* published by Mark Ludwig. One of the first books to provide detailed instructions and accompanying source code to teach people how to write computer viruses.
1991	Tequila virus: First polymorphic virus capable of changing its appearance to avoid detection by antivirus programs.
1992	Michelangelo virus: First computer virus that caused a major media alert. Despite claims that millions of computers were in danger, the Michelangelo virus actually caused relatively little damage.

1992	Dark Avenger Mutation Engine (DAME): First toolkit designed to turn any computer virus into a polymorphic virus. Despite its threatening appearance, its widescale use was prevented by the toolkit's complexity and bugs in the program.
1992	Virus Creation Laboratory (VCL): First toolkit for creating a virus using pull-down menus.
1996	Boza: First Windows 95 virus released.
1996	Concept virus: First macro virus released that infects Word documents.
1996	Laroux virus: First macro virus released that infects Excel spreadsheet files.
1996	Staog virus: First Linux virus released.
1998	Strange Brew virus: First Java virus released.
1998	Back Orifice: First remote administration Trojan Horse that allows others to completely take over a target computer through the Internet.
1999	Melissa virus: First virus to spread by email through Microsoft Outlook and Outlook Express address books.
1999	Tristate virus: First macro virus capable of infecting Word, Excel, and PowerPoint files. First large-scale denial of service attacks to shut down major Web sites including Yahoo, Amazon.com, CNN, and eBay.
2000	Love Bug worm: The fastest spreading worm in history, causing an estimated $2 to $15 billion in damages.
2000	Timofonica worm: First worm to attack mobile phones using calls generated from an infected computer.
2000	Life Stages worm: First worm to spread as an SHS (Microsoft Scrap Object) file, which appears as a harmless text file.

THE PARTS OF A COMPUTER VIRUS

A typical computer virus (see Figure 13-2) consists of two essential and three optional parts. The essential parts are a search routine and an infection routine; the optional parts are a trigger routine, a payload, and an anti-detection routine.

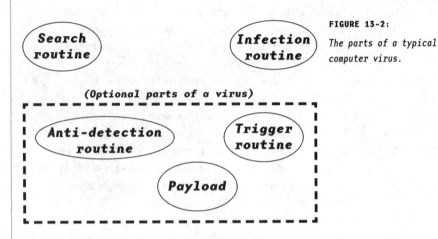

FIGURE 13-2:

The parts of a typical computer virus.

The *search routine* scans a floppy or hard disk for a target. The two most likely targets are files (created in such programs as Microsoft Word, WordPerfect, and Lotus 1-2-3) or the boot sector of a floppy or hard disk. The search routine must also identify previously infected files or disks to prevent the virus from repeatedly re-infecting the same target.

The *infection routine* takes over once the search routine has found a target. It makes the virus infect the selected target. A clumsy infection routine can destroy the target, blowing the virus's cover—like a burglar who picks a lock by blowing the door off its hinges.

The *trigger routine* tells the virus when to strike. Typical triggers can be a date (such as Friday the 13th or April Fool's Day) or some significant event (such as when the hard disk is 80 percent full or once the virus has infected a certain number of files).

The trigger releases the *payload*. Typical payloads tell the virus to erase a file, scramble a hard disk, display an obscene message, or disable a certain key on the keyboard.

The *anti-detection routine* prevents the user or an antivirus program from detecting the virus. This routine may work very simply, by modifying the date, time, and size of an infected file, or it may be more sophisticated, burrowing itself into memory and trapping all attempts to examine the boot sector of a floppy or hard disk.

For example, each time an antivirus program checks an infected boot sector, it asks the question, "Hey computer! Is the boot sector all right?" If the computer would respond, "No, it's infected," a virus might intercept this message and replace it with the message, "I'm okay." So although the boot sector is infected, the antivirus program believes everything is okay, and the virus avoids detection.

Before scanning your floppy or hard disk for viruses, most antivirus programs first check your computer's memory (RAM). Only after the antivirus program has determined that your computer's memory is free from viruses does it check for virus infections on your floppy and hard disks. Checking your computer's RAM first allows the antivirus program to examine the hard disk without fear of deception by a virus.

HAVE YOU GOT A VIRUS?

Your computer may be crawling with viruses, and you may not know it. Many viruses lie dormant, surreptitiously spreading around your hard disk and any disks you insert into your floppy drive. Other viruses make their presence known as soon as you run an infected program.

Obviously, the sooner you detect an infection, the sooner you can remove the virus before it "explodes" and does its damage (see Chapter 15 for how to cure an infected computer). There are two common ways to detect a virus infection:

→ Run one or more antivirus programs periodically.

→ Watch your computer for erratic behavior.

The more antivirus programs you have, the more likely at least one of them will catch any viruses that might infect your computer. Since a few viruses know how to slip past the more popular antivirus programs, relying on just one antivirus program is like locking all of the doors and windows of your house except one. A new or particularly tricky virus may even slip past all of your antivirus programs, in which case your only protection will be watching your computer for obvious signs of infection.

No antivirus program can be 100 percent effective at detecting and removing all viruses. Fortunately, no virus can be 100 percent effective in hiding itself either, no matter what stealth techniques, polymorphism, or retaliating tactics it uses.

Even if you run an antivirus program, it's important to watch your machine for unusual behavior that might spell V-I-R-U-S.

Computer slows to a crawl

Just because your computer responds slower than usual doesn't mean that you have a virus. You may simply have too many programs loaded at the same time. Generally, the more programs loaded into your computer's memory, the slower your computer will run. Try closing the programs you aren't using to free up some memory. If this solution doesn't speed up your computer, you might have a virus. Some viruses slow your computer down, eventually bringing it to a complete standstill as the virus spreads.

Strange pictures or messages appear

To announce their presence, many viruses display a message ("You're screwed") or a picture (such as an ambulance driving across the bottom of the screen). A harmless virus might display a message or a picture and nothing more, as shown in Figure 13-3. A malicious virus would display a message or a picture to distract you and delete a file or wreck part of your hard disk.

FIGURE 13-3:
The VBS Monopoly virus displays a picture of Bill Gates after infecting a hard disk.

Anytime you see an obviously strange picture or message on your screen, you can assume that your computer has been infected by a virus.

A virus is operating system—specific. For example, MS-DOS viruses can only display a strange picture or message on your screen if you're using MS-DOS. If you only run Windows programs, an MS-DOS virus won't be able to run or display any weird pictures on your screen.

Computer plays music for no reason

Some of the more playful viruses will beep or play a musical tune (such as Yankee Doodle Dandy) through the computer's speaker. Unless you've loaded a program to play musical tunes periodically (such as a screensaver or a contact manager that beeps to remind you of an appointment), assume that any strange music coming from your computer is from a virus.

Programs mysteriously fail to load

If a program that you've used before suddenly fails to load, and the computer displays an error message saying that you don't have enough memory, be careful. Many viruses hide themselves in your computer's memory, thereby reducing the total amount of memory available to run your programs.

Before concluding that you have a virus, try booting from a clean floppy disk (one that you're absolutely sure isn't infected by a virus) and loading the program again. Sometimes when you install a new program, it grabs part of

your computer's memory for itself. Then when you try loading a program you've used before, the program suddenly
won't work because a new program you just installed is hog-
ging too much of the memory.

If your computer will not load a new program the first
time because of insufficient memory, first check that your
system has the minimum amount of memory required by the program. If it does, but you still can't load a program, make
sure you don't have any other programs loaded into memory.

If you still have trouble running a program, even
though your computer has enough memory to run it and you
don't have any other programs running at the same time, you
may have a virus lurking in your computer's memory.

Keyboard doesn't work right

If your keyboard suddenly fails to work, you probably have
a dead keyboard—most viruses prefer to mess up keyboards,
not kill them. One common sign of a virus infection is when
you press a key and suddenly that same letter or number
repeats itself several times. Another common sign is when a
certain key fails to work.

Before you panic, try cleaning your keyboard. Dust,
crumbs, and sticky liquids can slip into a keyboard, gum-
ming up the keys and preventing them from working right.
Try switching keyboards and see if the same keys still act
weird. If so, your problems may be due to a virus.

Time and date stamps on files have changed

When you create or modify a file, your computer stamps the
file with the exact time and date that the file changed.
The same is true for changes that viruses make when they
infect a file.

A quick way to check for some older virus infections
is to examine the time and date stamps on your program
files. Program files, such as WordPerfect or Lotus 1-2-3,
show the time and date the program was finally finished by
the programmers. This date should never change, so if it
suddenly shows yesterday as the time and date stamp—something is wrong.

But remember that checking a file's time and date stamp can only catch the older viruses. More sophisticated recent viruses can infect a file without appearing to change its time and date stamp.

To check the time and date stamp of a file using MS-DOS, type the DIR command followed by the file name at the DOS prompt, such as:

DIR RESUME.DOC

This will display information such as the following:

RESUME   DOC   4,509   01-03.98   10:21a

In this example, the file name is RESUME.DOC, it's 4,509 bytes in size, and it was last modified on January 3, 1998, at 10:21 in the morning.

To check the time and date stamp of a file using Windows 95/98/Millennium Edition/NT/2000:

1. Load the Windows Explorer.
2. Right-click on the file you want to examine.
3. Choose Properties from the pop-up menu.
4. Click OK.

Unknown files appear or existing files disappear

Rather than wreck your hard disk right away, some viruses erase files one by one instead. If you notice that some files seem to be missing, make sure that nobody has been using your computer and moving files around. Also check that you haven't stored your files in a different directory by mistake. If you're absolutely sure that no one has moved or erased a file, then you might have a virus infection.

Also be wary if new files suddenly appear for no apparent reason. Some viruses (known as companion viruses) create new files rather than infect an existing file. Because companion viruses don't modify existing files, many antivirus programs have trouble detecting them.

Just because a new file appears on your computer, don't assume it's a virus at work. Each time you install a new program, it scatters a handful of new files in various directories across your hard disk. And each time you use a program, it may create a temporary or backup file. Unless a really strange file mysteriously appears on your hard disk, you can probably assume that you don't have a virus.

Hard disk fails to boot

If you turn on your computer and get an error message saying that your computer can't start, you might have a virus or you might just have a plain ol' run-of-the-mill hard disk failure. Despite the illusion of technical sophistication, hard disks tend to fail on a fairly regular basis. Generally, the older a hard disk is, the greater the chance of failure.

Before blaming a virus, run a utility program, such as Norton Utilities, to see if it can fix your hard disk. If it can't resurrect your hard disk, boot from a clean floppy (that you're certain isn't infected by a virus) and run an antivirus program.

If you're lucky, you may be able to copy files from a hard disk that fails to boot. If you're really unlucky, everything on your hard disk may be gone forever. That's why you should always back up your valuable files from your hard disk periodically.

Disk drive light goes on and off for no apparent reason

Each time a virus (or any program) accesses a floppy or hard disk to read or write data, your computer probably flashes a light to show you what's happening. (Some computers, including many Macintoshes, do not have a disk drive light that flashes when the computer accesses the disk.)

Of course, many programs have an automatic File Save feature that saves your data whenever you pause for a few seconds. Many Macintosh disk compression programs also wait patiently until you stop using your computer momentarily, then rush off to compress files on your floppy or hard disks. If you're using Windows 95 or higher, you may also see the hard disk light flash on and off as Windows stores and deletes files temporarily as you work.

Before deciding that a virus is infecting your computer, quit out of all programs. If you still see the disk drive light flashing way too often, you might have a virus lurking about.

Other computers at work have similar problems

If you are at work, perhaps the easiest way to determine if your computer is infected is to see if any other computers in your area are experiencing similar problems. For example, if three other people in your office complain that the "J" key on their keyboard isn't working or that their computer seems abnormally slow, check for a virus.

INFECTION METHODS

Like all computer programs, viruses can only work if you load and run them. Because nobody *wants* to run a virus (except perhaps virus and antivirus programmers), viruses have to load themselves without your knowledge. There are three types of viruses: file infectors, boot infectors, and macro viruses.

File infectors only infect programs, such as WordPerfect or Microsoft Excel. A file-infecting virus spreads whenever you run the infected program.

Boot viruses only infect the boot sector of a disk. Every floppy and hard disk contains a boot sector, which tells the computer how to use that particular disk. A boot virus spreads whenever you boot from (or access) an infected floppy or hard disk. (Some viruses, called multipartite viruses, know how to infect both files and boot sectors. This gives them twice as many chances to infect your computer.)

Macro viruses only infect files created by a specific program, such as documents created in Microsoft Word or spreadsheets created in Microsoft Excel. Macro viruses spread when you load an infected file, such as an infected Word document.

Viruses can spread using a variety of methods:

→ Direct infection

→ Fast infection

→ Slow infection

→ Sparse infection

→ RAM-resident infection

Direct infection means that the virus infects one or more files each time you run the infected program or open the infected document. If you don't do either, this virus can't spread at all.

Fast infection means that the virus infects any file accessed by an infected program. For example, if a virus infects your antivirus program, watch out! Each time an infected antivirus program examines a file, it can actually infect that file immediately after certifying that the file is virus-free.

Slow infection means that the virus only infects newly created files or files modified by a legitimate program. By doing this, viruses attempt to further mask their presence from antivirus programs.

Sparse infection means that the virus takes its time infecting files. Sometimes it infects a file, and sometimes it doesn't. By infecting a computer slowly, viruses reduce their chance of detection.

RAM-resident infection means that the virus buries itself in your computer's memory and, each time you run a program or insert a floppy disk, the virus infects that program or disk. RAM-resident infection is the only way that boot viruses can spread. Boot viruses can never spread across a network, although they can infect individual computers attached to a network.

File infectors

File-infecting viruses infect program files like games, word processors, databases, or spreadsheets. (If you're running MS-DOS, the typical files a virus can infect are .COM, .EXE, and .SYS files such as COMMAND.COM, 123.EXE, or CONFIG.SYS. With macro viruses, the virus infects Microsoft Word documents or Microsoft Excel worksheets.) Each time you run an infected file, the file-infecting virus searches for another program to attack.

File-infecting viruses can only spread within a specific operating system. Thus, a file-infecting virus designed to infect MS-DOS program files won't be able to infect Windows 95 program files and vice versa.

Parasitic program infectors

When a virus infects a file, it has three choices: It can attach itself to the front or back of a file or plant itself in the middle. (If the virus deletes part of the file it's infecting, it's known as an overwriting virus.)

When a virus attaches itself to the front or back of a file, it changes the file's size and usually doesn't harm the infected file. This virus is known as a parasitic program infector and can easily be spotted by the change in file size (see Figure 13-4).

Overwriting file infectors

Overwriting viruses are a bit more dangerous. Because they physically alter any files they infect—replacing some of the program's code with their own—they can damage or destroy files. If you run a program infected by an overwriting virus, the program usually won't work. Overwriting viruses can often escape detection because they infect a file without changing its size (see Figure 13-5).

Lehigh virus

One of the first file-infecting viruses struck Lehigh College in Bethlehem, Pennsylvania, in November 1987. Students borrowing software from the library soon found

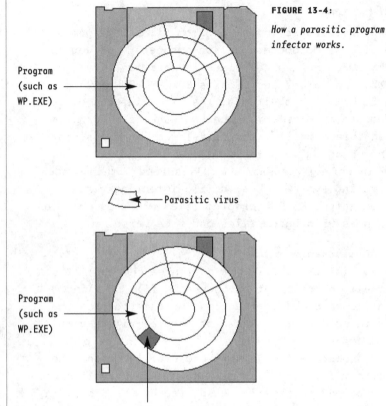

FIGURE 13-4:
How a parasitic program infector works.

Program
(such as
WP.EXE)

Parasitic virus

Program
(such as
WP.EXE)

The parasitic virus latches on to
the beginning or end of a program.

that an abnormally large number of floppy disks simply failed to work.

Several students quickly attributed the cause to a virus and dubbed it the Lehigh virus, which had originally infected one of the library's hard disks. As soon as someone inserted a floppy disk into the infected computer, that disk was infected with the Lehigh virus.

Although the Lehigh virus failed to spread much beyond the college, its existence helped prove once and for all that viruses really did exist and weren't the fanciful creation of a science fiction writer with a computer.

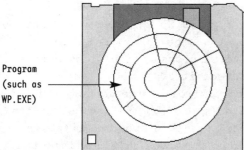

FIGURE 13-5:

How an overwriting file infector works.

Program
(such as
WP.EXE)

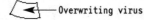
Overwriting virus

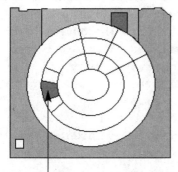

The overwriting virus copies itself
over part of an existing program.

Boot viruses

Every disk has a boot sector with instructions that tell
the computer how to use that particular disk. Because every
disk (including blank formatted floppy disks) has a boot
sector, every disk can be infected by a virus.

When you turn on your computer, it may check to see if
there's a floppy disk in the disk drive. If a disk is present, the computer reads the boot sector off the floppy
disk. If no floppy disk is present, then the computer uses
the boot sector on the hard disk, called the Master Boot
Record (MBR).

Boot viruses hide themselves in the boot sector of a floppy or hard disk (where else?). So while your computer frantically looks to the boot sector for instructions on what to do next, the boot virus grabs control long before an antivirus program can detect it.

Once the boot virus has control of the computer, it loads itself in your computer's memory, then passes control back to the real boot sector. As far as your computer is concerned, everything is fine, although it's now infected by a virus. That's why boot sector viruses can be some of the most dangerous viruses around.

But a boot sector is very small—only 512 bytes long—much too small for an entire virus to squeeze into. To get around this limitation, most boot viruses break themselves into two parts: One part infects the actual boot sector, and the rest of the virus hides elsewhere on the disk.

Some boot viruses hide in any empty space on a disk. To prevent other programs from overwriting them, they mark their location as bad sectors.

Once a boot virus buries itself in your computer's memory, it waits for a new disk to infect. Each time you insert a floppy disk into your computer, the boot virus infects that floppy disk.

To spread to a new hard disk, a boot virus has to infect a floppy disk. If you insert an infected floppy disk into an uninfected computer and then boot up or run a program from that floppy disk, the boot virus can copy itself to the uninfected computer's hard disk (see Figure 13-6).

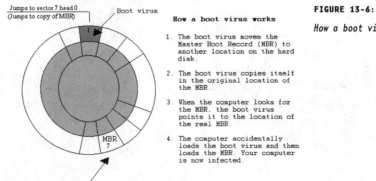

Jumps to sector 7 head 0
(Jumps to copy of MBR)

Boot virus

MBR 7

How a boot virus works

1. The boot virus moves the Master Boot Record (MBR) to another location on the hard disk.

2. The boot virus copies itself in the original location of the MBR.

3. When the computer looks for the MBR, the boot virus points it to the location of the real MBR.

4. The computer accidentally loads the boot virus and then loads the MBR. Your computer is now infected.

FIGURE 13-6:

How a boot virus works.

The infamous Michelangelo virus is a boot virus.
Although the Michelangelo virus gets all the publicity,
another boot virus called Stoned actually infects more computers worldwide every year. Michelangelo is really just a
modified version of Stoned.

By the way, you cannot transfer a boot virus through
the phone lines, so you'll never catch a boot virus by
dialing into a BBS, an online service, or the Internet.

Pakistani/Brain virus

As discussed earlier in this chapter, the earliest boot
virus was the Pakistani/Brain virus, which is generally
considered responsible for the world's first computer virus
outbreak. The creators were two brothers, Amjad Farooq Alvi
and Basit Farooq Alvi, who ran a software company in
Lahore, Pakistan, called Brain Computer Services.

Brain Computer Services developed proprietary software
and, like most software publishers, they soon fell victim
to rampant software piracy as people copied their programs
illegally. To punish these software pirates, the two brothers created the Pakistani/Brain virus, which would infect
any computer using an illegal copy of their program. To
remove the virus from their computer, software pirates
would have to call Brain Computer Services for help.

To supplement their software business, these two
"righteous" brothers also sold bootleg copies of popular
American programs such as WordStar, Lotus 1-2-3, and dBASE.
For the cost of a few dollars, anyone could buy a bootleg
copy of a program that normally retailed for $495 or more.
Eventually, many college students wound up with copies of
these bootleg programs and took them back to their schools.

But through a twisted sense of logic, the brothers
decided that people buying pirated copies of American programs should also be punished for their actions. So every
bootleg copy of an American program came infected with the
Pakistani/Brain virus. Eventually students brought the
Pakistani/Brain virus to America, where it promptly made
its presence known in 1987 at places such as George
Washington University and the University of Delaware,

infecting thousands of computers in classrooms, laboratories, and dormitories.

The original Pakistani/Brain virus is fairly primitive by today's standards, and its main flaw was that it could only infect 5.25-inch floppy disks—not the newer 3.5-inch disks. As users switched to the 3.5-inch floppy disk standard, the Pakistani/Brain virus could not spread as easily. As a result, the Pakistani/Brain virus is now practically extinct, although variants of it continue to spread.

Michelangelo virus

Almost everyone learned about computer viruses during the great "The Boy Who Cried Wolf" scare of 1992. The virus scare began when Leading Edge, a major computer manufacturer, accidentally shipped several hundred computers infected with the Michelangelo virus, another boot virus. Within a month, two software publishers, DaVinci Systems and Access Software, also shipped disks infected with the Michelangelo virus.

For some odd reason, the media quickly latched on to the Michelangelo virus story and spread hysteria far and wide, warning computer users that the Michelangelo virus would destroy their hard disks on March 6, Michelangelo's birthday. The *Houston Chronicle* called the virus "a master of disaster." *USA Today* warned that "Thousands of PCs could crash Friday." The *Washington Post* displayed its own scare tactic headline, "Deadly Virus Set to Wreak Havoc Tomorrow."

Estimates about the number of infected computers ranged wildly, from a low of five thousand to a high of five million. In the meantime, antivirus software publishers sold thousands of antivirus programs to a hysterical public. When March 6 arrived, computer users around the world braced themselves for the impending attack—and nothing happened.

Although the Michelangelo virus is real and did attack a few computers, the danger was nowhere near what the media proclaimed. Some experts say that if the media had failed to warn the public of the virus, the Michelangelo virus would have proven more disastrous. Others claim that the

Michelangelo virus was never widespread to begin with and that the media hype simply made antivirus program publishers wealthier.

Whatever the case, the great Michelangelo virus scare of 1992 did make the general public aware of the virus threat for the first time. And every year, around March 6, software publishers report that sales of their antivirus programs increase dramatically, much to the delight of their stockholders.

Multipartite viruses

Both file infectors and boot viruses have their strengths and weaknesses. File-infecting viruses can only spread if you run an infected program. If the virus happens to infect a seldom-used file, such as QBASIC.EXE or DEBUG.EXE, then the program may be infected, but the virus may never spread and can never do any damage. Some computers can be infected for years without ever having any problems.

Similarly, boot viruses spread only when you boot up from an infected floppy or hard disk. If you don't boot up or use an infected disk, the virus can't spread.

A new breed of viruses combines the features of both file infectors and boot viruses. Multipartite viruses can infect either (or both) files and boot sectors to increase their chances of spreading. Although increasing their chances of infecting a computer, multipartite viruses also make themselves more vulnerable to detection by increasing the places an antivirus program can find them. They're also more complicated to write, so there are fewer multipartite viruses in the wild to worry about.

Natas virus

The Natas (Satan spelled backward) virus is one of the more common multipartite viruses, originally discovered running rampant in Mexico. Natas can infect files (.COM, .EXE, and overlay files) and boot sectors on both hard disks and floppies. It's one of the few known polymorphic stealth viruses that can change its appearance and hide from antivirus programs.

Besides being one of the more common and destructive viruses in the wild, Natas also has the odd distinction of being written by a hacker, dubbed Priest, who later worked for an antivirus company called Norman Data Defense Systems. After releasing Natas in the wild, Priest accepted a consulting job at Norman Data Defense Systems. The company later decided they could not trust a known virus writer and let him go, but not before the entire antivirus community screamed in protest and vowed that they would never stoop so low as to hire virus writers to help write antivirus software.

Macro viruses

Despite the fact that macro viruses can only infect files created by another program, they have quickly become the fastest spreading and most dangerous breed of viruses. Unlike other types of viruses that are written using an assembly language (C++, BASIC, or Pascal), macro viruses are written using the macro programming language in a specific program. Most of the new macro viruses are written using Microsoft's macro language, called Visual Basic for Applications (although a few older macro viruses are written in WordBasic, an older macro programming language for Microsoft Word).

Macro viruses infect the templates that define the margins, font, and general formatting for documents. Every time you create a new document from a template infected by a macro virus, the macro virus tries to infect another template and your new document.

Because most people share document files instead of template files, macro viruses cleverly convert infected documents into template files. So although you think you're opening up a document for editing, you're actually opening up a template instead.

Despite their prevalence in the wild, macro viruses (at least at the time of this writing) have been limited to infecting templates created by Microsoft products such as Word, Excel, or PowerPoint. Although some people have tried writing macro viruses to infect WordPro or WordPerfect doc-

uments, these don't spread as easily because WordPro and
WordPerfect documents store their macros in a separate
file. But when you copy a Word or Excel document file onto
a floppy disk, through a network, or over the Internet,
you're automatically copying both your document and any
macros in a single file, which gives the macro virus a
chance to spread.

The Concept macro virus

The world's first macro virus, dubbed the Concept virus,
can infect Microsoft Word documents on both Windows and the
Macintosh. This virus was written in the macro language
found in Microsoft Word version 6.0, although it can also
infect Word documents created by other versions.

The Concept macro virus appears to have been written
to prove that viruses really could be written using a macro
programming language. As a result, Concept simply displays
a dialog box announcing its existence, but it won't deliberately wreck any files on your disk.

The Laroux Excel macro virus

A year after the Microsoft Word Concept macro virus
appeared, the first Microsoft Excel macro virus, dubbed
Laroux, was found in July 1996. The Laroux macro virus was
written in Visual Basic for Applications (VBA), allowing it
to infect Excel files created under Windows, although it
can't spread to older versions of Excel or to Macintosh
Excel files.

Like the Word Concept macro virus, Laroux is not
intentionally destructive, does not visibly announce its
presence, and contains no payload; it just replicates and
spreads to all your Excel worksheet files.

Melissa

Taking macro virus programming one step further was the
Melissa virus, which made headlines in early 1999 by becoming the fastest spreading virus in history. This virus
infects Word documents and then uses Visual Basic macro
commands to read the address book of Microsoft Outlook, a
common email program that comes with Microsoft Office.

The Melissa virus then creates an email message and sends it to the first 50 names in the Outlook address book, where each message appears with the subject "Important Message From" (followed by your name), with a body text that states, "Here is that document you asked for . . . don't show anyone else ;-)." The virus then attaches a copy of the infected Word document to the email message.

As soon as the recipient opens the infected Word document, the virus spreads to that computer and repeats the process of emailing itself to another 50 people stored in that person's Microsoft Outlook address book.

If you peek inside the macro virus source code, you'll find the following message:

> *'WORD/Melissa written by Kwyjibo*
> *'Works in both Word 2000 and Word 97*
> *'Worm? Macro Virus? Word 97 Virus? Word 2000*
> *Virus? You Decide!*
> *'Word --> Email | Word 97 <--> Word 2000 . . .*
> *it's a new age!*

The original Melissa virus didn't do anything destructive, but variants do cause damage by erasing files.

Companion viruses

Companion viruses are a dying breed, most common to the ancient MS-DOS operating system. A companion virus takes advantage of a strange quirk in MS-DOS that causes .COM programs to run before .EXE programs.

For example, the QBasic program is stored in a file called QBASIC.EXE. If you want to run QBasic, you could type either one of the following:

```
C:\>QBASIC
```

```
C:\>QBASIC.EXE
```

Either command loads and runs the QBasic program. This abbreviation works with all MS-DOS applications.

Because it's shorter to type the program name without the .EXE file extension, most people use the former method and just type the program name, such as WP for WordPerfect, 123 for Lotus 1-2-3, or DBASE for dBASE.

So what happens if there are two files called WP.COM and WP.EXE? When confronted with identical file names, MS-DOS always runs the .COM program first. If you type WP at the DOS prompt, MS-DOS will always run the WP.COM file and ignore the WP.EXE file.

Companion viruses use this principle to their advantage. Instead of infecting a file, a companion virus creates an identically named file that ends with the .COM file extension. So rather than infect the actual file such as DBASE.EXE, a companion virus hides itself inside a file called DBASE.COM.

As a result, the next time you type DBASE at the DOS prompt, thinking you are loading the actual DBASE.EXE program, the DBASE.COM file (containing the virus) loads first. After infecting another file, the DBASE.COM file then runs the DBASE.EXE program, which is the file you wanted to run in the first place. Because your chosen program loads with no apparent problems, you might not even know that a virus is on your computer.

Antivirus programs have a tough time detecting companion viruses because companion viruses never modify files. Of course, if you suddenly notice multiple .COM files popping up all over your hard disk, you may catch a companion virus before your antivirus program does.

Fortunately, companion viruses are only effective on computers that use MS-DOS. If you use Windows, companion viruses won't spread because Windows programs always have the .EXE file extension. For example, to load Microsoft Word, Windows uses the complete file name WORD.EXE. Even if a companion virus has created a file called WORD.COM, Windows won't use it, which keeps the companion virus from loading and spreading.

The Goldbug virus

Goldbug is a complex virus and can spread as a boot virus that infects the boot sectors of hard and floppy disks or as a companion virus that creates a .COM companion file each time you run an .EXE program.

Although not especially dangerous or common, the Goldbug virus has the unique ability to avoid antivirus software. If Goldbug has managed to hide itself in your computer's memory, it can prevent the execution of .EXE programs whose names have the letter a as their second-to-last character (such as many antivirus programs with names like SCAN, CLEAN, NETSCAN, CPAV, NAV and TBAV).

Windows viruses

When Microsoft introduced Windows 95/98/Millennium Edition/NT/2000, they effectively killed the breeding ground for many viruses that relied on the MS-DOS operating system. Although DOS-based viruses could still replicate under Windows, they had more difficulty if the user never ran any DOS-based programs.

Virus writers quickly took up the challenge and began writing Windows-specific viruses. As more people began using only programs designed for Windows, these Windows-specific viruses began appearing on more computers throughout the world.

Boza virus

The Boza virus was first discovered in January 1996 and holds the distinction of being the first virus to spread only under the Microsoft Windows 95 operating system. Written by an Australian virus writers group called VLAD, Boza tries to infect .EXE files, but a bug prevents the virus from working correctly. As a result, the Boza virus poses virtually no threat to Windows users.

Chernobyl virus

On April 26, 1999, a virus struck in Korea and infected as many as one million computers, resulting in more than $250 million in damages. Dubbed the Chernobyl virus (or the CIH virus), this virus was written by 24-year-old Chen Ing-hau and is considered one of the most destructive viruses ever written.

The virus can infect 32-bit Windows 95 and higher executable files but can only run under Windows 95/98/ Millennium Edition. If you run an infected program, the virus resides in your computer's memory and infects every file that your computer accesses.

To avoid detection, the CIH virus never alters the size of any files it infects. Instead, it searches for empty space in the infected file, breaks itself up into smaller pieces, and inserts those pieces in the unused spaces.

There are three known variants of the CIH virus. Version 1.2 and Version 1.3 attack on April 26 (the date of the Chernobyl Soviet nuclear disaster) and Version 1.4 attacks on the 26th of every month.

When the CIH virus triggers, it launches two separate attacks. The first attack overwrites the hard disk with random data until the computer crashes, ultimately preventing the computer from booting up from the hard disk or floppy disk and making the overwritten data on your hard disk nearly impossible to recover. The second attack targets the data stored in your computer's Flash BIOS (the Basic Input Output System, which is the part of your computer that controls all system devices, including the hard drive, serial and parallel ports, and the keyboard). To fix this problem requires replacing or reprogramming the BIOS.

While every antivirus program can protect against the CIH virus, the 26th of every month still finds some companies getting their data wiped out.

Linux viruses

With the growing popularity of the Linux operating system, don't expect it to remain virus-free for long. Already a handful of virus writers have targeted the Linux operating system, so expect more Linux viruses to appear in the near future. However, viruses can only do limited damage to Unix systems, since it is a proper multi-user operating system, with security mechanisms that prevent users or programs from wreaking widespread havoc across an entire computer hard disk.

Staog virus

The Staog virus first appeared in 1996 and was written in assembly language by the VLAD virus writing group, the same group responsible for creating Boza, the first Windows 95 virus.

Like the Windows 95 Boza virus, the Staog virus is a proof-of-concept virus for demonstrating the potential of Linux virus writing without actually causing any real damage. As of yet, the Staog virus hasn't posed much of a threat to any Linux computers. Still, with the Staog assembly language source code floating around the Internet, other virus writers are likely to study and modify the code to create new Linux viruses that could be more dangerous.

Bliss virus

Unlike the Staog virus, the Bliss virus not only spreads in the wild, but also possesses a dangerous payload that wipes out data. Although reports of Bliss virus infections appear low, this virus poses a definite threat to Linux systems, especially since few antivirus companies have released Linux versions of their antivirus programs.

Macintosh viruses

Because the Macintosh is such a challenging programming environment, most virus programmers find it easier to write MS-DOS, Windows, or macro computer viruses instead. As a result, the main threat to Macintosh users are macro viruses, but other types of Macintosh viruses do exist.

So far, most Macintosh viruses simply display a message on the screen or make a noise. Almost no Macintosh virus will purposely wreck your files or scramble your hard disk, although their existence may still cause your Macintosh to crash or act erratically. Here are some examples:

MacMag virus

One day, Richard R. Brandow, the publisher of the Montreal-based computer magazine *MacMag*, decided to write a benign virus to spread a message of peace on the anniversary of the Macintosh SE and Macintosh II. His virus, dubbed the MacMag virus, was programmed to spread and then display the following message on March 2, 1988:

> *Richard Brandow, publisher of MacMag, and the entire staff would like to take this opportunity to convey their universal message of peace to all Macintosh users around the world.*

After displaying this message, the MacMag virus would erase itself out of existence. The MacMag virus eventually wound up at Aldus Corporation, the publishers of a graphics program called FreeHand.

Unknowingly, Aldus distributed several thousand copies of FreeHand that were infected with the MacMag virus. Once the company discovered its existence, they yanked back their programs, but not before several thousand copies had been sold and the MacMag virus had spread to Macintosh computers all over the world.

Although the MacMag virus currently poses no threat, its appearance alerted the industry to how quickly a single virus could spread among computers.

Scores virus

The Scores virus is the first known virus written out of revenge. Apparently, a programmer got fired from Electronic Data Systems (EDS) in 1987, and to get back at the company, this programmer created the Scores virus specifically to wreck two programs the company was developing at the time. It's unknown whether this virus ever successfully attacked its original target, but it eventually wound up infecting Macintosh computers at NASA and Apple Computer.

Apple Computer quickly responded with an anti-Scores virus program called Virus Rx, which they distributed free of charge. Like other Macintosh viruses, the Scores virus doesn't intentionally wreck anything, although its presence may keep your Macintosh from working properly.

To check your Macintosh for the Scores virus, look in your System Folder and examine the NotePad and Scrapbook files. If your Macintosh is virus-free, both files will appear as a cute little Macintosh icon. If your Macintosh is infected by the Scores virus, both files will appear as dog-eared pages (see Figure 13-7).

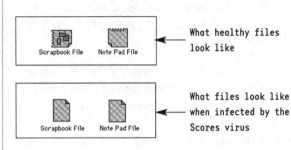

What healthy files look like

What files look like when infected by the Scores virus

FIGURE 13-7:

How to detect the Scores virus.

CAN A VIRUS EVER BE GOOD?

To many people, asking if viruses can ever be good is like asking if politicians can ever be trusted. Although the answer to the politician question is always no, the answer to the virus question is a possible yes. (Naturally, antivirus companies vehemently claim that there is no such thing as a good virus, despite the fact that without viruses none of these antivirus companies would have a single product to sell.)

The worm in Microsoft Word

When Microsoft introduced its word processor, they copy-protected the floppy disks. This was fairly common back in the early 1980s, so no one really cared. However, copy-protected disks also kept legitimate program owners from making backup copies of their $495 programs. One cup of coffee spilled on a floppy disk could ruin your entire $495 investment.

To allow legitimate program owners to copy a copy-protected disk, several companies sold special disk-copying programs, which of course defeated the copy-protection schemes. Naturally, software pirates bought these same programs and resumed illegally copying copy-protected programs. So how did the software publishers fight back?

According to one story, Microsoft fought back by planting a worm (which is similar to a virus, except a worm can't infect other programs) in their Microsoft Word program. Periodically, this worm would check to see if the program was running off a legitimate copy of Microsoft Word. If so, the worm remained dormant. But if the worm noticed that it was running off an illegal copy of Microsoft Word, it woke up, displayed a message stating that, "The seeds of crime bear bitter fruit," and then trashed that person's data in retaliation.

This worm was only supposed to punish software pirates, but one day it woke up, mistook a legitimate copy of Microsoft Word for a pirated one, and trashed a legitimate user's data.

Microsoft denied that it had ever planted a worm in its program, then quickly placed the blame on a summer intern who had worked for them. Whatever the truth, Microsoft soon dropped copy protection from all of their programs, and many other software publishers followed suit to avoid being associated with such a lethal worm.

Was the worm "good" or "bad"? You have to decide for yourself.

Cruise viruses

Cruise viruses get their name from cruise missiles, which are capable of delivering a payload thousands of miles into enemy territory virtually undetected because they fly at low altitudes, underneath the range of most radar systems. Likewise, the purpose of a cruise virus is to sneak into a computer undetected and, instead of destroying its target, slip away with a copy of a password or an important file stored on the hard disk.

With such a capability, cruise viruses have become the darling of military and corporate espionage agents. The military is actively studying the use of viruses as a weapon, and their related spy agencies are equally intent on using cruise viruses as yet another way to steal secrets from an unsuspecting target.

Depending on what side you happen to be on, cruise viruses can be an important tool or a fearful weapon. Although the governments of the world publicly denounce the existence of viruses, you can bet that their top-secret spy agencies are more than happy to study viruses and recruit virus programmers for their own uses. Think virus writers are all deranged individuals who lack the social skills to deal with society? You might think again if you found out that a computer virus saved your country.

With the Soviet threat gone, espionage agencies are turning against each other, stealing corporate secrets in an effort to boost their own nation's industries at the expense of their so-called allies. It's no secret that American companies spy on French companies, French companies spy on Japanese companies, and Japanese companies spy on American companies.

The German government even funded a project, dubbed Project Rahab, which hired hackers to study the feasibility of spying and crashing computer systems in Russia, Japan, France, Italy, Great Britain, and the United States. If you think all governments and corporations play by the rules and deal with one another fairly, there's a bridge in Brooklyn you might be interested in buying. . . .

The KOH encryption virus

The Potassium Hydroxide (KOH) virus is of a rare breed: a beneficial computer virus. The KOH virus can spread and infect computers like any other computer virus, but instead of wiping out files or displaying silly messages like other computer viruses, it asks for your permission to encrypt all the data on your floppy or hard disk instead.

If you say no, the KOH virus does nothing, but if you give it permission, it will encrypt every file on your hard disk. Even better, any new files that you create or copy onto your KOH-encrypted hard disk will be encrypted as well. The KOH virus thus ensures that all of your data is protected, not just the few files you might remember to encrypt using a separate encryption program.

When you insert a floppy disk into your computer, the KOH virus asks for your permission to infect (and encrypt) that floppy disk as well. If you want, you can use a different password to infect your floppy disks so you can share encrypted floppy disks with others and still retain a separate password to protect your hard disk. (You can always remove the KOH virus encryption later.)

When you create a new file or copy a file onto a KOH-encrypted floppy disk, the KOH virus encrypts that file as well. If you insert a KOH-encrypted floppy disk into a new computer, the KOH virus asks for permission to infect and encrypt the data stored on that new computer's hard disk too. By spreading like a virus, KOH makes sure all of your data gets encrypted so you don't have to worry about encrypting separate files or floppy disks yourself.

The KOH virus is freeware and has been tested on various computers to ensure compatibility with all versions of MS-DOS, Windows 3.0 and 3.1, and various disk compression technologies like Stacker and DoubleSpace. But, the KOH virus has not been tested under any of the newer operating systems so take care when using it with Windows 95/98/Millenium Edition/NT/2000 or OS/2.

The future of "good" viruses

Even if you consider all computer viruses "bad," the technology used to create computer viruses can be beneficial. For example, some people have proposed using software "agents" (miniature programs) that can be programmed to search the Internet based on specific criteria. Much of the research on agents borrows ideas from both viruses and worms.

Whatever your own feelings, the fact is that viruses are real. Some are destructive, and nearly all are unwanted. If you use a computer, it's in your own best interest to know how viruses work, how to detect them, and how to get rid of them. After all, the chances of getting a computer virus infection may be minimal, but that doesn't mean you shouldn't take appropriate safety precautions.

VIRUS MYTHS AND HOAXES

Since each new outbreak of a virus causes hysteria and panic among computer users, you can cause nearly as much trouble by inventing a fictional virus than creating a real one. To learn more about specific virus hoaxes, visit the Virus Myth Page (http://kumite.com/myths) for the latest news about virus hoaxes and outbreaks. The following are some examples of some of the more common virus hoaxes.

The chain letter virus

Viruses often cause more havoc by just existing and spreading panic than through any actual damage they may cause. Thus some of the more annoying virus hoaxes are those that encourage you to email copies of the hoax to your friends. Not only does this spread the virus hoax, but it creates undue panic and confusion.

To convince people to propagate the hoax, virus hoaxes often contain information that sounds valid and threatening. One virus hoax, dubbed the Disney hoax, consists of this message:

Hello Disney fans,

And thank you for signing up for Bill Gates' Beta Email Tracking. My name is Walt Disney Jr. Here at Disney we are working with Microsoft which has just compiled an email tracing program that tracks everyone to whom this message is forwarded to. It does this through an unique IP (Internet Protocol) address log book database. We are experimenting with this and need your help. Forward this to everyone you know and if it reaches 13,000 people, 1,300 of the people on the list will receive $5,000, and the rest will receive a free trip for two to Disney World for one week during the summer of 1999 at our expense.   Enjoy.

Note: Duplicate entries will not be counted. You will be notified by email with further instructions once this email has reached 13,000 people.

Your friends,

Walt Disney Jr., Disney, Bill Gates & The Microsoft Development Team.

A similar virus hoax, dubbed the Good Times hoax, consists of a message urging people to forward the message to others:

Happy Chanukah everyone, and be careful out there. There is a virus on America Online being sent by E-Mail. If you get anything called "Good Times", DON'T read it or download it. It is a virus that will erase your hard drive. Forward this to all your friends. It may help them a lot.

Be suspicious of a message that urges you to send copies of itself to as many people as possible. It might be a hoax. Take some time to verify the information before blindly sending it out to others.

Also be suspicious of any email that says it contains a virus. An email virus in impossible for two reasons: A virus can only travel through the phone lines if it has infected a program. Second, a virus cannot infect email (but it can infect an email attachment!) because email is simply text displayed on your screen. Catching an email virus would be like becoming sick from touching a photograph of a biological virus.

The JPEG virus

Similar to the "Good Times" email hoax is another virus hoax dubbed the JPEG virus, which supposedly activates whenever you view a JPEG graphic file. Occasionally, you may find a message on a BBS or online service such as the following:

WARNING:

If you are using a DOS or Windows machine, then you are vulnerable to attack from the JPEG virus. THIS IS NOT A JOKE! The JPEG virus has already destroyed the hard disk of a major BBS in Chicago and has caused much grief to several users already.

The JPEG virus supposedly hides in the comment field of a JPEG file. When you view the graphic file, the JPEG virus allegedly uses an undocumented (and nonexistent) feature of DOS to spread and attack your computer.

Because this undocumented feature of DOS is entirely fictional, it's impossible for a virus to hide in a graphic file and spread when the graphic file is displayed. (Of course, a virus could still infect your graphic viewing program. If you run an infected graphic viewing program, the virus could spread and give the illusion that it popped out of your JPEG file. But now that you've read about this, you'll know where to look for the virus, and it won't be inside your JPEG graphic files.)

The fax machine virus

No, fax machines can never get infected by a computer virus. However, occasionally someone will send a fax with the words FAX MACHINE VIRUS—GOTCHA!!! printed in bold letters. Anyone who hasn't taken the time to learn about computer viruses will usually panic at the sight of these harmless words scrolling out of their fax machine.

If this happens to a co-worker, calm the person down and explain that it's impossible for a virus (which is a computer program) to transfer itself inside a fax machine over the phone lines.

The Iraqi printer virus

According to an article in *U.S. News & World Report* in 1992, the National Security Agency (NSA) planted a virus-infected computer chip into a printer sent to Iraq shortly

before the Gulf War. According to this story, the virus
spread from the printer and eventually infected the Iraqi
computers connected to it. Each time an Iraqi technician
tried to use an infected computer, the contents of the
screen would appear briefly, then disappear, rendering the
computer useless.

Although the Pentagon has never officially admitted or
denied the existence of this printer virus, the story
resembles an April Fool's joke published by *InfoWorld* magazine in 1991. Apparently someone (who didn't know anything
about viruses) took this April Fool's joke seriously—with
the result that Ted Koppel, a news broadcaster, reported
the existence of this virus on the popular news show
Nightline.

LEARNING MORE ABOUT VIRUSES

Here's a list of some Web sites with additional information
about viruses: AVP Virus Encyclopedia (http://www.avp.ch/
avpve), F-Secure Computer Virus Info Center (http://www.
europe.f-secure.com/vir-info/, Sophos (http://www.sophos.
com), Symantec (http://www.symantec.com/avcenter), and
Trend Micro (http://www.antivirus.com/vinfo). These Web
sites list all known viruses, their characteristics, what
damage (if any) they cause, and how to detect them.

To exchange messages about computer viruses, visit the
comp.virus or alt.comp.virus Usenet newsgroups.

14

Viruses II:
Writing a Computer Virus

IF THE THOUGHT THAT SOMEONE WOULD DELIBERATELY WRITE A COMPUTER VIRUS HORRIFIES YOU, REMEMBER THAT EVERY DAY SOMEONE ON THIS PLANET WAKES UP AND DELIBERATELY DUMPS TOXIC WASTE INTO THE ENVIRONMENT, BRIBES A GOVERNMENT OFFICIAL, OR SELLS WEAPONS TO UNSTABLE COUNTRIES. Virus writing is just one of many horrible things that people do to hurt others.

WHO WRITES COMPUTER VIRUSES?

IBM's antivirus Web site (http://www.av.ibm.com) provides a collection of research papers related to computer viruses including discussions about the use of neural networks to identify virus signatures (the code that uniquely identifies a particular virus), developing a computer immune system against present and future viruses, and the theory behind identifying and removing viruses.

But the most interesting studies on the IBM site are three papers written by Sarah Gordon: The Generic Virus Writer I, The Generic Virus Writer II, and Inside the Mind of the Dark Avenger (an infamous virus writer from Bulgaria). According to the virus writers themselves, people write viruses:

→ Out of boredom.
→ To become famous for writing a well-known virus such as the Michelangelo or Melissa virus.
→ To see if they can defeat the latest antivirus programs.

Bungling NATO scientists have created a computer virus "by mistake"...called Anti-Smyster 1... They were seeking protection from virus attacks similar to those launched at NATO by the Serbs during the Kosovo conflict. But the experiment went wrong, and scientists unleashed the virus on themselves.

—THE SUNDAY TIMES
(JUNE 18, 2000)

→ To punish others who may be pirating software, playing games at work, and so on.

→ To point out the weakness or flaws in certain operating systems or programs and "force" the company responsible to make changes.

Because viruses have received so much publicity, many people want to know how viruses (and antivirus programs) work—so they write their own out of sheer curiosity. Usually these people don't intend to screw up somebody else's computer; they just want to test their programming skills. They've just happened to choose virus writing as their way of expressing their creativity.

Similarly, just as some people collect Barbie dolls, autographs, or parts of dead animals to display as trophies, some people also collect computer viruses. Some virus collectors have even sold their collections to government agencies and also (surprise!) to companies that publish antivirus programs.

Still other people see writing new viruses as a form of electronic graffitti. Rather than waste time marking up walls and freeway overpasses with spray paint, they waste time by writing viruses to see how far they can spread a piece of themselves around the world. Many of these viruses simply display a political message or the nickname of the person who wrote the virus. Unfortunately, some of these viruses can be really destructive, such as the Chernobyl (CIH) virus or variations of the Love Bug worm.

When asked why he wrote viruses that could attack innocent users, the infamous Bulgarian virus writer, the "Dark Avenger," replied, "The innocent users would be much less affected if they bought all the software they used (and from an authorized dealer) and if they used it in the way they are allowed to by the license agreement. If somebody plays pirated computer games all day long instead of working, then it's quite likely that at some point they will get a virus. Besides, there's no such thing as an innocent user, but that's another subject."

The Dark Avenger further justified virus writing by claiming that "Antivirus products are as useless as viruses. The users spend much more money on buying such products and their updates rather than on the losses of data damaged because of viruses. The a-v products only help the users to empty their wallets. Besides, viruses would spread much less if the 'innocent users' did not steal software, and if they worked a bit more at their workplace, instead of playing games. For example, it is known that the Dark Avenger virus was transported from Europe to the USA via some (stolen) games."

Another reason people write viruses is to expose the flaws or weaknesses in products to embarrass certain companies. Past targets have included nearly all of the major antivirus programs (from vendors such as Symantec, McAfee Associates, and Trend Micro) and operating system vendors including Red Hat Software, Sun Microsystems, and Microsoft.

Since Microsoft is a particularly tempting target, virus writers have shifted their focus to writing macro viruses, which affect only files created by Microsoft products such as Word, Excel, PowerPoint, and Outlook. Joel McNamara, who created one of the first macro viruses to explore the theory and danger of viruses that could infect Word documents, reached this conclusion:

> Because of the simplicity in creating DMVs
> (Document Macro Viruses), it is likely only a mat-
> ter of time before the method is discovered and
> disseminated among the more malicious virus writ-
> ers. A concerted effort needs to be made to
> educate users of this threat. While this is hap-
> pening, the virus research community should
> examine all applications that feature automatic
> macros so their characteristics can be understood.
> Based on this information, existing virus detec-
> tion tools should be modified to scan for
> automatic macros in data files. Finally, software
> manufacturers need to add functionality to future

*versions of their applications to limit potential
damage DMVs can cause.*

Although McNamara wrote his DMV macro virus in 1994 to
warn application developers (such as Microsoft) that they
should modify their programs to limit the spread of macro
viruses, years later nothing much has changed. Anyone using
Microsoft products is still vulnerable to macro viruses.
With each revision, Microsoft adds additional security
patches to Microsoft Office, but the vulnerability still
exists. In the wake of the Love Bug worm (but not the initial Melissa virus attack), Microsoft finally released a
patch to prevent rogue programs from accessing the address
book in Outlook.

The Bulgarian virus factory

In the early days, the first computer viruses appeared
in countries such as Pakistan and Bulgaria. How did these
relatively tiny countries wind up with so many skilled
virus programmers? It started with cracking copy-protected
software.

More people use IBM-compatible computers than any
other computer type in the world. Unfortunately for many
people who live outside of North America, software prices
are outrageously high, sometimes equaling three months'
salary. Given the choice between making an illegal copy of
a program or sacrificing months to save up to buy a legal
copy, many foreigners choose pirated software (as do many
Americans).

To combat this piracy, most American programs sold
overseas are copy-protected. Essentially, this copy protection acts like an electronic lock that keeps people from
copying the floppy disks containing the program. However,
as with all human creations, anything that can be created
can be destroyed.

Picking the electronic locks of a copy-protected
floppy disk is no simple matter. But with the cost of

legitimate software so high in poorer countries, a surprisingly large number of people have taught themselves how to crack a copy-protected floppy disk. And the same knowledge required to dig into the guts of a floppy disk and remove copy protection also comes in handy when writing viruses. With so many skilled programmers, such countries soon became a fertile breeding ground for viruses.

Because the Bulgarian programmer called the Dark Avenger became so prolific at writing and spreading viruses, Bulgaria soon became known as the Bulgarian virus factory.

Today, virus writers can be found in all parts of the world, and software piracy is common practically everywhere. So if you happen to travel through a foreign country and someone hands you a floppy disk, be careful. It just might be infected with a new virus that nobody has ever seen before.

The fall of Communism and the rise of viruses

Of the more than 5,000 known computer viruses, approximately 1,000 originated in Russia and Eastern Europe. Some were written by typical teenaged hackers, but many others come from disgruntled Russian programmers living in the former Eastern Bloc countries.

Russian and Eastern European programmers earn much less than their Western counterparts. Whereas a programmer in the West can earn a six-figure salary along with lucrative stock options, programmers in Eastern Europe generally work for much less, ranging from the equivalent of a few hundred dollars up to a few thousand dollars a month—if they're lucky.

Such a wide gap in salaries between East and West angers many Eastern European programmers, so they vent their frustration by writing and spreading ever-more-sophisticated viruses to the West. If you ever catch a computer virus, examine it closely. It might have come from as near as your neighbor's house, or from as far away as Russia.

THE QUICK WAY TO WRITE A VIRUS: MODIFY AN EXISTING VIRUS

It's often easier to copy someone else's work than it is to create your own, and the same holds true for virus writing. Rather than take the time to learn how to write their own computer virus, most virus programmers take an existing virus, modify it slightly, and then release it in the wild as a new virus. Of course, because modified viruses tend to retain much of the original code, antivirus programs usually have few problems detecting them (assuming, of course, that the antivirus programs could detect the original virus).

Modifying an existing virus is a quick way to create a new virus without much effort or technical know-how. As a result, many "new" viruses are simply modified variations that people trade with other virus collectors through a *BBS* (Bulletin Board System) or a Web site (see Figure 14-1).

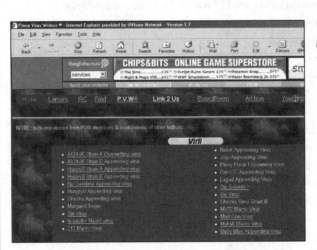

FIGURE 14-1:

Many Web sites provide viruses for everyone to share.

A virus Bulletin Board System (often called Virus Exchange Bulletin Board Systems or VX BBS) or Web site exists as a place for virus creators and collectors to trade viruses, but not everyone is welcome. Some won't let you join without the recommendation of a current member; others ask for a fee or that you upload a new virus before you can download one from their collection (another reason why it is such a popular practice to pass off a modified virus as new).

The key ingredient in modifying a virus is access to the source code—the instructions that make the virus work. You can get the source code either by downloading the virus from a virus exchange Web site or by disassembling an existing virus. (Note that although the antivirus industry frowns on spreading information about where to find live computer viruses, virus source code, or virus-writing tutorials, we've included this information to help you to understand and prevent viruses from ravaging your own computer at home or at work.)

To find live viruses to disassemble or actual virus source code, visit a hacker Web site like http://hackersclub. com/, or browse the directories in your favorite search engine: Hotbot and Yahoo, for example, list hacker Web sites in their directories. (Check their Security and Encryption categories.) Once you find a hacker Web site, you can often download live computer viruses and their source code.

What the heck is disassembling?

If you're lucky enough to find a Web site with virus source code, the next step is to modify its code. If you can only find live viruses but not any source code, you'll have to disassemble the live virus (macro viruses, for example, include their source code whenever they infect a file such as a Word document or an Excel spreadsheet).

To disassemble a virus, you use a disassembler (clever name, huh?). A disassembler is the opposite of an assembler or a compiler. If these terms mean nothing to you, here's a crash course on how people write computer programs.

To write a computer program (such as a database, game, or computer virus), you first choose a programming language such as C, BASIC, Pascal, or an assembly language. A programming language gives you commands that you can string together as a list of instructions that tell your computer to do something.

Unfortunately, computers know only one language, called machine language, which consists of nothing more than a collection of 0's and 1's. Because writing programs as a series of 0's and 1's is impractical, people have invented compilers.

A *compiler* acts as a translator. You write a program in BASIC, for example, and the compiler converts your BASIC instructions into machine language instructions. (If you write a program in assembly language, you convert it into machine language using a compiler called an assembler.)

Once you've compiled a program, that program is stored in an executable file. In the world of MS-DOS and Windows, an executable file has the extension .EXE (older programs for MS-DOS may have the .COM file extension). Once a program has been converted into an executable, the original programming instructions (known as source code, because it represents the original source of the program) is no longer needed.

So when you want to study the source code for a particular program, such as a computer virus, you use a disassembler which dissects an executable file and converts it into assembly language instructions. (Since macro viruses are written in the macro programming language of a particular program, such as Visual Basic for Applications for Microsoft Word, disassemblers won't dissect them.)

A disassembler can't convert an executable file into C or Pascal source code because it has no idea what programming language was used to write the program. To a computer, an executable file created by a C compiler looks identical to one created by a Pascal, Ada, C++, or FORTRAN compiler. So rather than torture themselves trying to figure out the language someone used to write a program, disassemblers take the easy way out and just convert an executable file into assembly language source code instead. (Except that programs created using Microsoft Visual Basic, Computer Associate's Clipper, or Java create distinct executable files that can be dissected and converted back into their original source files.)

Finding a disassembler

Many companies sell disassemblers as shareware or as commercial products, depending on the features you want. The majority of disassemblers work only on MS-DOS executable files (which is what most viruses are), but a growing number will now disassemble Windows executables. The most popular Windows disassembler is called Windows Disassembler Program, abbreviated as WDASM or Win32DASM.

When you disassemble a program, the disassembler tries to create assembly language source code that captures the original source code as closely as possible. But because there are a zillion ways to write a program, disassembling the same program with two different disassemblers will likely create two different versions of the assembly language source code. Even worse, assembly language source code created from a disassembler isn't always accurate. This means that you may need to modify, edit, or rewrite chunks of the assembly language source code before you can assemble the source code back into an executable program.

To find a disassembler, try these Web sites: IDA Pro (http://www.datarescue.com), Letun Disassembler (http://users.gazinter.net/letun), Programmer's Heaven (http://www.programmersheaven.com), or Sourcer and Windows Source (http://www.v-com.com).

Assembling virus source code

No matter how you get the source code for a computer virus, the final step is to convert the code into an executable file. To do this, you need an assembler. The three most popular assemblers are Turbo Assembler (TASM), Microsoft Macro Assembler (MASM), and A86.

Of the three, Borland International's Turbo Assembler has rapidly become the assembler of choice for virus programmers. If you can't find a copy of TASM anywhere, you can try the less-popular Microsoft Macro Assembler or the shareware A86 assembler (http://eji.com/a86/index.htm).

Once you have an assembler and the source code, you can start modifying the virus (assuming you know how to write assembly language instructions). Good luck, and if you have this much time on your hands, you're lucky already.

VIRUS-WRITING TOOLS AND TOOLKITS

Since writing a computer virus is neither easy nor financially rewarding, many virus programmers have developed virus-writing toolkits to make virus writing easier. Sporting names like the Virus Creation Laboratory, The Instant Virus Production Kit, or the Macro Virus Development Kit, all simplify the process of virus writing by letting you custom design a brand-new virus through pull-down menus (see Figure 14-2).

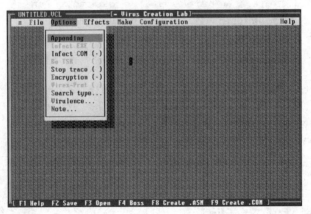

FIGURE 14-2:

The user-friendly interface of the Virus Creation Laboratory.

Although these toolkits lend credibility to the antivirus industry's claims that "thousands of viruses are released every month (so buy our antivirus program now)," most viruses created by virus-writing toolkits pose few threats.

Just as modern-day programs are plagued with bugs, many virus-writing toolkits are riddled with bugs that keep them from working properly. Even if the virus-writing toolkit does work correctly, many of the viruses it produces won't. Or if they do, they don't work exactly as intended (and so aren't as dangerous as they might first appear).

Even better (from an antivirus point of view), virus-writing toolkits tend to create similar types of viruses. Thus, once an antivirus program figures out how to recognize one virus created by a specific virus-writing toolkit, it can usually recognize variations created by that same toolkit. So no matter how many billions of viruses you create with a virus-writing toolkit, they will all be detected and removed easily by antivirus programs.

Mutation engines are a variation on virus-writing toolkits. These programs, like the Dark Avenger's Mutation Engine or the Trident Polymorphic Engine, are not viruses themselves but add-on programs used to create viruses. The idea is that you write a virus, then link it to a mutation engine. With a linked mutation engine, each time your virus spreads, the mutation engine changes the virus's identifying "signature," theoretically making it impossible for antivirus programs to identify and detect it.

Although a cunning attempt at foiling antivirus programs, mutation engines have their own flaws. First of all, using a mutation engine requires a fairly detailed knowledge of programming. Second, these engines have bugs, which often result in the creation of "sterile" viruses that are unable to spread. Even if mutation engines do occasionally create live computer viruses, they all will tend to have the same characteristics, making them easily detected by antivirus software.

WRITING A VIRUS FROM SCRATCH

If mutation engines and virus-writing toolkits can't increase the number of live, dangerous, and highly infectious computer viruses in the wild, how do people create the deadly new computer viruses that make the headlines every few months? The answer is easy: They write them from scratch.

But writing a computer virus from scratch isn't easy. Not only do you have to know how to write a computer program, but you also need detailed knowledge of your computer's operating system. These two challenges weed out most prospective virus writers, leaving only a handful skilled and determined enough to write a deadly new virus.

To write a virus, you need to use an assembler (such as Turbo Assembler) or a compiler (such as Visual C++). To write a macro virus, you need a copy of Microsoft Word or Microsoft Office.

VIRUS-WRITING NEWSLETTERS

Unless you happen to know assembly language, C, Pascal, or WordBasic, downloading the source code to a particular virus probably won't do you a bit of good, because you may not have the slightest clue how to modify it. Not surprisingly, many virus programmers distribute notes, tips, and complete virus-writing tutorials through newsletters. These newsletters almost always appear as ASCII or Word documents under a variety of names, such as 40Hex, SLAM, VLAD, or the NuKE Informational Journal.

A typical newsletter might contain actual virus source code that demonstrates a new technique for avoiding anti-virus programs, lists of known flaws in popular antivirus programs, reviews of useful books for virus writers, and news stories ignored by the popular press (see Figure 14-3).

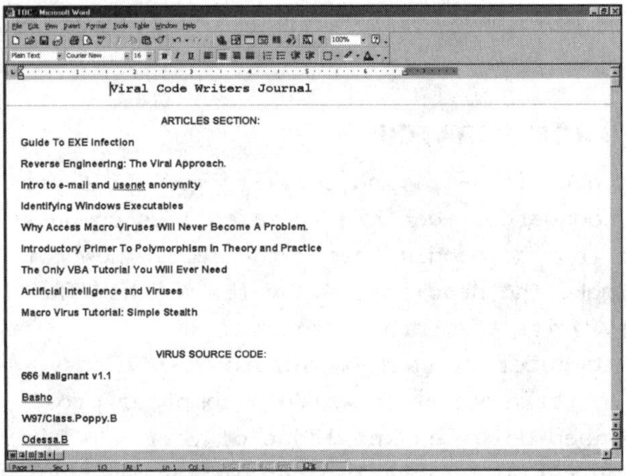

FIGURE 14-3:

Virus newsletters often provide source code to the latest viruses along with other news of interest to virus writers.

Some of these newsletters can be found on hard-to-find virus BBSs, and many are easily available through the Internet. Not only do these newsletters help keep virus writers informed on the latest developments, but they also provide antivirus programmers (along with the average person) with information for detecting and removing the latest generation of computer viruses.

To find a copy of a virus-writing newsletter, search for 29A, 40-Hex, CodeBreakers, HEX-FILES, Infectious Disease, Insane Reality, Living Turmoil, NuKE Info Journal, Plasma Mag, RSA, SLAM Mag, Source of Kaos, VLAD Magazine, VX United, or Xine.

HOW VIRUSES AVOID DETECTION

Viruses can only survive if they remain undetected. The longer they remain undetected, the greater the chances they can spread and deliver their payload. To write viruses that protect themselves, you can use a variety of defensive tactics.

Stealth

Viruses normally reveal their presence during infection. For example, a file-infecting virus typically changes the size, time, and date stamp of the file that it infects. However, file-infecting viruses that use stealth techniques may infect a program without modifying the program's size, time, or date, thus remaining hidden.

Boot viruses always use stealth techniques. When the computer reads a disk's boot sector, the boot virus quickly loads the real boot sector (which it has safely stashed away in another location on the disk) and hides behind it. This is like having your parents call you at home to make sure you're behaving yourself, but you really answer the phone at the neighborhood pool hall by using call forwarding. As far as your parents are concerned, they called their home number and you answered. But in reality, their call got routed from your home phone to the pool hall phone. Such misdirection is how boot viruses use stealth techniques to hide their presence from the computer.

In most cases, stealth techniques mask the virus's presence from users but cannot fool an antivirus program. To hide from an antivirus program, viruses may use polymorphism.

Polymorphism

To keep from infecting the same program or boot sector over and over again (and revealing itself), viruses must first check to see whether they have already infected a particular file or boot sector. This involves detecting themselves. To do so, viruses look for their signature—a set of instructions that make up that particular virus. Virus signatures are as unique as human fingerprints. Of course, antivirus programs can also find viruses by looking for these signatures. But as long as a virus has never been caught and examined, an antivirus program will never know its signature.

If convicted criminals could modify their fingerprints each time they committed a crime, they would be harder to catch. That's the idea behind polymorphism.

Theoretically, a polymorphic virus changes its signature each time it infects a file, which means that an antivirus program can never find it. However, because polymorphic viruses need to make sure they don't infect the same file over and over again, polymorphic viruses still leave a small distinct signature that they (and an antivirus program) can find.

Retaliators

The best defense is a good offense. Rather than passively hiding from an antivirus program, many viruses actively search out and attack them. When you use your favorite antivirus program, these retaliating viruses either modify the antivirus program so that it can't detect the virus, or they infect the antivirus program so that the antivirus program actually helps spread the virus. In both cases, the attacked antivirus program cheerfully displays a "Your computer is virus-free" message while the virus is happily spreading throughout your computer.

Although more than a dozen companies market antivirus programs, MS-DOS 6.0 came with a copy of Microsoft's own antivirus program. So it's no surprise that this program quickly became the number-one target for retaliating viruses.

Some retaliating viruses simply turn off Microsoft's antivirus program, which is supposed to detect viruses the moment they try to attack your computer. You continue to think that the antivirus program is protecting you, but it isn't—and the virus is busy infecting your computer. Others infect Microsoft's antivirus program, so each time you use it, the virus infects another file on your hard disk.

Besides Microsoft's antiquated antivirus program, other favorite targets for retaliating viruses include Norton AntiVirus and VirusScan. In other words, the most popular antivirus programs are always popular targets for retaliating viruses.

DO VIRUSES EVER ATTACK THEIR CREATORS?

When programmers write a word processor program or a game, they test it to see if it works correctly. When virus programmers write a new virus, they also may want to test it to see if it works right.

Of course, testing a word processor program means making sure it edits, prints, and formats text correctly. Testing a virus means making sure it spreads. If you're writing a destructive virus, you also need to make sure that it destroys its target. How do you determine whether a virus can successfully infect, spread, and ultimately destroy a file or hard disk? You have to test it on a computer.

Because viruses are computer programs, they almost always have bugs that keep them from working correctly or cause them to behave in ways that the programmer didn't expect. This means that many viruses prove too successful and manage to infect and attack their creator's own computer. If a virus gets out of control, the virus writer must track it down or it might just keep attacking the computer again and again.

Writing computer viruses is like handling nitroglycerin. If you're careful, nothing will happen. But make one mistake, and you may regret it for a long time afterward. Because viruses can turn around and attack their creators, viruses will always remain one of the more difficult types of programs to write. That explains why the better virus writers tend to be highly skilled programmers.

THE ANTIVIRUS COMPANY WARS

Antivirus companies spend most of their time battling virus writers, but they also spend a considerable portion of their time attacking each other. Although antivirus companies cooperate by sharing the latest computer virus discoveries, they're always fighting one another for market share and profits, publicly attacking one another for making misleading claims that one antivirus program is far superior to another one.

Every time a new virus appears, antivirus companies rush to be the first to issue a report and discredit the reports of their rivals. For example, when a new worm appeared disguised as a game based on the *South Park* cartoon, Computer Associates issued a report describing the worm as "dangerous" and (naturally) promoted its antivirus software as the solution for protecting your computer. But rivals at Trend Micro issued their own report claiming that the South Park worm wasn't a threat at all.

Another source of friction between antivirus companies is that some hire former virus writers. The theory is that a virus writer is already skilled in writing a virus and so should also be skilled in detecting viruses. Although such logic may make sense, the idea of hiring the "enemy," so to speak, makes other antivirus companies cringe. To many people, this is as reprehensible as the CIA cooperating with organized crime to launder illegal drug money.

So even though antivirus companies loosely cooperate with one another, they like their rivals only a little bit better than they like the virus writers themselves. The next time a major magazine gives a particular antivirus program an award or recommendation, watch the sparks fly among the losing antivirus companies as their public relations departments churn out flaws in the magazine's conclusions. Watching antivirus companies fight one another can be nearly as amusing as watching them battle computer viruses and their creators.

LEGAL CONCERNS

With viruses threatening the lucrative world of e-commerce, government organizations have stepped up their efforts to track down and prosecute virus writers. While tracking down the original virus writer is extremely time-consuming and difficult, the FBI did manage to catch the suspected Melissa virus creator, David L. Smith. If convicted, Smith could face five to ten years in prison and a fine of up to $150,000.

In early 2000, Pennsylvania Governor Tom Ridge signed into law a new bill that makes computer hacking and the willful spreading of computer viruses a crime. Anyone who intentionally spreads a computer virus could face a seven-year prison sentence and a $15,000 fine. Look for other states and countries to pass similar laws in the near future.

To learn more about the government's efforts in stopping computer crimes, visit the Computer Crime and Intellectual Property Section (CCIPS) of the Criminal Division of the U.S. Department of Justice (http://www.cybercrime.gov); you'll find information on recently prosecuted cases, Federal criminal codes related to computer crime, and how to report Internet-related crimes. CCIPS attorneys play a leading role in some computer crime and intellectual property investigations and coordinate many national investigations.

Of course, the threat of legal prosecution won't stop virus writers any more than the threat of prison has stopped bank robbers, murderers, or embezzlers. For the foreseeable future, virus writers are likely to continue their virus-writing rampage simply because they can.

THE NEXT GENERATION OF VIRUSES?

In the old days, viruses spread rather slowly, either by infecting a floppy disk that someone passed around or by infecting a file that people downloaded off an online service or the Internet. With the introduction of the Melissa virus and its many variants including the Love Bug worm, viruses soon found a new way to spread through email.

With the use of email growing so rapidly, experts fear that this trend of spreading viruses through email will continue, and soon viruses will spread to more than just personal computers. As cellular phones and personal digital assistants (PDAs) gain wireless communication and email capabilities, the next generation of viruses may soon start targeting smart phones and other handheld devices. Viruses could destroy data, reroute phone calls, record conversations, access contact information, or generate huge phone bills for the owners of an infected handheld device.

So the next time your cellular phone, Palm handheld, WebTV, or PocketPC device starts acting erratically, you may have a simple breakdown, technical problem, or the symptoms of a new virus attack that nobody has ever seen before.

15

Viruses III:
Prevention and Cure

THE BEST WAY TO PREVENT AND CURE A COMPUTER VIRUS IS TO BUY AN ANTIVIRUS PROGRAM. Basically, antivirus programs do the following:

→ Stop viruses before they can infect your computer

→ Detect viruses that may have already infected your computer

→ Remove viruses before they can do any damage

Not all antivirus programs provide all three features: Some can only detect and remove viruses but will do nothing to stop them from infecting your computer in the first place. Many shareware antivirus programs will only detect viruses but won't remove them until you pay for the program.

THE COMMON PARTS OF AN ANTIVIRUS PROGRAM

An antivirus program typically consists of three separate parts that work together to detect and prevent viruses:

→ Virus monitors

→ Scanners

→ Integrity checkers

Virus monitors

An antivirus *monitor* (also called a behavior blocker) does nothing more than bury itself in your computer's memory and watch for suspicious behavior in your computer's workings. Virus monitors are able to detect how programs like word processors or spreadsheets behave. When you run a word processor or spreadsheet, you typically save and modify certain files on your hard disk.

Viruses also behave in predictable ways. To infect or attack your computer, a virus must modify existing program files, the boot sector, the Master Boot Record (MBR), or the File Allocation Table (FAT) of your hard disk. The boot sector tells your computer how to use a floppy or hard disk and the MBR tells the computer how a hard disk has been divided.

Ordinary programs, such as spreadsheets or games, almost never need to modify program files, boot sectors, or the MBR. When you run these types of programs, the virus monitor watches their behavior to be sure that these programs are safe.

But the moment the virus monitor senses a program modifying a program file, boot sector, or FAT, it assumes a virus is at work and displays a warning. You then have the option to stop whatever program is accessing the sensitive parts of your disk or ignore it and assume it's a legitimate program at work.

The biggest advantage of antivirus monitors is that they work against all types of viruses—today's viruses and any viruses that come out tomorrow—because they look for typical virus behavior.

Their biggest disadvantage is that few people can tell whether the virus monitor has actually caught a virus or is confused by a legitimate program. As a result, virus monitors can be annoying—flagging a warning every time they detect a possibility that your computer could be in trouble. With so many false alarms (known as "false positives" in the antivirus business), it's easy to get disgusted by the virus monitor and either turn it off or simply ignore its warnings.

Scanners

Like all programs, computer viruses contain a unique set of
instructions known as a *signature*. A program's signature is
as unique as a fingerprint. If you know a particular
virus's signature, you can find that virus by looking for
its signature buried on your hard disk. An antivirus *scanner* works by examining each file on your hard disk for
known virus signatures. If it finds a virus signature
inside a file, it knows it has found a particular virus
(see Figure 15-1).

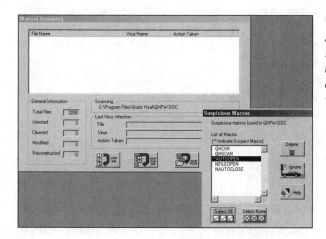

FIGURE 15-1:

*A virus scanner exam-
ines every file on your
hard disk for signs of
a known virus signa-
ture.*

Scanners are extremely dependable in protecting your
computer against known viruses. But if the scanner's list
of virus signatures is incomplete or out of date, the scanner may not detect a newer virus. This is why most
antivirus programs offer frequent updates (and may charge
you a lot for them). As new viruses appear, antivirus programmers update the scanner's list of recognizable virus
signatures.

Always make sure you have the latest version of your
antivirus scanner. If your antivirus scanner's list of
virus signatures is older than six months, it's time to get
an update. For optimal protection, you might consider using
two or more different antivirus scanners. That way if one

scanner misses a new virus, one of the others (hopefully) will catch it.

Integrity checkers

Integrity checkers examine each file on your hard disk and calculate a mathematical value (called a checksum) that uniquely identifies that particular file, based on the file's size and structure. The moment a virus infects a file, it changes the file's size or internal structure. The next time the integrity checker examines that file, it calculates a new checksum and compares it with the previous one. If the checksums match, the integrity checker assumes that the file is virus-free. If they differ, the integrity checker displays a warning that the file has been altered and may be infected.

Because integrity checkers look for changes in existing files, they can work against both existing viruses and future ones. But integrity checkers have two fatal flaws:

→ They can be fooled.

→ They raise frequent false alarms.

Each time you run an integrity checker, it examines the files on your hard disk and calculates a checksum, which it stores along with other checksum calculations in a file on your hard drive. To avoid detection, many viruses simply search out and destroy these checksum files. Now what happens on your hard drive when this file containing all the checksums gets wiped out?

Surprisingly, some integrity checkers in this situation simply create a new checksum file, and so the virus goes undetected.

Even worse, integrity checkers have no way of differentiating between legitimate program modifications to a file and virus-induced modifications. So each time an integrity checker runs across a modified file, it may flash a warning. And, once again, after several of these false alarms, people begin to distrust the integrity checker and ignore its warnings or stop using it.

For example, when you update an existing program on your hard disk, you must also tell the integrity checker what you've done. If you're using WordPerfect version 7.0 and update the program to version 8.0, your integrity checker notices that the WordPerfect program files are different. It may squawk out a warning that a virus could be infecting your updated WordPerfect program. Inexperienced users might immediately panic and tell the integrity checker to wipe out the suspected file, which would wipe out a legitimate program file.

If you're a programmer using a compiler such as Symantec C++, Delphi, or Visual Basic, integrity checkers may irritate you with constant false alarms. Each time you modify your program and compile it, the integrity checker may notice that it was modified and may incorrectly signal the presence of a virus. As a result, making a tiny change in a program and compiling it will start the integrity checker screaming out a warning.

To avoid this problem, you can tell your integrity checker to ignore the directories where you compile your programs. (Of course, if a real virus infects any programs in that same directory, then the integrity checker won't notice.)

HEURISTIC ANALYSIS

Many antivirus programs use a technique known as *heuristic analysis*. Heuristic analysis looks for suspicious program instructions. For example, an ordinary word processor would never need instructions to format a hard disk. But if that same word processor were infected by a virus, the virus might contain instructions for formatting a hard disk, and those instructions would then be embedded inside the infected word processor file.

Any time an antivirus program using heuristic analysis runs across files containing suspicious instructions, it flashes a warning that a virus may be present. Unfortunately, because heuristic analysis is nothing more than informed guesswork, it can mistake legitimate, uninfected files for infected ones. As a result, antivirus programs that use heuristic analysis may raise occasional false alarms.

Many antivirus programs use a scanner with heuristic analysis. That way, if a scanner doesn't recognize a virus, it uses heuristic analysis to check the file just in case. A file must pass both inspections to be proclaimed virus-free.

"FISHING" FOR VIRUSES

Rather than rely on scanners, integrity checkers, virus monitors, or heuristic analysis, some antivirus programs try to trick viruses into revealing themselves by offering special "bait" files for viruses to infect.

For example, an antivirus program might set up constant surveillance on two simple .EXE and .COM files. The moment a virus infects one of these files, the antivirus program immediately captures the virus's signature so it can recognize that particular virus later.

Bait files are the digital equivalent of Roach Motels. No matter what immunities cockroaches develop against insecticides, they can always get stuck in glue. However, because there is no guarantee that a virus will infect the bait file, most antivirus programs do not use the "fishing" technique.

RESCUE DISKS

If a virus thoroughly trashes your hard disk, what can you do? Usually nothing but weep and curse the person who wrote the virus.

To prevent you from ever reaching this sorry state of despair, many antivirus programs will create a rescue disk, to be used in case a virus destroys your hard disk (see Figure 15-2).

Although a rescue disk won't recover your destroyed files (backups will), it can restore your operating system and possibly many of your files.

Make a rescue disk as soon as you install your

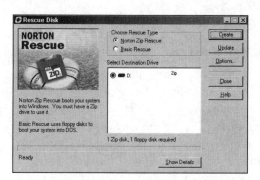

FIGURE 15-2:

If a virus totally dis-
ables your computer, an
antivirus program can use
a rescue disk to help you
recover.

antivirus program, then update it every time you add new
hardware or software to your computer. Keep your rescue
disk current so that it can restore your computer to its
most current state.

HOW ANTIVIRUS PROGRAMS FAIL

Not all antivirus programs offer virus monitors, scanners,
integrity checkers, heuristic analysis, virus removal, or
the ability to create a rescue disk. Most offer some of
these features, and those that offer all don't always perform very well.

Antivirus programs become obsolete quickly

Most versions of programs, like spreadsheets and databases,
can be used (almost) indefinitely. In fact, some people are
perfectly happy using software they bought in the early
1980s.

But antivirus programs become obsolete about six
months after release. Because new viruses appear every day,
an antivirus program older than six months is about as useful as a manual typewriter in a modern office.

Antivirus programs are extremely effective against
viruses they know. But each time antivirus companies update
their programs, virus writers study the updates for weaknesses and write new viruses specifically to exploit any
flaws. Because virus writers are always one step ahead of
the antivirus programmers, no antivirus program can ever

guarantee that your computer is 100% free from viruses.

Antivirus programs can be fooled

Antivirus programs are not perfect. Many people write viruses specifically designed to evade the popular antivirus programs. Some viruses even search and infect the more popular antivirus programs. If an antivirus program claims that your computer is virus-free, it might actually be infected by a virus that slipped through its defenses.

No matter how many antivirus programs you use, there's always a chance that your computer can be infected by a new virus strain that none of the antivirus programs knows how to detect and remove yet. Unfortunately, by the time the antivirus companies update their programs to detect a new virus strain, the virus may already have attacked your computer and wiped out your data.

The only sure way to protect yourself against a virus attack is to make backup copies of all your important files. That way, if a virus does wreck your hard disk, you'll still have all your data tucked away somewhere safe.

WHAT TO DO IF YOU FIND A VIRUS

Most people will never see a computer virus. However, if your computer is unlucky enough to catch a virus, your first indication could be a crashed computer and an empty hard disk.

But if you've been using antivirus programs regularly and correctly, you may be fortunate enough to stop the virus before it can cause any damage. What should you do when an antivirus program says that your computer has a virus (see Figure 15-3)?

Verify that it's a virus

The moment an antivirus program warns that it has found a virus, stop using your computer! The program will usually identify the virus by name (see Figure 15-4), provide a brief description of it, and then offer to remove it for you.

Often an antivirus program won't be able to remove a

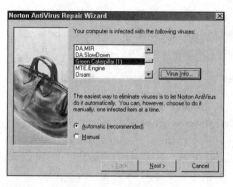

FIGURE 15-3:

Antivirus programs always alert you when they find a virus.

Virus Information

Virus name:	Green Caterpillar (1)	Close
Aliases:	1575, 1577, 1591, Find	Print...
Infects:	.COM and .EXE files	Help
Likelihood:	Common	
Length:	1575 bytes	

Characteristics
- ✓ Memory resident
- ○ Size stealth
- ○ Full stealth
- ✓ Triggered event
- ○ Encrypting
- ○ Polymorphic

Comments:
About two months after initial infection, a green caterpillar may appear and move across the screen. The program's time and date stamp are changed.

<< Previous virus   Next virus >>

FIGURE 15-4:

Antivirus programs often give short descriptions of the virus infecting your computer.

283

virus without wrecking the file that the virus is infecting. In that case, you'll just have to erase the infected file or move it to a temporary directory.

If you suspect that your computer may have a virus, try running two or more antivirus programs. If none of them finds a virus, then either your system is clean, or you have been infected by a new virus that your antivirus programs aren't noticing. This is especially possible if your antivirus programs are not up-to-date.

For additional help in identifying a virus, send any suspect file to your favorite antivirus publisher, who will examine it and determine whether it's really infected. Believe it or not, this service is (usually) free because antivirus publishers are in the business of finding new viruses so they can modify their programs to detect them. Of course, modifying and publishing a revised antivirus program that can detect and remove a new virus may take a long time, ranging from a few days to a few weeks, depending on the severity of the particular virus.

Remove the virus

Once you're certain that you've found a virus (or if you just want to play it safe), you can remove the virus by deleting the program it's infecting. (If you have a boot virus, you may have to reformat the hard disk as a last resort.)

A gentler measure is to let your antivirus program remove the virus for you. (Just remember that removing the virus may wreck the infected file.) When an antivirus program deletes a virus, it erases it and then overwrites its location with random data to kill the virus for good.

Although it is possible to remove a virus from a file, the success rate of disinfecting files depends on the virus and the technical abilities of the antivirus program. When a virus infects a file, it may either attach itself to the front or back of the file or bury itself somewhere inside. If the virus attaches to the front or back of a file, the antivirus program can separate the virus from the file and then eliminate it. But if the virus has buried itself inside the file, removing that virus is like curing a stomach ache by ripping out the stomach. In this case, removing the virus physically destroys part of the file in the process, rendering the file useless.

Despite the chances of ruining the infected file, removing a virus is far easier than deleting any infected files (which could number into the hundreds) and then copying clean versions of those same files back to your hard disk all over again.

Check other computers

If you've found a virus and successfully removed it, immediately check all floppy disks you may have used with the infected computer. Also check nearby computers and any other computers at home or at work that might have exchanged floppy disks with the infected computer.

Although it can be difficult, try to isolate the virus's origin. Did it come on a floppy disk that someone brought from home? (If so, then who brought it and where did they get it?) Or did the virus come over the network? From the Internet, maybe? If you can isolate where the virus came from, you can make sure that you don't get infected by that same virus (or a different one) from the same source, and you can warn others of the virus.

Of course, keeping your computer safe from viruses might not be as much fun as playing video games, but virus prevention is a fact of life. Any antivirus plan should allow for prevention, detection, and recovery from viruses.

PREVENTING VIRUSES

Keeping viruses out is much more effective than detecting and removing them after they've infected your computer. Although no computer can be completely safe, some computers may be more vulnerable than others. For example, a computer that several people share will be more vulnerable than a computer in your boss's office that gets used only once a month.

Educate people around you

The more people know about how viruses work, what they can and cannot do, and how they might infect a computer, the more likely someone can stop a virus before it spreads too far. Everyone who uses a computer should know that the threat of viruses is real.

Never boot from a floppy

Boot viruses spread whenever someone turns on a computer with an infected floppy disk in the disk drive. To completely eliminate this risk, always make sure everyone removes any floppy disks from a computer before turning it on.

If you know how to change your CMOS settings, you can tell your computer never to boot up from the A: drive. Use this option to keep novices from booting from a floppy disk.

There are, though, two good reasons to boot up from a floppy disk. One, if you suspect you have a virus, boot up from a clean, virus-free boot disk. That way you can prevent a virus from gaining control over your computer before your antivirus program can try to track it down.

A second reason to boot up from a floppy disk is if you have created a rescue disk to restore any files damaged by a virus. That way you can restore the files on your hard disk after a hard disk crash.

Check your email

Fast-spreading macro viruses often spread themselves by infecting a Word document that someone unwittingly sends as a file attachment via email, so you need to be careful with what you receive by email. Any time someone sends you a Word document, save it first and then scan it with your antivirus program. Or, better yet, configure your antivirus program to automatically scan all files sent to you by email. That way the antivirus program can detect the virus before it has a chance to arrive on your hard disk.

Know who uses your computer

If you're the only one who uses your computer, then you have only yourself to blame if your computer gets infected by a virus. But unless your computer is locked away, chances are it's wide open to anyone who happens to walk past.

Always make sure you know who uses your computer. To control access, you can use a security program that locks your keyboard with a password. Of course, you can't rely on passwords alone to keep people out, but they can be useful for stopping most who try using your computer without your permission.

DETECTING VIRUSES

There's always the chance that, no matter what precautions you take, a virus will still infect your computer. So check your computer periodically to be sure it's not already infected.

Unfortunately, checking for viruses can be as rewarding as scanning the skies for UFOs—most of your time will
be spent looking at nothing. But all it takes is one virus
exploding on your computer, and you'll kick yourself for
not checking more diligently.

Scan every disk periodically

Even if you don't think it's possible for a virus to infect
your computer, scan your disks with two or more antivirus
programs. Scan your hard disk and all your floppy disks
periodically. To make this task easier, many antivirus programs offer an option that lets you schedule automatic
scans.

Some people scan their hard disk every time they turn
on their computer. Others scan once every few days or once
a week. If losing two weeks' worth of data is okay, then
scan every two weeks. If you can't afford to lose even one
day's worth of work, run an antivirus program daily.

Scan every suspicious disk

Scan every removable disk (floppy, CD, ZIP, Superdisk, and
so on) if you're not absolutely sure where it's been or
whether it's virus-free. Scan the disks you get from
friends, the free ones with demos, even the ones you buy
shrink-wrapped.

Keep your antivirus programs up-to-date

Antivirus programs age rapidly. As new viruses appear, publishers release updated versions to detect new viruses. If
you're using a program older than six months, get an
updated version right away.

Some commercial antivirus programs offer a quarterly
update plan: You send them a wad of money (often totaling
more than the program's initial cost), and they send you
updated versions every few months. Many also offer free
updates at their Web sites or post their updates on commercial online services such as America Online.

RECOVERING FROM A VIRUS

No matter how careful you are, a virus could still wipe out your computer's hard disk. When all else fails, it pays to be prepared.

Make backup copies

Always make backup copies of your important data. Losing a one-page letter to your mother-in-law might not be important, but losing your company's financial records for the past five years can be disastrous.

Ask yourself how much data you're willing to risk losing and then make backups accordingly. For example, if you can afford to lose a week's worth of data, make backups once a week. If you can't afford to lose any data, make backups every night.

If you've got a hard disk larger than a few hundred megabytes, back up to a tape. (Many tape backup units can automatically back up your hard disk every night.) Backups can be your most important defense against viruses: If you lose everything, at least you'll always have your most recent backup. Now if your most recent backup occurred three years ago. . . .

Save your CMOS settings

The CMOS is a special chunk of memory in which your computer stores vital information like the time, date, hard disk type, boot options, and other features provided by your computer's motherboard. If your CMOS settings are incorrect, your computer may not work. So rather than mess up your computer, some viruses deliberately alter its CMOS settings. Then when your computer doesn't work, you'll blame the CMOS settings rather than the virus.

To view your CMOS settings, turn your computer off and then turn it back on again. For a brief moment before your operating system can grab control of your computer, you'll see a message like the following:

Press <DEL> to enter SETUP

If you act fast and press the DEL key, you'll see your CMOS settings or a menu, letting you choose the settings you want to view (see Figure 15-5). Write these settings down and keep them in a safe place. Then if your CMOS settings get wiped out, you'll be able to fix them yourself.

```
System Date     July 19 2000         F1      Help
System Time     13:47:11             ESC     Back
                                     Enter   Select
Floppy Options                       Press Enter

Primary IDE Master    WDC AC32100H    ↑       Previous Item
Primary IDE Slave     CS-R38 0        ↓       Next Item
Secondary IDE Master  Maxtor 83500D4  ←→      Select Menu
Secondary IDE Slave   Not Installed
                                      F5      Setup Defaults
     Language          English (US)   F6      Previous Values
     Boot Options      Press Enter    F10     Save & Exit
     Video Mode        EGA / VGA
     Mouse             Installed
     Base Memory       640 KB
     Extended Memory   31744 KB
     BIOS Version      1.00.06.CS1
```

FIGURE 15-5:

A typical cryptic menu for modifying your CMOS settings.

Or, instead of copying down all of your settings (which can be as exciting as reading a computer manual), many shareware and commercial utility programs will save your CMOS settings on a floppy disk. You can then load them back into your computer right from the floppy disk.

Make a clean boot disk

If your computer acts flaky, you may or may not have a virus. To determine if you have one, you need a clean boot disk.

A clean boot disk lets you start up your computer without accessing the files on your hard disk, thus bypassing any virus that may have infected your hard disk. You can then scan your hard disk with confidence.

Many commercial antivirus programs can create a clean boot disk for you, but you can make one yourself by using DOS or the Windows File Manager.

Making a clean boot disk with DOS

MS-DOS is the most primitive way to create a boot disk, but for PCs that don't run Windows, it's the only way. Here's what you do:

1. Exit out of Windows or display the DOS prompt if you're running Windows. (If you're running DOS, skip to Step 2.)

2. Stick a blank floppy disk in drive A, type **FORMAT A:/S**, and press **ENTER**. DOS displays the following message:

Insert new diskette for drive A: and press ENTER when ready...

3. Press **ENTER**.

4. Lock your disk as shown in Figure 15-6 by putting a sticky tab over the disk notch (for 5.25-inch floppy disks) or pushing the tab open (for 3.5-inch floppy disks).

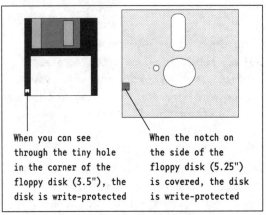

FIGURE 15-6:

How to lock a floppy disk.

When you can see through the tiny hole in the corner of the floppy disk (3.5"), the disk is write-protected

When the notch on the side of the floppy disk (5.25") is covered, the disk is write-protected

5. Scan your floppy disk with as many antivirus programs as possible. If all of them claim your floppy disk isn't infected, store your new boot disk in a safe place and label it clearly.

Making a clean boot disk with Windows 3.1

If you're using Windows 3.1, you can make a clean boot disk using the File Manager. Here's how:

1. Load the File Manager by double-clicking on the **File Manager** icon in the Main window group.

2. Insert a blank floppy disk in drive A.

3. Click on the **A**: drive icon in the File Manager.

4. From the Disk menu, click on **Make System Disk**. The Make System Disk dialog box appears.

5. Click on **OK**.

6. From the File menu, click **Exit** to exit the File Manager.

7. Lock your disk as shown in Figure 15-6 by putting a sticky tab over the disk notch (for 5.25-inch floppy disks) or pushing the tab open (for 3.5-inch floppy disks).

8. Scan your floppy disk with as many antivirus programs as possible. If all of them claim your floppy disk isn't infected, store your new boot disk in a safe place and label it clearly.

Making a clean boot disk with Windows 95 or higher

If you're using Windows 95 or higher, you can make a clean boot disk by following these steps (see Figure 15-7):

1. Choose **Control Panel** from the Settings menu. The Control Panel window appears.

2. Double-click on the **Add/Remove Programs** icon. The Add/Remove Programs Properties window appears.

3. Click on the **Startup Disk** tab.

4. Click on **Create Disk**. Eventually, an Insert Disk dialog box appears (see Figure 15-7).

5. Stick a blank floppy disk in drive A and click on **OK**.

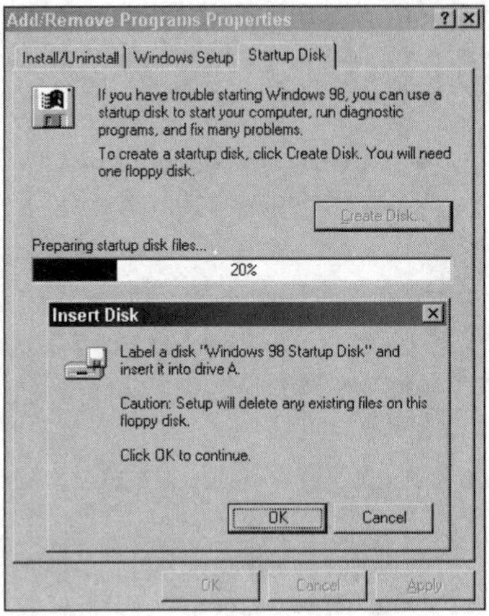

FIGURE 15-7:

Making a boot disk (start-up disk) from Windows 98.

6. Lock your disk as shown in Figure 15-6 by putting a sticky tab over the disk notch (for 5.25-inch floppy disks) or pushing the tab open (for 3.5-inch floppy disks).

7. Scan your floppy disk with as many antivirus programs as possible. If all of them claim your floppy disk isn't infected, store your new boot disk in a safe place and label it clearly.

Using your clean boot disk

Once you've created a clean boot disk, check your CMOS settings for the order in which your computer boots up. Some computers check the C: drive for a disk first and then the A: drive; others do the opposite. If you want to boot from a floppy disk, you may have to change the CMOS boot sequence to check the A: drive first and then the C: drive.

LEARNING MORE ABOUT POPULAR ANTIVIRUS PROGRAMS

To get shareware or trial versions of the more popular antivirus programs, or to learn more about the companies that sell antivirus programs, visit the following Web sites:

AntiViral Toolkit Pro (http://www.avp.com), F-Secure (http://www.datafellows.com), The Norton AntiVirus (http://www.symantec.com/avcenter), Sophos Anti-Virus (http://www.sophos.com), or VirusScan (http://www.nai.com or www.mcafee.com).

With a little diligence, you can prevent and eliminate most virus threats, but don't forget to make backups of all your important data. Even though you may never become the victim of a computer virus, there are many other ways you can lose valuable data, and you will be very relieved you took the trouble to make backups.

REALLY TECHNICAL WAYS TO SEARCH FOR A VIRUS

Although an antivirus program can be handy for detecting a possible virus infection, you might want to experiment with detecting viruses on your own. If you aren't afraid of bytes, disk sectors, hexadecimal, or other bizarre terms like that, there are more sophisticated (and complicated) ways to check whether your computer has a virus (even if your antivirus program says your computer is virus-free).

The DOS Debug program

MS-DOS has a seldom-used program buried on your hard disk called DEBUG.EXE. Back in the early days of computers, before OS/2 or Windows, programmers used this DEBUG.EXE program to help them write, edit, and correct their programs.

Today, there are better tools available to programmers, so the DEBUG.EXE program is an anachronism. Still, nearly every computer that uses MS-DOS 6.2 or earlier has a copy of the DEBUG.EXE file, and if you're serious about hunting down viruses, you can use it as a virus-hunting tool.

WARNING! The DEBUG.EXE program can modify the contents of your computer's memory or physically alter the contents of your disk. If you're not careful, the DEBUG.EXE program can mess up your computer worse than any virus attack. Use the DEBUG.EXE program with caution. When in doubt, don't use it.

Checking files with the DOS Debug program

Most virus writers can't resist adding comments or messages in their viruses, such as "Now trashing your hard disk, bozo! Ha, ha, ha!" Obviously such remarks will never be found in legitimate programs (see Figure 15-8).

```
CODE_SEG      SEGMENT
ASSUME CS:CODE_SEG, DS:CODE_SEG, ES:CODE_SEG, SS:CODE_SEG
ORG 0100
TEQUILA PROC NEAR

JMP START

  DB 000, 000, 000, 000, 000, 000, 000, 0FFH, 0FFH
  DB 009, 005, 001H, 010H, 000, 000, 002H, 0FAH, 000, 00CH

  DB 00DH, 00AH, 00DH, 00AH
  DB "Welcome to T.TEQUILA's latest production.", 00DH, 00AH
  DB "Contact T.TEQUILA/P.o.Box 543/6312 St'hausen/"
  DB "Switzerland.", 00DH, 00AH
  DB "Loving thoughts to L.I.N.D.A.", 00DH, 00AH, 00DH, 00AH
  DB "BEER and TEQUILA forever !", 00DH, 00AH, 00DH, 00AH
  DB "$"
```

FIGURE 15-8:

Part of the assembly language source code to the Tequila virus.

So if you suspect that your computer has a virus, you can run an antivirus program and hope that it finds the virus, or you can verify it yourself by examining suspect files individually using the MS-DOS DEBUG.EXE program.

To use the DEBUG.EXE program, load MS-DOS (either exit out of Windows or display the DOS window) and follow these steps:

1. Type **CD /DOS** and press **ENTER**. (This assumes that the DEBUG.EXE program is stored in your \DOS directory.)

2. Type **DEBUG** followed by the name of the file you suspect may be infected. Then press **ENTER**. (For example, if you suspect the WP.EXE file in your C:\WP directory is infected, type **DEBUG C:\WP\ WP.EXE.**) The DEBUG.EXE displays a cryptic little dash as a prompt.

3. Type **D** and press **ENTER**. Each time you type D and press **ENTER**, the Debug program displays the different parts of the file. If you see suspicious-looking messages (like the one shown in Figure 15-8), congratulations! You've just detected a possible virus!

4. Type **Q** and press **ENTER** to exit out of the DEBUG.EXE program.

Remember, not all viruses blatantly advertise their presence with suspicious messages; but if you do find such a message, it's almost always a virus or another malicious program—like a Trojan Horse or logic bomb. If you find a malicious program lurking on your hard disk, wipe it out right away with an antivirus program. (For the curious, you might want to save the program on a floppy disk to study it and just wipe out the copy located on your hard disk.)

Checking the boot sector with the DOS Debug program
Many virus writers can't resist leaving a nasty message in the boot sector as their calling card. You can also use DEBUG.EXE to examine your hard disk's boot sector. Here's how:

1. Start up the Debug program as described in the previous section.

2. Type one of the following to examine the boot sector on a disk:

```
L 100 0 0 1   (Examines the boot sector on drive A)
L 100 1 0 1   (Examines the boot sector on drive B)
L 100 2 0 1   (Examines the boot sector on drive C)
L 100 3 0 1   (Examines the boot sector on drive D)
```

3. Type **D** and press **ENTER**. Each time you type D and press Enter, the Debug program displays the different parts of the boot sector. If you see suspicious-looking messages, congratulations! You've just detected a possible virus!

Although using the MS-DOS Debug program is an ancient and somewhat clumsy method for examining viruses, you might learn a lot by dissecting a virus, especially if you want to know as much as possible about threats that could attack your computer. For safety, always keep an updated antivirus program around just in case you run across a particularly nasty virus that could get out of control and completely wreck your hard disk.

16

Trojan Horses:
Beware of Geeks Bearing Gifts

TROJAN HORSES WERE AROUND LONG BEFORE COMPUTER VIRUSES AND WORMS BECAME POPULAR. Trojan Horses are named after the famous ruse in which the ancient Greeks left a giant wooden horse by the gates of Troy and sailed away as if they had given up after 10 long and grueling years of war. Thinking the Trojan Horse was a gift to the gods and a symbol of the Greek defeat, the people of Troy pulled the horse into their city. Later that night, Greek soldiers—who had been hiding inside the wooden horse—snuck out, attacked the Trojan guards and opened the gates of the city to their returning army.

A Trojan Horse is any program that masquerades as something that it's not. The main difference between a virus, a worm, and a Trojan Horse is that a Trojan Horse does not need to spread itself. Unwary users will spread it far and wide.

The only way to get rid of a temptation is to yield to it.

—OSCAR WILDE

HOW TROJAN HORSES SPREAD

Before a Trojan Horse program can attack, it must first find a way to entice the victim to copy, download, and run it. Since few people knowingly run a malicious program, Trojan Horses must disguise themselves as other programs that the victim believes to be harmless (such as games, utilities or popular applications). Trojans can also be linked (also called "wrapped" or "bound") to an existing, legitimate program. This method of disguise uses a variety of wrapper or binder programs with names like Saran Wrap, Silk Rope or The

Joiner. You can use a wrapper or a binder to disguise a Trojan Horse in any type of program, thereby reducing the likelihood that someone will discover it. Trojans can even be linked to custom programs created by large, well-known corporations. Since most users don't suspect that programs from large, well-known publishers contain Trojans, the victim is likely to install the linked program.

Once someone has written a Trojan Horse, the next step is to spread it. This is far easier than it used to be. It can be posted to Bulletin Board Systems (BBSs) or Web sites, sent as a file attachment via email, distributed through IRC and online service chat rooms, or sent through ICQ and other instant messaging services. These days a Trojan Horse writer does not have to take the risk of physically installing it on someone's computer.

Downloading software from a BBS or Web site

Trojan Horses are commonly found on BBSs or shareware Web sites where unsuspecting victims download them. These communal gathering spots on the Web give Trojan writers a degree of anonymity along with the chance of attacking as many random victims as possible. Since BBS or Web site operators rarely have time to thoroughly examine every file posted, Trojan Horses will usually slip through the checking procedures unnoticed.

Of course, as soon as the BBS or Web site operator discovers the existence of the Trojan Horse, he can delete it to prevent others from downloading it. However, between the time that the Trojan Horse was available and the time the BBS operator deletes it, many people may have downloaded the Trojan Horse and suffered the consequences. Even worse, many of these victims will have copied and sent the Trojan Horse to other people or even other BBSs or Web sites. So although Trojan Horses are as easy to wipe out as ordinary files, finding and deleting all of them is time-consuming, difficult, and nearly impossible. Efforts to track them down are often as ineffective as shutting the stable door after the Trojan Horse has bolted.

Rather than post a Trojan Horse to someone else's BBS or Web site, some people set up their own Web sites and pretend to offer hacker tools or pornographic files for others to download. Naturally, some of these files will be Trojan Horses, so the moment an unwary user downloads and runs them, they are free to cause whatever damage their writer intended.

Opening a Trojan Horse as an email file attachment

Another common way to spread a Trojan Horse is through a file attachment to email. To get you to open these file attachments, someone may send you a Trojan Horse disguised as a message from a legitimate organization (such as Microsoft or America Online); a tempting program such as a hacker tool for gaining illegal access or privileges to a well-known computer; or a contest announcement, porno-graphic file or similar message designed to pique your curiosity. It is always prudent to save file attachments to disk and let your antivirus program check them out before you run them.

Catching a Trojan Horse from a chat room or instant messaging service

Many people send Trojan Horses to people visiting online chat rooms because they can do so without having to find an email address. The hacker typically strikes up a friendly conversation with a potential victim and then offers to send the person a hacker program or pornographic file. When the victim accepts the file and tries to open it, the Trojan Horse attacks.

Hackers also send Trojan Horses to people who use an instant messaging service such as ICQ. Like email, instant messaging services allow an attacker to send a Trojan Horse directly to a particular person, based on the person's instant messaging ID, which is readily available through member directories.

Physically copying a Trojan Horse to a computer

Sending Trojan Horses is easiest if an attacker has physical access to your computer. He can simply copy a Trojan Horse to your hard disk. If the attacker is particularly skilled, he can create a custom Trojan Horse that mimics the appearance of a program that's unique to that particular computer, such as a corporate log-in screen or a company database program. Not only would such a Trojan Horse be more likely to trick its victim, but the Trojan Horse could also perform an action specific to that particular computer, such as stealing a company's list of credit card numbers or copying the source code of a game company's unreleased products and posting them on the Internet.

TYPES OF TROJAN HORSES

Once a Trojan Horse has copied itself onto your computer, it can unleash a variety of different payloads, much like a computer virus. These attacks range from harmless to destructive, including:

- → Displaying taunting or annoying messages.
- → Wiping out data.
- → Stealing information such as a password.
- → Placing a virus or another Trojan Horse on your computer.
- → Allowing remote access to your computer.

To help Trojan Horses avoid detection, many hackers simply rename the Trojan Horse file. While this won't fool an antivirus program or a Trojan Horse detector, a simple name change is often enough to trick an unsuspecting user into running the Trojan Horse.

Joke Trojans

A joke Trojan causes no damage but may play an annoying sound from your computer's speaker, warp the appearance of your computer screen, or display a taunting message on the screen, such as "Now formatting hard drive!" Although irritating and unwanted, joke Trojan Horses are harmless and easily deleted.

NVP Trojan

NVP Trojan is a Macintosh Trojan Horse that modifies the system file so that when the user types any text, the vowels (a, e, i, o, and u) fail to appear. To entice victims to run this Trojan Horse, the NVP Trojan masquerades as a utility program that can customize the look of the computer display.

IconDance Trojan

The IconDance Trojan minimizes all application windows and then starts rapidly scrambling all the desktop icons. Beyond scrambling your desktop icons, it does nothing more than make you take the time to reorganize your Windows desktop.

Destructive Trojans

A destructive Trojan can either wipe out your hard drive or selectively delete or modify certain files. Although these are the most dangerous Trojans, their very nature tends to limit their spread: In the process of attacking your computer they reveal their presence, often by displaying a taunting message on the screen. And, if they reformat your hard drive they also wipe themselves out.

The only warning you may have that you've been hit by a destructive Trojan may be a blinking light or grinding noise from your hard disk. But by the time you notice this suspicious sound at least some of your files will likely already be wiped out.

Feliz Trojan

When the Feliz Trojan runs, it displays the image shown in Figure 16-1. If the victim clicks the Exit button, a series of message boxes appears, warning the user not to run programs. At the end, the program displays a message wishing the user a Happy New Year.

FIGURE 16-1:

The Feliz Trojan Horse displays a threatening image to warn users that the program is about to attack.

FELIZ ANO NOVO !!! EXIT

While the program displays its message boxes, it deletes the core Windows files, thus preventing the computer from rebooting.

AOL4FREE Trojan

In 1995, a Yale student named Nicholas Ryan wrote a program called AOL4FREE, which allowed users access to America Online without having to pay the normal subscriber fee. Immediately following news of the AOL4FREE program, someone started a hoax, warning that the AOL4FREE program was actually a Trojan Horse:

> *Anyone who receives this [warning] must send it to as many people as you can. It is essential that this problem be reconciled as soon as possible. A few hours ago, someone opened an Email that had the subject heading of "AOL4FREE.COM". Within seconds of opening it, a window appeared and began to display all his files that were being deleted. He immediately shut down his computer, but it was too late. This virus wiped him out.*

Inevitably, someone actually wrote a Trojan Horse, called it AOL4FREE, and on March 1997, began distributing it to America Online users by email. Attached to the email message was the archive file named AOL4FREE.COM, which claimed to provide the original AOL4FREE program for allowing access to America Online for free.

Once executed, the Trojan runs the DOS program DELTREE.EXE and wipes out all files from the hard drive. After deleting the files, it displays "Bad Command or file name" along with an obscene message.

Trojans that steal passwords and other sensitive information

One of the most common uses for a Trojan Horse is to steal passwords. Hackers often build custom Trojans to gain unauthorized access to a computer. For example, if a school computer requires a password before anyone can use it, a hacker can install a program that looks like the log-in screen, asking the user to type in a password.

When an unsuspecting victim comes along and types a password, the Trojan stores the password and displays a message like "Computer down" to convince this person to go away or try another machine. The hacker can then retrieve the saved passwords and use them to access other people's accounts.

If hackers can't physically access a targeted computer, they can always trick a victim into loading the Trojan under the guise of a game or utility program. Once loaded, the Trojan steals passwords and other information, which it can then transmit back to the hacker. Since you may not even be aware that the Trojan is on your computer, it can continue stealing information every time you use your computer.

Once someone has stolen your password or other vital information (like a credit card number), guess what? The thief can now access your account and masquerade as you without your knowledge, using it to harass others online in your guise or run up huge charges on your credit card.

RegForm Trojan

The RegForm Trojan tries to steal Internet account passwords and send them by email to a free Web-based email account for any hacker to retrieve. The RegForm Trojan consists of a DOS program and a Windows program. The DOS program displays a registration application (in Russian) on the screen, offering its victim the chance to test-drive a free Internet access in Moscow.

Dear Sirs,

The Softnet Euro company provides you with a free dial-up access to Internet via Moscow telephone lines. This is done to test the quality of phone lines and certain remote access servers. We are inviting you to take part in testing. To get a free access you need to fill in registration form (see below) and to specify your login and password that you will use. This information will be saved to REG_FORM.DAT file in encrypted format. You will have to send this file to our automatic mail robot to the following address: euro.softnet@usa.net. After that your password will be enabled and the Internet access phone numbers will be sent to you. This free service is provided from 13:00 till 23:00 during working days only. If you want to get a commercial Internet access please call (095) 911-3535.

Press any key

The next screen asks the following:

Please fill in the registration form.

Your last and first names and initials:

Operating system you are using:

Modem type you are using:

Your login to access our system:

Your private password:

Please re-enter your password:

*Registration is complete. Your information has
been saved.*

*Please send the created file to the above speci-
fied email address.*

Press any key

If the victim fills in the requested information, the
Trojan Horse runs a Windows program which stores *all* log-ins
and passwords the user types for any programs or accounts to
the REG_FORM.DAT file. When the user sends this file to the
specified email address, the hacker can retrieve this information and use all the saved log-ins and passwords.

ProMail Trojan

In 1998, a programmer named Michael Haller developed an
email program dubbed Phoenix Mail. Eventually, he tired of
maintaining the program and released it as freeware, even
to the point of providing the Delphi language source code
so that anyone could modify it. Unfortunately, someone took
the Phoenix Mail source code and used it to create a Trojan
Horse dubbed ProMail v1.21.

Like Phoenix Mail, ProMail claims to be a freeware
email program, which has been distributed by several freeware and shareware Web sites including SimTel.net and
Shareware.com as the compressed file, proml121.zip.

When a victim runs ProMail, the program asks for a
whole bunch of information about the user's Internet
account—similar to the information you'd enter when setting
up email software to download your email:

→ User's email address and real name

→ Organization

→ Reply-to email address

→ Reply-to real name

→ POP3 user name and password

→ POP3 server name, and port

→ SMTP server name, and port

Once the user provides this information, ProMail encrypts it and attempts to send it to an account (nagga-manteh@usa.net) on NetAddress (http://www.netaddress.com), a free email provider.

Since ProMail allows users to manage multiple email accounts, it's possible that this Trojan Horse can send information about each account to the waiting hacker, allowing that person complete access to every email account the victim may use.

Remote access Trojans

Remote access programs are legitimate tools that people use to access another computer through the telephone or the Internet. For example, a salesman might need to access files stored on a corporate computer or a technician could troubleshoot a computer online without having to physically access that computer. Some popular remote access programs include pcAnywhere, Carbon Copy, and LapLink.

Remote access Trojans (RATs) are simply remote access programs that sneak onto a victim's computer. While people knowingly install remote access programs like pcAnywhere on their computer, RATs trick a victim into installing the Trojan on their computer first. Once installed, the RAT allows an unseen user (who may be anywhere in the world) complete access to that computer as if he were physically sitting in front of its keyboard; he can see everything that you do and see on your computer.

Using a RAT, a hacker could erase files on your hard disk, copy files (including viruses or other Trojan Horses) to your machine, type messages in a program that the user is currently running, rearrange your folders, change your log-on password, open your CD-ROM drive door, play strange noises through the speaker, reboot the computer, or watch and record every keystroke that you type including credit card numbers, Internet account passwords, or email messages.

RATs come in two parts: a server file and a client file. The server file runs on the victim's computer while the client file runs on the hacker's computer. As long as a hacker has the right client file, he can connect to any computer that has inadvertently installed the server file of that particular Trojan Horse.

To fool someone into installing the server file of a Trojan Horse, hackers often disguise this file as a game or utility program as shown in Figure 16-2. When the victim runs the Trojan, the server file installs itself and waits for anyone with the right client file to access that computer.

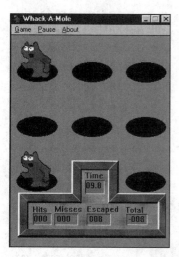

FIGURE 16-2:

To trick a victim, many hackers disguise the server file of a Trojan Horse as a game for the victim to play.

Once the server file has been successfully installed, it opens a port on your computer which allows your computer to send and receive data, at which point anyone with the client file of the Trojan can access that computer. Many hackers methodically probe a network of computers (such as those connected to cable or DSL modems) and try client files from different Trojan Horses. The hope is that if they or another hacker has managed to infect a computer with a server file, they'll be able to connect to it.

To automate the process of checking for infected computers, hackers can use a port scanning program, such as Trojan Hunter, which scans a range of IP addresses to search for any computers already infected by a Trojan. When it finds an infected computer, the port scanner saves that computer's IP address so the hacker can return to that computer again at his leisure.

Some Trojans will even secretly email the hacker once they're installed, notifying him that the server file has successfully installed on a target computer, and often sending along the target computer's IP address so the hacker knows how to find his target. Once a hacker has found a computer infected by a particular Trojan Horse, he can password-protect the port so only he can access the Trojan. Or if he's particularly devious, he can publicize his find and let any hacker with the right Trojan Horse keep returning to that computer again and again and again. . . .

Back Orifice (BO)

The most famous remote access Trojan is Back Orifice (dubbed BO), named to mock Microsoft's own Back Office program. Back Orifice is one of the few Trojan Horse programs with its own Web site (http://www.bo2k.com) as shown in Figure 16-3.

FIGURE 16-3:

The Back Orifice Web site provides the program, source code, and plug-ins for anyone to download and use.

An underground computer group, called the Cult of the Dead Cow (http://www.cultdeadcow.com), originally wrote Back Orifice as a Trojan and released it in 1998. The program caused an immediate uproar as hackers around the world began infecting computers with the Back Orifice server file and accessing other people's computers.

In 1999, the Cult of the Dead Cow released the updated version of Back Orifice called Back Orifice 2000 (or BO2K). Unlike the previous release, Back Orifice 2000 came with complete C/C++ source code so that anyone could examine how the program worked. In addition, Back Orifice 2000 provided a plug-in feature so programmers around the world could extend its features by adding their own.

With the release of Back Orifice 2000, the Cult of the Dead Cow moved the program away from its hacker roots and promoted BO2K as a remote administration tool for Windows, putting it in the same class of remote access programs as pcAnywhere and Carbon Copy. Besides giving away Back Orifice 2000 for free along with its source code, the Cult of the Dead Cow further embarrassed the commercial vendors by comparing the features of BO2K with other remote access tools.

Besides charging you money, commercial remote access programs also hog up disk space and memory. While BO2K requires just over 1MB of disk space and 2MB of RAM, Carbon Copy requires about 20MB of disk space and 8MB of RAM and pcAnywhere requires about 32MB of disk space and 16MB of RAM. Perhaps more surprising is that both BO2K and Carbon Copy offer a stealth remote installation feature, which means that both programs could be used to remotely access a computer without the user's knowledge!

Although the computer community shuns Back Orifice 2000 as a cheap hacker tool, it's really no more a hacker tool than Carbon Copy. Yet considering the group that made it and its original intent, Back Orifice treads the fine line between a Trojan and a legitimate remote access tool for administrators. Used carefully, Back Orifice can be an invaluable program. But used recklessly it can become a dangerous weapon.

SubSeven

SubSeven (see Figure 16-4) is another Trojan that has been growing in popularity. It too boasts its own Web site (http://subseven.slak.org) where you can download a copy for your own "amusement." Besides the standard features of remote access (deleting, modifying, or copying files and folders), SubSeven can also steal ICQ identification numbers and passwords, take over an instant messaging program such as AOL Instant Messenger, and make the victim's computer read text out loud in a computer-generated voice.

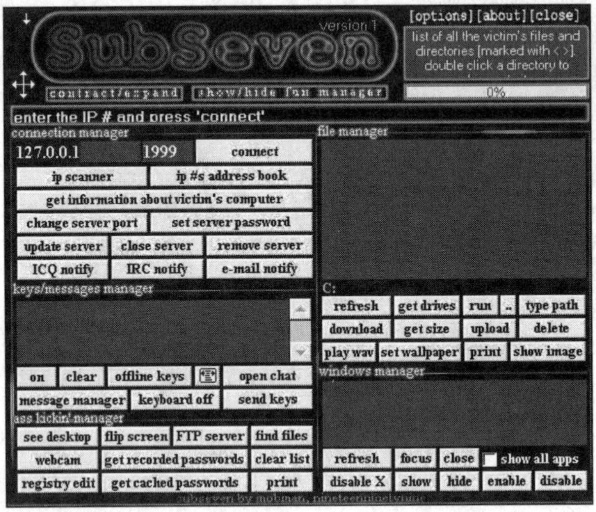

FIGURE 16-4:

The SubSeven client program lists all the Trojan Horse features in a user-friendly interface.

The Thing

Many RAT server files can range in size from 300KB up to 1.2MB or more. Trying to hide such a large file may be difficult, so hackers sometimes use smaller Trojans like The Thing.

The Thing takes up only 40KB of space, thus ensuring that it won't be detected when linked or bound to another program. Unlike other RATs, The Thing won't give you complete access to a victim's computer. Instead, it only opens a port for the hacker to upload a larger RAT, like Back Orifice or SubSeven, which does provide complete control over a victim's computer. Once a hacker has uploaded and installed one of the more sophisticated RATs, he can erase The Thing off the victim's computer and use the other RAT to wreak havoc.

HOW HACKERS WRITE A TROJAN HORSE

Hackers have written Trojan Horses in practically every programming language, including MS-DOS batch files and BASIC. The choice of programming language isn't as important as creating a Trojan that can avoid detection, install itself without the victim's knowledge, and do its work. Still, the two most popular programming languages for writing RATs are C/C++ (Back Orifice for example) and Delphi (NetBus), because both languages can create small programs that can be stored in a single executable file.

While it's possible to write a RAT in a language like Visual Basic, the chances of such a Trojan running are much lower since Visual Basic programs require special, large run-time files, while C/C++ and Delphi programs do not. If a computer lacks the correct run-time files, Visual Basic programs won't run.

Before you can write a Trojan, you need to identify its type. RATs are far more difficult and time-consuming to write than simple password-stealing ones. Many hacker sites provide source code for a variety of Trojans, which is a good way to learn to write one yourself. You can study the source code and then try to write one from scratch, or modify it to create a new variant.

Another way to get source code is to copy the code from any open source project. (Linux is the most famous open source project, but there are other ones as well such as Phoenix Mail, which was used to create the ProMail Trojan Horse.) Once you have the source code to a legitimate program, you can add your own code to turn the program into a Trojan Horse. Given the complexity of computer virus writing, more hackers are turning to writing either macro viruses or Trojan Horse programs.

STOPPING A TROJAN HORSE

Like computer viruses, Trojan Horses can infect your computer without your knowledge. Fortunately, you can protect yourself against them through a combination of different protective tools and a little common sense.

First of all, be careful where you get your software. Any time someone tries to give you a program by email, a chat room, or through an instant message, watch out! That program could be infected with a Trojan Horse, either with or without the sender's knowledge.

When downloading software, download only from the software publisher's official Web site. If you download a program from another Web site, someone could have inserted a Trojan Horse into that program. Many hacker Web sites even post pirated software and hacker tools for others to download, and some of those files could be infected with a Trojan Horse as well.

But no matter how careful you may be with your computer, someone could still slip a Trojan Horse on your computer in your absence. To further protect yourself, install a defensive program, including a rollback program, antivirus program, firewall, and an anti-Trojan Horse program, described later in this chapter.

ROLLBACK PROGRAMS

One of the biggest problems with today's software is that much of it, once installed, seems to muck up even perfectly fine computers. Rollback programs guard against these problems by tracking changes made to your hard disk and taking periodic "snapshots" of the contents of your hard disk. As such, if a newly installed program crashes your computer, you can run the rollback's Undo program to undo the changes you made to your hard disk and return your computer to its prior condition.

Although originally designed to protect against software conflicts, rollback programs can also protect your computer against viruses or Trojans. The moment a Trojan wipes out your data, run your rollback program to turn back time on your hard disk.

Rollback programs only let you recover from damage caused by a Trojan Horse, virus, or other problem; they can't prevent problems from happening in the first place. But when used together with frequent backups, a rollback program can provide valuable insurance for your important data and reduce the chance that a Trojan Horse attack will prove catastrophic.

Some of the more popular rollback programs that you can buy include ConfigSafe (http://www.imagine-lan.com), CoreSave (http://www.innovativesoftware.com), FlashBack (http://www.aladdinsys.com), GoBack (http://www.adaptec.com), PictureTaker (http://www2.lanovation.com), Second Chance (http://www.powerquest.com), and Undelete (http://www.execsoft.com). Most any one will do the trick.

ANTIVIRUS PROGRAMS

Although antivirus programs are designed to detect and remove computer viruses, most can also detect and remove the client files of the more popular RATs. But don't rely exclusively on an antivirus program to protect you against all Trojans. They recognize only the most popular ones, usually RATs, so they may not protect you against lesser-known, destructive Trojans, RATs, or custom Trojans. Consider an antivirus program a supplement to the defense of your computer. (For more information about the different antivirus programs available and how they work, see Chapter 15.)

FIREWALLS

A firewall is designed to isolate your computer network from any outside threats (see Figure 16-5). While a firewall can't remove a Trojan Horse, it can monitor and shut down external traffic flowing through any open ports on your computer. By shutting down a port, a firewall prevents hackers from accessing your computer while also keeping any Trojans already on your computer from sending messages. Firewalls can also track and log all attempts to access your computer, trace an intruder probing your computer for openings, and sound an alarm whenever someone tries to access your computer without your permission.

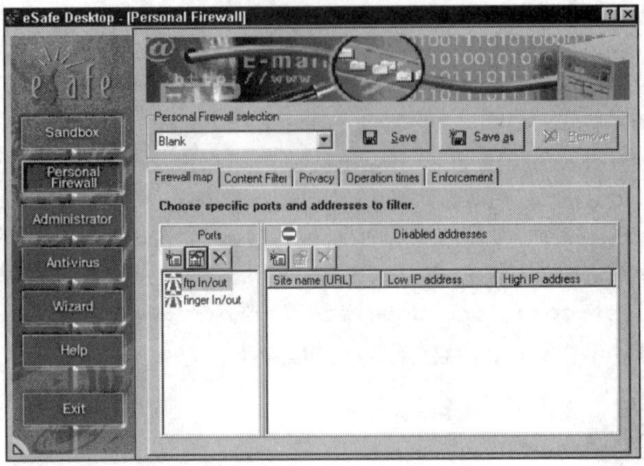

FIGURE 16-5:

A firewall can monitor specific ports and notify you if any are being used without your knowledge.

314

We've included a selection of the more popular firewalls on the CD. Here's a list of the more popular ones: BlackICE Defender (http://www.networkice.com), McAfee.com Personal Firewall (http://www.mcafee.com), Norton Internet Security (http://www.symantec.com), and ZoneAlarm (http://www.zonealarm.net).

ANTI-TROJAN HORSE PROGRAMS

Your best defense against a Trojan Horse is to install a program specifically designed to scan and remove any Trojans from your computer.

These anti-Trojan Horse programs work like antivirus programs, maintaining a database of Trojan Horse signatures which are unique to particular Trojan Horses (see Figure 16-6). The program scans your hard disk and checks to see if the contents of any file matches a known Trojan Horse signature stored in its database. If the program finds a match, it knows it has found a Trojan Horse, and can then remove the offending program and fix any changes it might have made to other parts of your hard disk, like the Windows registry.

Like antivirus programs, anti-Trojan Horse programs must be constantly updated to protect you against the latest Trojans. We've included a number of the more popular

FIGURE 16-6:

An anti-Trojan Horse program can detect and remove dangerous Trojan Horses before they have a chance to attack your computer.

ones on the CD; here's where to download or register the latest versions of the more popular ones: LockDown 2000 (http://www.lockdown2000.com), Tauscan and Jammer (http://www.agnitum.com), TDS-2: Trojan Defence Suite (http://tds.diamondcs.com.au), and The Cleaner (http://www.moosoft.com).

HACKER ANTI-TROJAN TOOLS

Since hackers often target each other, many hackers have written their own tools designed to remove specific Trojan Horses from their computers. Unlike general purpose anti-Trojan Horse programs that scan for all known Trojan Horses, hacker Trojan Horse-removing programs are meant to detect and remove a specific Trojan Horse. (Just be careful that some malicious hacker doesn't infect an anti-Trojan Horse program with a real Trojan Horse and trick you into downloading it.)

To find a hacker anti-Trojan Horse program, look for programs with names such as Back Orifice Eradicator, Busjack, NetBus Remover, Nemesis, Anti Socket, Anti BD, Backfire, BO2K Server Sniper, TW-Trojan Scanner, or Toilet Paper.

Trojan Horses may be dangerous, but by avoiding unknown programs and protecting yourself with a handful of defensive programs, you should be able to keep your computer free of them.

PART 5

PROTECTING YOURSELF

17

Waging War on **Spam**

NO MATTER HOW INFREQUENTLY YOU USE THE INTERNET, YOU'RE GOING TO GET SPAMMED. Instead of finding important messages from business associates, friends, or your favorite newsgroup, you find a long list of junk email from companies advertising totally useless products, like bogus vitamins or money-making schemes. Unlike newspaper or magazine advertisements that you can ignore without losing a moment's thought, spam just doesn't seem to leave you alone.

Spamming means sending unsolicited messages to multiple email accounts or Usenet newsgroups. Victims of spamming must then take time to delete the unwanted messages so they can make room in their emailboxes for useful email. Some of the more common spams are chain letters or other suspicious "business opportunities" like this:

$$$$$$$$ FAST CASH!!!! $$$$$$$$

Hello there, Read this it works! Fellow Debtor: This is going to sound like a con, but in fact IT WORKS! The person who is now #4 on the list was #5 when I got it, which was only a few days ago. Five dollars is a small investment in your future. Forget the lottery for a week, and give this a try. It can work for ALL of us. You can edit this list with a word processor or text editor and then convert it to a text file. Good Luck!!

What this country needs is more free speech worth listening to.

—HANSELL B. DUCKETT

Dear Friend,

My name is Dave Rhodes. In September 1988 my car was repossessed and the bill collectors were hounding me like you wouldn't believe. I was laid off and my unemployment checks had run out. The only escape I had from the pressure of failure was my computer and my modem. I longed to turn my avocation into my vocation.

This January 1989 my family and I went on a ten day cruise to the tropics. I bought a Lincoln Town Car for CASH in February 1989. I am currently building a home on the West Coast of Florida, with a private pool, boat slip, and a beautiful view of the bay from my breakfast room table and patio.

I will never have to work again. Today I am rich! I have earned over $400,000.00 (Four Hundred Thousand Dollars) to date and will become a millionaire within 4 or 5 months. Anyone can do the same. This money making program works perfectly every time, 100 percent of the time. I have NEVER failed to earn $50,000.00 or more whenever I wanted. Best of all you never have to leave home except to go to your mailbox or post office.

I realized that with the power of the computer I could expand and enhance this money making formula into the most unbelievable cash flow generator that has ever been created. I substituted the computer bulletin boards in place of the post office and electronically did by computer what others were doing 100 percent by mail. Now only a few letters are mailed manually. Most of the hard work is speedily downloaded to other bulletin boards throughout the world.

If you believe that someday you deserve that lucky break that you have waited for all your life, simply follow the easy instructions below. Your dreams will come true.

And so on.

WHY COMPANIES SPAM THE INTERNET AND HOW THEY DO IT

Nobody likes to receive spam because it wastes time and clogs their email account, yet many companies continue to send it anyway because, unlike direct mail advertising, spamming is essentially free. For the cost of a single Internet account, anyone can reach a potential worldwide audience numbering in the millions. In the eyes of spammers, even if they upset 99 percent of the people on the Internet, having 1 percent buy your product can make spamming worth it.

When sending spam, you don't need to type multiple email messages either; just as bulk mailers never lick their stamps, many companies use bulk emailing software that automates the multiple addressing process. Click a button and you, too, can scatter unwanted email messages across the Internet.

Many ISPs respond to users' outrage at spam by blocking mail from the accounts of known spammers, though some groups question the legality of doing so since it amounts to a form of censorship.

Spammers are often stereotyped as scammers and con artists, but that's not necessarily the case. Many are like you or me, just trying to make a buck—but just going about it the wrong way.

There are lots of places on the Web to learn more about how spammers think and the techniques and software they use. A visit to the Bulk Email Forum (http://www.easybiz.com) will give you a quick introduction.

Retrieving email addresses

Before bulk email programs can start spamming, they need a list of email addresses. Although lists of email addresses can be bought, they are not always accurate or up-to-date. Rather than rely on these lists, spammers use email address extracting programs to build their own lists. These programs are of three different types: newsgroup extractors, Web site extractors, and database directory extractors.

Newsgroup extractors

When you post a message to a CompuServe forum or Usenet newsgroup, your message appears with your email address. Newsgroup extractors download the messages from online services (like CompuServe or America Online) and Usenet newsgroups, strip away the text, and store the return emails in a list, to produce a free, up-to-date email list. Figure 17-1 shows the options available to a typical newsgroup extractor.

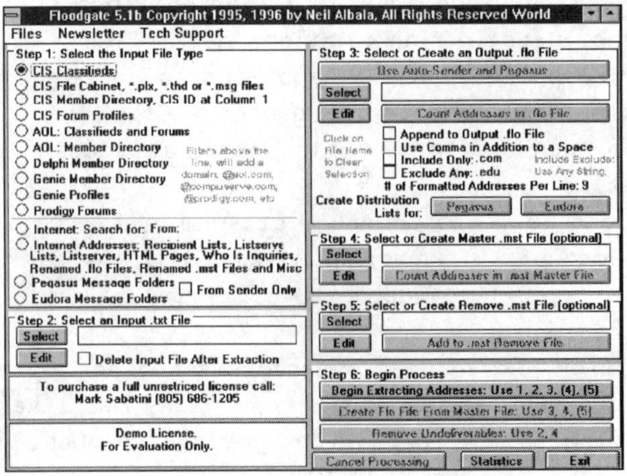

FIGURE 17-1:

Bulk email programs offer several options for retrieving email addresses.

Even better (from the bulk emailer's point of view), online service forums and Usenet newsgroups focus on specific topics, such as health and fitness, computer programming, or sports. So if, for example, they're selling vitamins, they can simply visit any CompuServe or America Online forum or Usenet newsgroup related to health and fitness and bingo! They've got a list of prospective customers' email addresses.

Web site extractors

Web site extractors work like newsgroup extractors except that they pull their email addresses from Web sites. They first search for Web sites on the topics you specify and then pull the email addresses from the sites they find.

Database directory extractors

Database directory extractors pull email addresses from
people-finding directory services like Bigfoot. While the
list they produce can't be as tightly targeted as those
produced by Web site or newsgroup extractors, they can produce useful lists targeted toward specific geographical
groups or people with particular surnames.

Masking your identity

Spammers often incur the wrath of several hundred (or several million) irate victims. Some respond with angry
messages; others launch their own email bombing attacks,
sending multiple messages to the spammer's email address,
clogging it and rendering it useless.

Unfortunately, crashing or clogging the spammer's ISP
can also punish innocent customers who happen to use the
spammer's ISP as well. To avoid such counterattacks, many
spammers create temporary Internet accounts (on services
such as Hotmail or Juno), send their spam, and then cancel
the account before anyone can attack them. Of course, this
means constantly creating and canceling multiple Internet
accounts, but getting kicked off an ISP and opening new
accounts is just part of the game bulk emailers play. When
an interested customer responds, the spammer sends out an
actual email address, phone number, or postal address so
the prospective customer can learn more.

Of course, for those spammers who can't be bothered
opening and closing email accounts, there's an easier way.
Many bulk emailing programs, like Email Magnet, simply omit
or forge the sender's email address to avoid counterattacks.

Finding a bulk emailing program

You probably won't find a bulk emailing program sold at
your local computer store, but you'll find lots of them
on the Web. Some of the more popular ones are BrainTree
(http://www.braintree.com), which pulls email addresses into
a reusable database for successive mailings; Desktop Server
2000 (http://www.desktopserver2000.com), which saves your

addresses in a database and will cloak your real email address; Email Magnet (http://www.emagnet.com); and Express Mail Server (http://www.homeuniverse.com) (see Figure 17-2).

Publishers of bulk emailing programs are often the target of spam avengers, so, to protect their identity, many don't post their own Web sites. Instead, they sell their programs through individual distributors who create their own Web sites and then, in typical pyramid scheme fashion, sign up others to sell the program through their Web sites too. By using this multi-level marketing approach to selling their software, bulk emailing publishers can remain relatively anonymous while ensuring that their software will be available from multiple locations no matter how many times anti-spam activists try to attack and shut down a Web site offering spamming software.

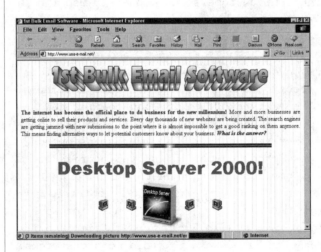

FIGURE 17-2:

You can buy or download a demo of a bulk emailing program from a variety of Web sites.

PROTECTING YOURSELF FROM SPAMMERS

Now that you know some of the tricks spammers use, how can you fight back? Depending on your mood and temperament, your response may range from politeness to hostility. While you may ignore and simply delete most spam, some may enrage you.

Complain to the spammer

When you receive spam, the message may include an email address that you can write to to remove your address from the spammer's email list. Sometimes this works, but more likely this email address itself is phony, or replying simply alerts the spammer that your email address is valid, which can encourage him to sell your email address to others and keep sending spam to you.

Complain to the spammer's ISP

To protect themselves against retaliation, most spammers either strip out or fake their return email address. But even if you can't find a valid return address in the email to respond to, you may still be able to uncover one. To do so, search the spam's header for the ISP's address, such as netcom.com, earthlink.net, or cris.com, buried in the From or Message-ID heading. Once you identify the ISP, you can complain directly to them.

In the following example, a quick search of the email header reveals that the spammer's ISP is hidden.com.

> Subject: Absolutely NOT Risky ! Nothing to lose !!!
>
> From: Hidden <noname@hidden.com>
>
> Date: Fri, 01 Aug 1997 00:02:54 +0800
>
> Message-ID: <33E0B72E.3796@hidden.com>

Because spam is so annoying, most ISPs prohibit their subscribers from sending bulk email. If they receive complaints, the ISP will often cancel the spammer's account.

To notify an ISP of a spammer, email your complaint to postmaster@spammer.site, root@spammer.site, admin@spammer.site, or abuse@spammer.site, where "spammer.site" is the site the spammer used to send the junk email.

ISPs can't monitor all of their users, but if they receive a flood of complaints about one of their customers, they can take action against the spammer and stop future abuses.

Complain to the Internal Revenue Service

Since many spammers promote get-rich-quick schemes, there's a good chance they may not keep proper tax records of their earnings. So one way to take revenge on these spammers is to contact the Internal Revenue Service (or your own government's tax agency) so they can investigate whether the spammer is properly reporting all income. American citizens can forward spam to either net-abuse@nocs.insp.irs.gov to report fraudulent make-money-fast (MMF) schemes or to hotline@nocs.insp.irs.gov to report tax evaders. Reports of tax fraud should be sent directly to your regional IRS Service Center; there is currently no Internet email address for reporting those suspected offenses.

Use an email filter

Email programs like Microsoft Outlook, Eudora Pro, and the Web-based Hotmail, let you filter incoming email based on FROM addresses, subjects, and keywords. You can set the filtering rules to search for particular spammer email addresses or keywords in messages or subjects (like "MAKE MONEY FAST") and have the filter automatically delete the message or route it to a special folder. Some of the more common keywords found in spam include: "to be removed," "not mlm," "serious inquiries only," "earn $2000-$5000 weekly," "sent in compliance," "at no cost to you," "spam," "work from home," "dear friend," "not multi-level marketing," "xxx," and "call now" so try using these.

Or, subscribe to an email filtering service like SpamCop (http://spamcop.net) or Msgto.com (http://msgto.com). Both screen your email for spam and route suspicious messages to a designated location so you can review it just in case a legitimate message got routed there by mistake. Anti-spam programs like SpamBuster automatically filter suspicious email, analyze email headings, and track down spammers' ISPs by checking received email against a database of known spammer addresses or searching for keywords (see Figure 17-3). When the program finds a likely match, it moves the suspect email to a special folder where you can review or delete it later.

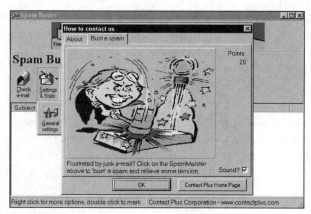

FIGURE 17-3:

SpamBuster can help you track down and locate spammers.

Locating the spammer's postal address

Perhaps the most satisfying way to deal with spam is to find the spammer's actual email address, phone number, or postal address—and use it. If you have the domain name of the spammer's Web site, visit the Network Solutions registry at http://www.networksolutions.com/cgi-bin/whois/whois, type in the domain you want to search, and the Network Solutions database cheerfully provides you with the postal address of the person who registered the domain name along with the server currently hosting the Web pages (see Figure 17-4). Then have at it.

FIGURE 17-4:

The Network Solutions registry can reveal the postal address and Web hosting server of any domain address.

```
Registrant:
Spellbound Erotic and Fantasy Costume Design (CENTERFOLD-DOM)
    1847 Centinela Avenue
    Santa Monica, CA 90404

Domain Name: CENTERFOLD.COM

Administrative Contact, Billing Contact:
    CostumeGuy, Bill (BC2772)   costumeguy@AOL.COM
    Spellbound Erotic and Fantasy Costume Design
    7551 Sunset Bl. #100
    Hollywood, CA 90046
    310-716-3333 (FAX) 323-850-0201
Technical Contact, Zone Contact:
    Corporation, Network XXIII (NXC2)   network23@NETWORKXXIII.COM
    Network XXIII Corporation
    Attn: Bill
    7551 Sunset Blvd #100
    Hollywood, CA 90046
    310-716-3333 (FAX) 323-850-0201

Record last updated on 13-Jun-2000.
Record expires on 28-Apr-2003.
Record created on 27-Apr-1995.
Database last updated on 3-Jul-2000 20:04:42 EDT.

Domain servers in listed order:

NS.TMNINC.COM               207.240.74.251
NS2.TMNINC.COM              207.240.74.250
```

If the spammer doesn't list a Web address but gives you his real email address, strip away the spammer's ID to find the domain he's using. For example, if his address is spammer@isp.com, remove "spammer" and you're left with the domain name of the spammer's ISP, which in this case is isp.com. By typing this domain into the Network Solutions registry, you can find out how to reach the ISP by mail or phone, or you can add "www" to the front of the domain, such as http://www.isp.com, to visit its Web site, which should list an email address that you can complain to.

Dealing with forged email addresses

If a spammer opens a temporary email account just to spam the Internet, there's not much you can do about it—the spammer can keep opening up new email accounts and shutting them down afterwards. However, if he forges a return email address, there's still hope.

Forged email addresses may hide the spammer's email address, but the email itself can reveal the spammer's ISP if you know how to decipher its cryptic-looking headers which contain information on the route the email traveled.

Most email programs hide email headers to avoid burying you in irrelevant technical email-routing details. But by revealing these headers, you can trace the route a spam email has taken and possibly identify the spammer. For more information about displaying email headers from a variety of email programs including Outlook, AOL, Eudora, Pegasus, Netscape, and WebTV, visit the SpamCop site (http://spamcop.net).

Let's take a look at some headers sent from a valid email account to see what they mean.

Received: from db3y-int.prodigy.net [127.0.0.1] by

wflda-db3y-int.prodigy.net; Sat, 9 Dec 2000 10:38:19 -

0500

Received: from yorktown.stratfor.com (yorktown.stratfor.com

[207.8.81.2]) by db3y-int.prodigy.net
(8.8.5/8.8.5)

with ESMTP id KAA45964 for <BOTHECAT@prodigy.
net>; Sat,

9 Dec 2000 10:36:04 -0500

Received: from verdun.stratfor.com (verdun.
stratfor.com

[207.8.81.26]) by yorktown.stratfor.com
(8.8.7/8.8.5)

with SMTP id JAA07105 for <BOTHECAT@prodigy.
net>; Sat,

9 Dec 2000 09:38:25 -0600 (CST)

Received: by verdun.stratfor.com with Microsoft
Mail id

<01BD0485.F3790CC0@verdun.stratfor.com>; Sat,
9 Dec

2000 09:36:39 -0600

The Received headings describe where the email came
from along with the time and date it was sent. Starting
with the bottom Received heading, we see that this email
came from a domain named stratfor.com sent on Saturday,
December 9, 2000, at 9:36 a.m.

The next Received heading (starting from the bottom and
working your way up) shows that the email was transferred
within the stratfor.com domain (from verdun.stratfor.com
to yorktown.stratfor.com) on Saturday, December 9, 2000,
at 9:38 a.m. Notice that the stratfor.com domain is also
identified by its numeric (IP) address in square brackets,
[207.8.81.26].

The following Received heading shows that the stratfor.
com domain sent the email to the prodigy.net domain on
Saturday, December 9, 2000, at 10:36 a.m.

The top Received heading shows that the email was transferred within the prodigy.net domain to the receiving email inbox on Saturday, December 9, 2000, at 10:38 a.m. Notice that the prodigy.net domain is also identified by its numeric address in square brackets, [127.0.0.1].

This example shows how each Received heading records the transfer of the email from one domain to another. Forged email often omits all the Received headings that show the route of the email, or displays too many Received headings in an attempt to confuse you.

The following example of spam is obviously a forgery, because the Received headings do not show how the email got from the Sender domain (infosonic.com) to the receiving email account, a CompuServe account.

Sender: info@infosonic.com

Received: from Blaze.cscent.net ([206.98.109.9]) by

    arl-img-10.compuserve.com (8.8.6/8.8.6/2.9) with ESMTP

    id TAA09818; Sun, 3 Dec 2000 19:52:30 -0500 (EST)

Date: Sun, 3 Dec 2000 19:52:30 -0500 (EST)

From: info@infosonic.com

Message-Id: <199712040052.TAA09818@arl-img-10.compuserve.com>

To: info@infosonic.com

Subject: "Earn Insane Profits At Home!"

Besides not showing enough Received headings to trace the email's route, another big clue that the email address has been forged is the use of a single capital letter ("B") in the Received heading, listing Blaze.cscent.net. (Most Received headings use either all lowercase or all upper-case, but rarely a mix of both.)

NOTE From first appearance alone, you might conclude that the spammer is using either infosonic.com or cscent.net to send the spam, but in both cases these domain addresses could be forged. Unless you know for sure, you shouldn't complain to either domain, because they might be completely innocent.

Here's another example of a forged email address:

Return-Path: <More.Info.1ooooooo@bigger.net>

Received: from relay27.mail.aol.com (relay27.mail.aol.com

   [172.31.109.27]) by air27.mail.aol.com (v36.0) with

   SMTP; Wed, 13 Dec 2000 14:09:15 -0500

Received: from ul1.satlink.com (ul1.satlink.com [200.0.224.2]) by

   relay27.mail.aol.com (8.8.5/8.8.5/AOL-4.0.0) with ESMTP

   id MAA21540; Tue, 12 Dec 2000 12:23:29 -0500 (EST)

From: More.Info.1ooooooo@bigger.net

Received: from 34lHT27yw (sdn-ts-003nynyorP15. dialsprint.net

   [206.133.34.66]) by ul1.satlink.com (8.8.8/8.8.8) with

   SMTP id OAA13401; Tue, 12 Dec 2000 14:23:04 - 0300

   (GMT-3)

Received: From j1dqu3p1J (sdn-ts-003nyorP04. dialsys33.net

[306.203.08.10]) by cor.ibuyitnow22.net
(8.8.5/8.7.3)

with SMTP id JJA109; Tue, 12 Dec 2000
12:20:35 -400

(EDT)

You can tell this email has been forged because the last
Received heading sports three glaring flaws. First, you can't
trace the email from the recipient's email address to the
sender's email address (in this case it's an America Online
email account). The first three Received headings show that
America Online received the email from ul1.satlink.com, which
in turn received it from sdn-ts-003nynyorP15.dialsprint.net.
The last Received heading is garbage designed to confuse you,
because it doesn't trace any email being sent to the sdn-ts-
003nynyorP15.dialsprint.net domain.

The second flaw in the last Received heading is the sdn-
ts-003nynyorP15.dialsprint.net domain, which claims to have
an IP numeric address of [306.203.08.10]. The numbers used in
an IP numeric address can only range from 0 to 255, so any
number greater than 255 (306 in this example) immediately
reveals that this particular Received heading is forged.

The third flaw is that the word "From" begins with a capital letter; the other Received headings use "from" instead.

Because the last Received heading is obviously forged,
you can ignore it completely. Studying the remaining
Received headings, you can conclude that the email originated from the sdn-ts-003nynyorP15.dialsprint.net domain.
To verify that this is an actual domain and not a forged
one, look at its numeric address in square brackets. In
this case, the numeric address is [206.133.34.66].

DNS lookup programs

Once you have identified a spammer's name and numeric
address, you can verify the domain's existence using a
handy online tool called Whois. To run it, visit the Whois
Gateway (http://www.interlog.com/~patrick/cgi/whois.cgi),
the InterNIC site (http://rs.internic.net/cgi-bin/whois),

or the Network Solutions registry (http://www.
networksolutions.com/cgi-bin/whois/whois). Or run the
Whois command using a DNS lookup program like CyberKit
(http://www.cyberkit.net), DNS Workshop (http://www.evolve.
co.uk/dns), Domain Searcher (http://www.igsnet.com/igs/
dsearch.html), NetScan Tools (http://www.nwpsw.com), or
Sam Spade (http://samspade.org/ssw) (see Figure 17-5).

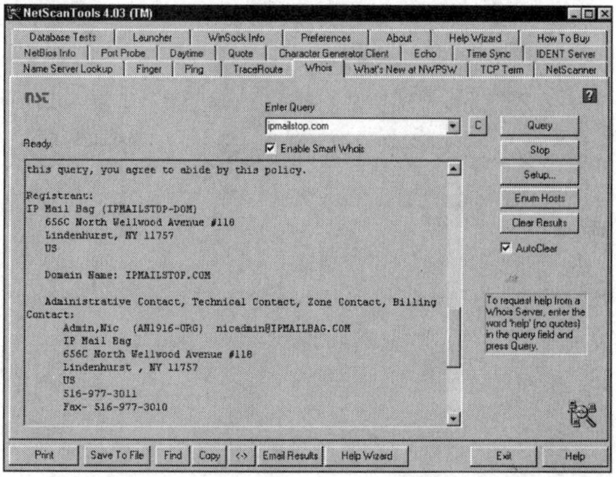

FIGURE 17-5:

*The NetScan Tools
program will probe the
Internet to find a
spammer or their ISP.*

Whichever version of Whois you use, it will tell you
whether the dialsprint.net domain really exists. In this
example, Whois reports the following:

Sprint Business Operations (DIALSPRINT-DOM)

> 12490 Sunrise Valley Dr.
> Reston, VA 22090
> US

> Domain Name: DIALSPRINT.NET

Administrative Contact, Technical Contact, Zone
Contact:

Sprint DNS Administrator   (SDA4-ORG)   dns-admin@
SPRINT.NET

(800)232-6895
Fax- (703)478-5471

Billing Contact:

Sprint Internic Billing
(SIB2-ORG) nicbills@SPRINT.NET

(800)232-6895
Fax- (703)478-5471

Record last updated on 23-Jan-00.
Record created on 12-Feb-96.
Database last updated on 22-Dec-99 05:27:44 EDT.

Domain servers in listed order:

NS1.DIALSPRINT.NET

206.134.151.45

NS2.DIALSPRINT.NET

206.134.79.44

NS3.DIALSPRINT.NET

205.149.192.145

This tells us that dialsprint.net is a valid domain and gives us the administrator's email address.

To further verify that the Received heading information is correct, do a DNS Name Server Lookup (http://www.interlog. com/~patrick/cgi/nslookup.cgi or try one of the DNS lookup programs like CyberKit or NetScan Tools) to see whether the IP address belongs to a specific domain name. In the example on page 333, the last valid Received heading:

from 341HT27yw (sdn-ts-003nynyorP15.dialsprint. net [206.133.34.66]) shows that the domain name has been masked by the garbled string of characters "341HT27yw." Examining the other Received headings shows that this string should list the same domain name as that which appears in parentheses (sdn-ts-003nynyorP15.dialsprint.net). Because the spammer deliberately scrambled this information, you can be pretty sure that this information reveals the address of the ISP they used to send the email.

Examining the [206.133.34.66] numeric address with the Name Server Lookup command confirms that it belongs to the sdn-ts-003nynyorP15.dialsprint.net domain. Thus, we can be pretty sure that the spammer sent email from the DIALSPRINT. NET domain. Of course, the spammer might have opened an account with DIALSPRINT.NET just to send spam and then canceled it, but at least you have the spammer's postal address.

For additional help dealing with forged email addresses, visit the Get That Spammer! Web site (http://kryten.eng. monash.edu.au/gspam.html) where you'll find additional tips for dissecting an email address, and several additional tools for tracing one. The UXN Spam Combat Web site (http:// combat.uxn.com) has even more robust tools for doing DNS lookups, traceroute, DNS probes, and so on (see Figure 17-6).

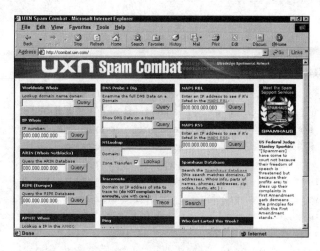

FIGURE 17-6:

The UXN Spam Combat Web site provides plenty of tools for helping you track down an elusive spammer.

One of the earliest methods for fighting spam was to maintain a database of known spammer email addresses and ISPs. Unfortunately, spammers can change ISPs rapidly, making most anti-spammer databases obsolete. To avoid this problem, the Kill the Spams program (http://www.zipstore.com) uses a list of rules to screen the headers of incoming email for signs of spam. If a header looks suspicious, the program can flag the email as possible spam or just delete the message automatically.

SpamBuster (http://www.contactplus.com) and SpamKiller (http://www.spamkiller.com) combine both filtering and a database of known spammers to help keep spam out of your email box. For more accuracy, SpamBuster can do a DNS lookup on email to verify that the header lists a real address. To avoid having the anti-spam program mistake valid email for spam, both programs offer a special Friends list, which tells the anti-spam program which email addresses you will always accept messages from.

Final tactics for avoiding spam

To reduce the chances of receiving spam in the first place, give out your email address sparingly. Create a separate email account with a free service such as Hotmail, and use it for posting messages in Usenet newsgroups or when buying online (many companies sell your email address when you register with them).

ANTI-SPAM RESOURCES

Despite laws, threats, and physical action taken against spammers, spamming is so cost-effective that it's probably here to stay. If spam really irritates you, consider joining and helping CAUCE (Coalition Against Unsolicited Commercial Email) at http://www.cauce.org, an organization consisting of Internet users who have banded together to lobby for new laws to regulate unsolicited email.

To show you how influential one person can be in the fight against spam, visit Netizens Against Gratuitous Spamming (http://www.nags.org). This Web site offers tips for identifying and dealing with spam and offers an example of "chaff," which is garbage data designed to fool spammers who retrieve email addresses off Web sites.

To keep up with the latest news regarding spam and to learn more about how to defeat spam, visit Death to Spam (http://www.mindworkshop.com/alchemy/nospam.html), Spam News (http://petemoss.com/spam), an e-newsletter provided to ISP administrators so they can learn different ways to fight spam on their own systems, or Junk Busters (http://www.junkbusters.com). Or try Fight Spam, an inter-national anti-spam group (http://spam.abuse.net/spam).

And for the latest news about different spammers, or to warn people about new ones, visit one of the following news-groups: alt.current-events.net-abuse, alt.current-events.net-abuse.spam, alt.spam, alt.privacy, news.admin.net-abuse.misc, news.admin.net-abuse.announce, or news.admin.net-abuse.email.

18

Computer Forensics: Recovering and Deleting Data

LIKE MOST CRIMINALS, HACKERS OFTEN BRING ABOUT THEIR OWN DOWNFALL BY FAILING TO REMOVE ALL TRACES OF THEIR CRIME. Not only do many hackers leave written notes and printouts of their latest exploits scattered around their computer, but they also can't resist bragging to others about their exploits in public chat rooms. Yet even this blatant disregard for secrecy and indiscretion wouldn't be so damaging if these same hackers didn't unwittingly also leave incriminating evidence on hard and floppy disks.

DELETING DATA

When a computer deletes a file, it takes a shortcut. Instead of physically destroying the file, the computer simply tells the system that the file no longer exists by replacing the first letter of the file name with a special character (hex byte code E5h); the contents of the file remain intact. This process is analogous to taking your name off an apartment building directory to make it look like you no longer live there but not cleaning out your old apartment until someone else needs it.

Only when the computer needs the space taken up by the deleted file will it actually overwrite the old file with a new file. But if your disk has plenty of extra space available, you could go weeks, months, or even years without ever overwriting previously deleted files. (Although defragmenting your hard disk will erase many of these "hidden" files.)

Reality is merely an illusion, albeit a very persistent one.

—ALBERT EINSTEIN

If you delete a file you can usually undelete it if you act quickly and run a utility like DOS's undelete or Norton Utilities' Unerase. (These programs simply give a previously deleted file a new name so the computer will recognize it again.) But the longer you wait, the more time your computer will have to overwrite some or possibly all of the deleted file with new data, making it difficult if not impossible to recover the original deleted file.

(Be especially careful when using utility programs like Norton SystemWorks. This utility suite, and others like it, come with a file deletion protection feature that saves any deleted files in a special folder so you can quickly and accurately undelete a file any time in the future. Obviously this feature can save you in case you accidentally delete something, but it can also work against you by preserving those sensitive files that you thought you deleted months ago.)

File shredders

If you deliberately erase a file and then overwrite it, most undelete programs will not be able to recover it. But since you can't be certain your computer has overwritten a deleted file, use a file shredder to be sure.

File shredders overwrite deleted files one or more times using random characters such as zeroes and ones. As a result, when an undelete program tries to recover the deleted file, the file shows only random data.

Levels of file shredding security

Not all file shredders are equal. A good one offers several ways to shred your files that balance speed and security (see Figure 18-1). To defeat ordinary undelete programs and wipe files quickly, a file shredder may make one pass at filling your deleted file with random data. While this quick wipeout defeats most undelete programs, it will not defeat specialized computer forensics tools.

For additional security, file shredders make multiple passes over a deleted file; the more passes, the longer the deletion takes, but the more likely you'll delete all data beyond hope of recovery. The Department of Defense (DoD) even has its own shredding standard, dubbed DoD 5220.22-M, which defines the government standards for deleting computer files. (The enclosed CD contains the full text of the official DoD 5220.22-M security procedures, stored as an Adobe Acrobat .PDF file.)

The DoD file shredding technique wipes a file seven times, each pass replacing the deleted data with a different set of random data. Since each additional pass adds another layer of random data to obscure the original, seven passes destroy virtually all traces of the original file, though not magnetic ones, which can always be examined by a magnetic sensor or electron microscope (discussed below).

FIGURE 18-1:

A file shredder can offer you different ways to shred your files, giving you a choice between speed and security.

Shredding temporary, Web cache, email, and slack space files

If you shred your sensitive files, don't forget to delete all your temporary and Web cache files too. A few file shredders, such as the Windows-based Kremlin (http://www.mach5.com) or the Macintosh-based The Eraser Pro (http://ospiti.imagica. it/yellowsoft/software), can automatically find and destroy these types of files with a simple click of the mouse. Two Windows-based shredders, BCWipe (http://www.jetico.com) and Shiva, Destroyer of Files (http://www.isis-software.com), can even wipe the slack space of specified files and simultaneously delete temporary and Web cache files.

For further security, you can even configure some file shredders, such as the Macintosh-based NetShred (http://www.arccom.bc.ca) and the Windows-based

Evidence-Eliminator (http://www.evidence-eliminator.com), to delete your old email messages.

If you're really paranoid, shred your files and then defragment your hard drive. Then shred the free space remaining on your hard drive to get rid of any traces of files you don't want others to find.

Integrating a shredder into your operating system

Loading the file shredder every time you want to delete a file can be a nuisance, and you may not use it as often as you need to. Fortunately, file shredders such as Shredder95 (http://www.gale-force.com), CyberScrub (http://www. cyberscrub.com), and Shred-X (http://www.bsoft.ic24.net) can integrate themselves into your operating system so that when you delete a file, the file shredder automatically shreds the file without any additional effort on your part.

Shredding swap files

One particularly vulnerable area of your computer is the swap file. A swap file allocates part of your hard disk for storing data so the computer can free up room in *random access memory* (RAM) for other programs that may be running.

Any time you run a program such as a word processor, your operating system may temporarily store your data in the swap file. When you save or delete the file, much of your information still remains in the swap file for anyone to look at. So for complete protection, make sure you shred your swap file regularly (ideally, every time you turn off your computer).

Shredding Windows NT/2000 swap files

If you're using Windows NT/2000, you can edit the registry to make Windows NT/2000 automatically shred your swap file when you turn off your computer. To do this, follow these steps:

1. Start the Registry Editor (REGEDIT.EXE).
2. Change the data value of the ClearPageFileAtShutdown value in the following registry key to a value of 1:

```
HKEY_LOCAL_MACHINE\SYSTEM\CurrentControlSet\
Control\Session Manager\Memory Management
```

3. If the value does not exist, add the following value:

Value Name: ClearPageFileAtShutdown Value Type: REG_DWORD Value: 1

This change does not take effect until you restart the computer.

Shredding Windows 95/98 swap files

Windows 95/98 constantly saves information to its swap file. To shred a Windows 95/98 swap file, restart your computer in MS-DOS mode to ensure that Windows won't store any more data in its swap file while you run your file shredding program. Once you're in MS-DOS mode, run an MS-DOS based file shredder such as Scour (http://www.bonaventura.free-online.co.uk/realdelete) or a file shredder that automatically restarts Windows in MS-DOS mode such as Clean Disk Security (http://www.ozemail.com.au/~ksolway/clndisk.html).

Panic mode shredding

Your file shredder may work great if you methodically delete incriminating files. But what happens if you're sitting at your computer and the police suddenly barge into your house? In an emergency, some file shredders offer a *panic mode*. To use it, you define ahead of time which files and directories you want to delete in an emergency; then you assign a unique keystroke combination to activate the panic mode (See Figure 18-2).

When the police (or other unwanted authorities) break in, press your magic panic mode keystroke and the file shredder starts deleting all your predefined important files. If you're serious about protecting your privacy, a panic mode feature is essential.

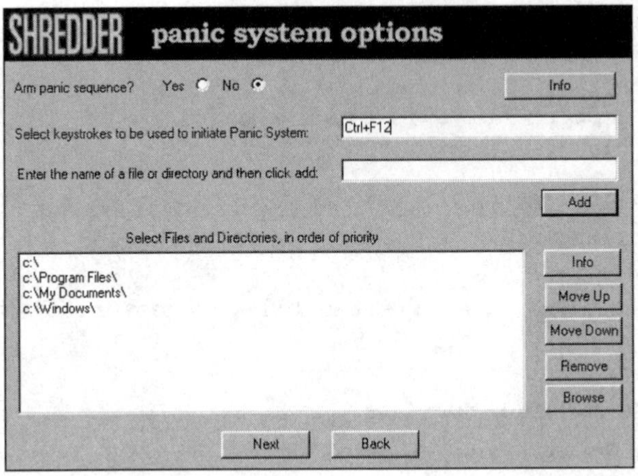

SHREDDER panic system options

Arm panic sequence?   Yes ◯ No ◉   [Info]

Select keystrokes to be used to initiate Panic System: [Ctrl+F12   ]

Enter the name of a file or directory and then click add: [   ]

                                                                    [Add]

Select Files and Directories, in order of priority

c:\	
c:\Program Files\	[Info]
c:\My Documents\	[Move Up]
c:\Windows\	[Move Down]
	[Remove]
	[Browse]

                    [Next]   [Back]

FIGURE 18-2:

Many file shredders offer a panic mode to wipe out your files quickly in an emergency.

Password protecting your shredder

Since file shredders make undeleting files nearly impossible, they can be powerful weapons in the hands of a particularly malicious person. Just run a file shredder on your enemy's computer and you can irreparably shred the contents of an entire hard disk in minutes. Even worse than having someone deliberately shred your files is if you accidentally shred files you really wanted to keep.

To protect against an enemy or your own clumsiness, some file shredders, such as Assure (http://www.alienseed.com), offer a *password protection feature*. Before you can shred any files, you have to type in your password. Not only does this keep you from shredding your own files by mistake, but it also keeps your enemies from turning your file shredder against you.

CAUTION Password protection can stop you from accidentally deleting any files, but you wouldn't want this feature turned on if you might need to use panic mode shredding where you might need to delete a bunch of files instantly.

Writing your own file shredder

If you want to see exactly how a file shredder works, download the source code to the file shredder called Eraser (http://www.tolvanen.com/eraser), written by Sami Tolvanen. Not only is this file shredder absolutely free for anyone to use, but it also includes Microsoft Visual C++ source code so you can examine how it works and even customize the program for your own particular needs.

Linux users can download a file-deleting program called Wipe (http://gsu.linux.org.tr/wipe). Like Eraser, Wipe is free to use and includes C source code so you can see how the program works and modify the program to add new features if you want.

Self-destructing email

Email can form a long incriminating trail of evidence, so you should also delete your email regularly and shred your email message directories. Since this can be a nuisance, several companies have come up with self-destructing email. The idea is that after a certain amount of time, the email message either shreds itself (using a secure file shredding method that can defeat ordinary undelete programs) or encrypts itself so it can't be read after a certain date.

Disappearing email

Disappearing Inc. (http://www.disappearing.com) offers a unique self-destructing version of email called Disappearing Email. When you send a message to someone and run the Disappearing Email program, you receive a unique encryption key from the special Disappearing Access server. Using this key, your copy of Disappearing Email encrypts your message (using the well-regarded Blowfish encryption algorithm) and sends it out on the Internet. When someone wants to read your email, the email has to get the encryption key from the Disappearing Access server, which opens the message.

However, once the expiration date of the message has passed, the Disappearing Access server destroys the encryption key needed to open the message, effectively locking out anyone who tries to read the message ever again. In this case the email isn't physically destroyed but rendered useless.

InThether

The problem with the Disappearing Email program is that it relies on a network of Disappearing Access servers to be available for sending out encryption keys. To avoid this reliance on other computers, Infraworks (http://www. infraworks.com) offers a program called InThether.

The InThether program consists of a Receiver and a Packager. To send a file (text, video, audio, etc.), you encrypt it using the Packager program. To read, view, or hear your file, another person needs the Receiver program. After a specified date or after someone opens the file a certain number of times, the Receiver package can delete and shred the file.

1on1Mail

1on1Mail, another email destruction program (http://www. 1on1mail.com), encrypts files that can expire (and self-destruct) after a certain time or date. Even if someone tries to undelete your self-destructive email, they'll still have to dig through the protection of the Blowfish encryption algorithm.

While self-destructing email can protect your information in transit and at its final destination, it still won't protect prying eyes from finding traces of your data on your hard disk in slack space, temporary files, and swap files on the computer where you created the email. Self-destructing email can be one step to protecting your privacy, but don't count on it to protect your privacy all by itself.

Securely deleting Windows registry entries

The Windows registry can save information about your files even after the files themselves have been securely deleted and shredded beyond recognition. To completely delete registry entries so they can't be examined and recovered, you have to rebuild (also known as *compressing*) your registry database. To do this under Windows 95/98, follow these steps:

1. Make a backup copy of your SYSTEM.DAT and USER.DAT files in case anything goes wrong since these files make up your registry. (Both files are normally hidden, so to view hidden files in the Windows Explorer program, choose **View · Folder Options**, click on the View tab, click in the **Show all files** radio button, and click **OK**. Click the **Start** button on the Windows taskbar and choose **Run**.

2. Type REGEDIT.EXE and press ENTER.

3. Choose **Registry · Export Registry File**. An Export Registry File dialog box appears.

4. Type a name for your registry file and click **Save**.

5. Restart your computer in MS-DOS mode.

6. Type the following command at the MS-DOS prompt and press ENTER:

   REGEDIT /c <filename of exported registry>

   (Where <filename of exported registry> is the name you typed in step 4.)

FINDING DATA

No matter how many times you've deleted a file, there are always ways to retrieve it again. While you could extract an overwritten file's data by analyzing its magnetic traces on your hard disk (discussed below), it's far easier to look for electronic traces of it.

Finding evidence in a file's slack space

The MS-DOS and Windows operating systems divide hard disks into partitions, which are further divided into clusters. In MS-DOS and older versions of Windows, the cluster size is 32K, meaning that if you save a 64K file it takes up two clusters. But if you save a file that's only 5K in size, your computer saves it in a 32K cluster, wasting 27K of space. This extra space is called the *slack space*. (Newer versions of Windows 95/98 use 4K clusters, thereby allowing more efficient use of your hard disk.)

The keyboard buffer

Most operating systems store everything you type in a portion of memory called the *keyboard buffer*; thus, when you create a text document (containing all the subversive actions you plan to take against your government), the keyboard buffer temporarily stores this information in your computer's memory. When you close the file, your computer clears the keyboard buffer by dumping its contents into the slack space of that particular file, which you can then view with a computer forensics tool (discussed below).

So if you're trying to get rid of evidence, simply encrypting or deleting a file is not enough. Encryption or file deletion protects your actual file, but does nothing to hide or erase information dumped in the slack space of your hard or floppy disk. To ensure you are not incriminated by the keyboard buffer, use your favorite file shredder to delete the slack space on your hard disk.

Finding evidence in temporary files

If slack space evidence isn't enough to convict you, computer forensic experts can examine the plethora of temporary files that programs like word processors or spreadsheet programs create to "recover" your data in case your computer suddenly crashes.

Although temporary files get deleted when you close the program that created them, they still exist on your hard or floppy disk until your computer physically overwrites them. By examining a disk for deleted files, a computer forensics expert can use an ordinary undelete program to recover any temporary files found on your disks, and expose any sensitive data you may have recently written.

To guard against temporary files revealing your secrets, you may need to shred any temporary files (often identified by the file extension .TMP) individually. Since temporary files are usually hidden, you may need to turn on the Show all files feature in the Windows Explorer program so you can spot your temporary files to shred.

Searching your Web browser cache

When you search the Internet, your Web browser stores (caches) the Web pages you visit in a directory on your hard disk called the *cache directory*. Since the cache directory records all the Web sites you've visited in the last two weeks, it can leave behind an incriminating trail if you've been visiting sites you're not supposed to visit.

In case you're curious what kind of information someone might find in your Web browser cache, run a program such as CacheX (http://www.mwso.com) for either Internet Explorer or Netscape. CacheX displays the contents of your cache files so anyone can see which Web pages you've looked at in the past few days.

Internet Explorer

To find the Web browser cache in the Windows version of Internet Explorer, look in the C:\Windows\History directory. To purge your cache, just delete all the files in this directory using the Windows Explorer program.

To find the Internet Explorer cache on a Macintosh, look in the System Folder and then the Preferences Folder. Microsoft Internet Explorer stores the cache in a folder called MS Internet Cache. If you want to purge your cache in the Macintosh version of Internet Explorer, follow these steps:

1. Choose **Edit · Preferences**. A Preferences dialog box appears.
2. Click **Advanced**.
3. Click on the **Empty Now** button.

Netscape

To find the Web browser cache from the Windows version of Netscape, look in the C:\Program Files\Netscape\Users directory. Each user has a folder and inside each user's folder is the Cache folder.

To find the cache on a Macintosh, look in the System Folder, then the Preferences folder, and finally the Netscape Users folder. Inside this Netscape Users folder will be additional folders for each user's name and inside these folders is the Cache folder for each user.

On Linux systems, Netscape stores the cache in a directory called .netscape/cache, which is often buried inside the /home/<user name> directory. For example, if the user name is bob, then the Netscape cache for Bob would be /home/bob/.netscape/cache.

To purge your cache in Netscape, follow these steps:

1. Choose **Edit · Preferences**. A Preferences dialog box appears.

2. Click on **Advanced** in the Category box.

3. Click on the **Cache** subheading underneath the **Advanced** heading as shown in Figure 18-3.

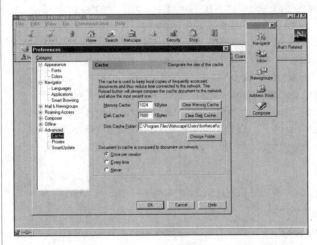

FIGURE 18-3:

All versions of Netscape allow you to purge your cache by clicking a Clear Disk Cache button.

4. Click the **Clear Disk Cache** button. A dialog box appears, asking if you really want to remove all the files in your cache.

5. Click **OK**.

As an alternative to purging your cache files manually, you can run special cache purging programs such as Cache and Cookie Washer (http://www.webroot.com), or IEClean/NSClean (http://www.nsclean.com), which can clean up the cache in both Internet Explorer and Netscape. Macintosh users running AOL or Netscape can also download WCCacheCleaner or AOL3CacheCleaner (http://www.whitecrest. com). Both programs automatically purge your cache every time you shut down your Macintosh. If you're a Windows user running AOL, Internet Explorer, Netscape, or even Opera, use the Internet Cleanup (http://www.ontrack.com) or Complete Cleanup (http://members.aol.com/softdd) program for purging your cache files.

Just remember that purging the cache simply deletes the files and won't physically remove them—anyone can undelete your erased cache directory file later. For more security, use a file shredder instead (see above).

If you think purging your cache, deleting old email messages, wiping out temporary files, clearing out slack space, and shredding all your files is too much trouble, guess what? That's exactly what computer forensics experts are counting on when they examine a suspect's computer—your finding it to be too much trouble to clean your cache frequently; and, in fact, most find all or part of the Internet cache intact when they examine it.

COMPUTER FORENSICS TOOLS

Depending on the seriousness of the crime and the skill of the criminal, computer forensics experts generally rely on four basic tools when searching for incriminating data: file undeleting programs, hex editors, magnetic sensors, and electron microscopes.

File undeleting programs

File undeleting programs, readily available in utility programs like Norton Utilities, are often sufficient to catch novices or people unfamiliar with the way computers work. As described above, they work by renaming undeleted files (if they have not yet been overwritten by your system) so that your system will recognize them again. But they only work if these files have not been overwritten on your hard disk, so undeleting programs are a relatively weak forensics tool.

Hex editors

If the suspect has deleted files and has overwritten them on his or her hard disk, you can always use a *hex editor* to view any data stored in (or deleted from) both files and disk sectors. A hex editor allows you to peek at the physical contents stored on a disk, regardless of the files, directories, or partitions. Hex editors are often used to crack copy-protected software, study how computer viruses work, or in the case of forensics, identify and retrieve information that can't normally be accessed by the operating system. To understand how hex editors can work, you need to know that all information saved on a hard disk gets recorded in tracks, which are concentric rings on the surface of each hard disk platter, like the rings on a tree. Each track is subdivided into sectors, each of which holds 512 bytes of data. These disk sectors are particularly important because they store the keyboard buffer. (For some great online information about how computers work, visit Charles Kozierok's "The PC Guide" at www.pcguide.com.) Figure 18-4 shows a hex editor at work. Hex editors read this physical media directly and don't rely on operating system services to read "files."

Forensics experts generally use a hex editor to search for evidence in specific parts of a disk; trying to use a hex editor to examine an entire hard disk would be like scouring the inside of a skyscraper for fingerprints. Still, hex editors can often recover some or all of the data in a deleted file that you might not otherwise be able to access.

Three popular hex editors are enclosed on the CD: Hex Workshop (http://www.bpsoft.com); UltraEdit (http://www.idmcomp.com); and VEDIT (http://www.vedit.com). You'll find more details about each, including user comments and features, at their Web sites.

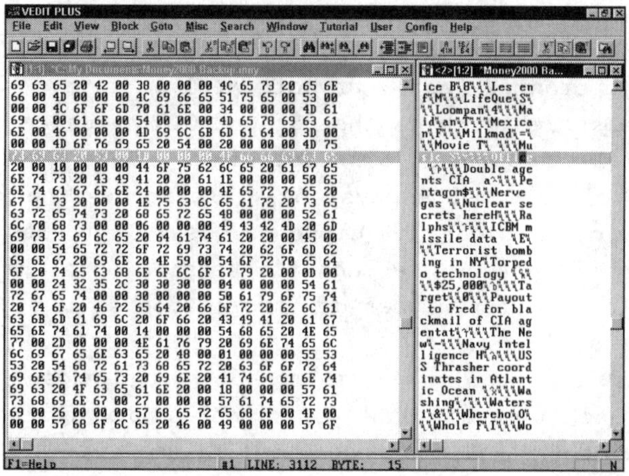

FIGURE 18-4:

A hex editor like VEDIT can display the hidden contents of any disk sector or file.

Magnetic sensors and electron microscopes

Every file you save leaves magnetic traces on the disk it was saved on. By measuring the changes in magnetic fields on a disk, forensics experts using magnetic sensors can reconstruct part or even all of a deleted file—or they can use an electron microscope (expensive, but available to almost all governments).

Electron microscopes can measure tiny changes in magnetic fields which not even overwriting a file can completely obliterate. Since each time the computer overwrites a file the disk heads may not be aligned directly over the file, fragments of the deleted file overwritten may remain, which an electron microscope can detect.

Disk splicing

No matter how many times you overwrite a file or format and partition a hard disk, traces of your original data may still remain. File shredders simply make it progressively more expensive and difficult to retrieve data, but not impossible.

Under the illusion that they'll have complete protection, many people burn floppy or hard disks, crush and mangle them, cut them into pieces, pour acid on them, and otherwise physically manhandle them so there's no possible way they could ever be used by another computer again. Unfortunately, physical destruction of floppy and hard disks still can't guarantee that your data will be safe since government agencies such as the FBI and CIA practice a specialized technique known as disk splicing.

With *disk splicing,* someone physically rearranges the pieces of a floppy or hard disk as close as possible to its original condition. Then they use magnetic sensors or elec- tron microscopes to scan for traces of information still stored on the disk surface.

Obviously, disk splicing is a time-consuming and expen- sive procedure, so don't expect that your local police force will have the knowledge, skill, or equipment to use disk splicing. But if you've destroyed evidence that involves national government agencies such as the NSA, CIA, or FBI, don't expect a mangled disk to hide your secrets from the prying electronic eyes of rich and powerful government agen- cies either. In fact, the American government even has a special laboratory called The Defense Computer Forensics Lab (http://www.dcfl.gov), located in Linthicum, Maryland, which specializes in retrieving information from computers, no matter what condition the hardware or disks may be in.

The ultimate lesson is that if you don't want to risk having certain information retrieved off your hard or floppy disk no matter what precautions you may have taken, don't store that information on a computer.

EXPERIMENTING WITH FORENSICS TOOLS

With so many different ways to leave behind a trail of incriminating evidence, you may want to examine your own hard disk for ways that someone could use your data against you.

Free forensics tools

To experiment with a variety of free forensics tools visit AntiCode (http://www.anticode.com) or the New Technologies site (http://www.forensics-intl.com/download.html). For example, the dirsnp program can recover previously deleted files, the dd program can read individual sectors off a disk and display their contents, and the readit program can search a file for a particular word or phrase, such as "nuclear missile," "nerve gas," or the name of your boss's mistress.

Since recovered files often contain non-alphanumeric characters (such as smiley faces, triangles, or odd mathematical symbols), the filter program can screen out such useless characters, allowing you to see more clearly the actual data buried inside. To preserve the contents of a suspect's computer, the disable program can turn off the keyboard.

Commercial forensics tools

To learn about some of the tools law enforcement agencies might use against you, visit the Digital Intelligence Inc. Web site (http://www.digitalintel.com), which sells a unique forensics tool called DriveSpy. DriveSpy accesses physical drives using pure BIOS (Int13 or Int13x) calls. Not only does this allow DriveSpy to access both DOS and non-DOS partitions, but it also insures that you won't risk having the operating system modify or erase data (for example modify the swap file) during normal use.

DriveSpy lets you do the following:

→ Examine hard disk partitions using a built-in Sector (and Cluster) hex viewer.

→ Copy files to a designated work area without altering file access/modification dates.

→ Unerase files to a designated work area without altering file access/modification dates.

→ Search drives, partitions, and files for text strings or data sequences.

→ Store all the slack space of an entire partition to a file for examination.

→ Save and restore one or more contiguous sectors to/from a file.

For those who need more power than DriveSpy offers, Digital Intelligence also sells dedicated computer forensics workstations (whimsically dubbed FRED, for Forensic Recovery Evidence Device) and a portable version called FREDDIE (for Forensic Recovery Evidence Device Diminutive Interrogation Equipment). If you ever see the police hauling a FRED or FREDDIE into your computer room, you'll know that they'll be able to copy data from any hard disk or any other removable storage device such as ZIP, JAZ, or SuperDisks; create images of your entire hard disk; connect directly to your computer and monitor any communications that your friends may be trying to send to you; examine any visible and hidden partitions for data; and capture video images from a camera to record the appearance and location of equipment at the scene of the crime.

Or visit Guidance Software (www.guidancesoftware.com) to learn about its EnCase program. Not only can EnCase examine MS-DOS/Windows computers, but it can also examine Macintosh and Linux computers. EnCase can hook up to a target computer through a parallel cable and scan the target computer's hard disk for graphic files (useful for hunting down child pornographers). Once it has retrieved all these graphic files and copied them to another computer, it can display or print the contents of these graphic files.

While searching graphic files may help find child pornography images, searching text and other files can help find evidence against ordinary criminals or terrorists. Since their information is likely to be stored in word processor documents or email messages, EnCase can search a hard disk for all files that contain certain words or phrases. Once EnCase finds a file containing a specific word or phrase, it can list or copy those files for further examination.

PROTECTING YOURSELF

Even if you use a file shredding program consistently, law enforcement officials can always use a variety of computer forensics tools to pry out any secrets your deleted files may be hiding. So how can you protect your computer from their prying eyes? Basically, you can't. While you can make recovering data harder by periodically purging your cache directory and only storing files on removable disks (such as floppy or ZIP disks) and physically destroying them afterwards, just remember that everything you do on your computer can be recovered and examined later.

Even if you use encryption, guess what? Any information that you encrypt could still be stored in slack space or temporary files, which means a forensics expert can avoid your encryption and uncover your information by finding the unencrypted version of your data elsewhere on your disks.

If you don't want your computer to incriminate you, learn what computer forensics experts are capable of recovering. Experiment with some of the free or commercial forensics tools to recover data on your computer or see what you can find on other people's computers. Try secretly examining a co-worker's computer. You might learn how to better protect your own data.

19

Protecting Your Computer, Your Data, and Yourself

WHEN USING YOUR COMPUTER, IT PAYS TO BE PARANOID.
Anything you store on it could be used against you. Write a
letter to a pen pal who lives in North Korea, Iran, or Cuba,
and you could be accused of transferring state secrets.
Email a friend about your work, and you might be accused of
leaking proprietary corporate information. Type personal
information in your word processor or address book, and a
spy could later use this information to blackmail you.

But you can keep your information private by

→ Physically locking up your computer so no one
   can access it

→ Password protecting it

→ Purging your machine of incriminating files

→ Encrypting your data

*If you haven't got
anything nice to
say about anybody,
come sit next
to me.*

—ALICE ROOSEVELT LONGWORTH

LOCKING UP YOUR COMPUTER

For many people, the most valuable part of their computer
is the data stored on its hard drive. But while that data
may be irreplaceable, you probably can't afford to lose
your computer either. More than 200,000 laptops are stolen
every year, and thousands of desktops are either stolen or
stripped of parts by thieves or dishonest employees. To
prevent their computers from disappearing, many people use
locking cables that attach to a laptop computer's security
slot or through a special loop that connects to the side of
the computer, monitor, or desk (see Figure 19-1).

While security cables will probably slow down a thief, they won't stop a determined one. Ordinary nail polish remover can dissolve the adhesives used to glue the cable's attachment to the computer, and laptop security locks can be easily broken with a few well-placed blows of a hammer. Wire cutters can snap the cable in half.

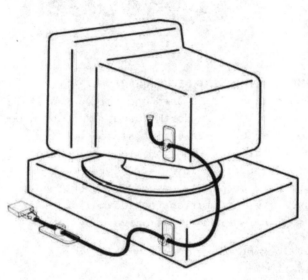

Disk drive locks and computer covers are other types of protective mechanisms. The drive lock fits into the floppy disk drive and prevents anyone from inserting a floppy disk. This prevents other people from accidentally (or deliberately) spreading a computer virus, loading a Trojan Horse, copying files, or booting from a floppy.

Protective computer covers are often metal shields that encase the computer, and are intended to stop a thief from opening the computer and removing valuable components like hard disks or memory. They also add bulk to a computer, making it more cumbersome to steal.

To purchase a restraining cable, disk drive locks, tamper-proof screws, alarms, or protective covers, visit one of these sites:

→ CompuGuard (http://www.compu-gard.com)

→ Computer Security (http://www.computersecurity.com)

→ PC Guardian (http://www.pcguardian.com)

→ Security Solutions (http://www.security-solutions. com)

Here's an interesting trick

Barracuda Security Devices (http://www.barracudasecurity. com) offers a unique security product that works like the exploding dye capsules used by banks to foil heists. (The capsules give a warning, and then they explode, spraying ink over the money and the bank robber so the police can later identify the perp and trace any attempt to put the money into circulation.)

The Barracuda Anti-Theft Device fits into an internal expansion slot in a desktop computer and detects changes in internal ambient light, signaling that the case has been opened. If the cover is removed without disarming the device with a PIN, an alarm sounds and the device sprays indelible ink across all of the internal components, making them easy to identify as stolen and impossible to resell.

PROTECTING YOUR LAPTOP

If you're traveling with a laptop in an airport, hide it. Think about it: Walk through any airport and you'll see many people carrying their laptops in distinctive black carrying cases, easily recognizable to a thief and nearly impossible to identify by sight if stolen. Instead of carrying your laptop in a case that screams out "laptop, steal me," put it in an ordinary briefcase or carrying bag, or even a paper shopping bag to disguise it as a souvenir from an overpriced airport gift shop.

If you're going to lose your laptop in an airport, the most likely place will be at the metal detectors. One person will step in front of you, loaded down with pockets full of metal objects (keys or coins), and wait until you pass your laptop on the conveyor belt for the X-ray machine.

Then, while he beeps the metal detector and delays the passengers behind him (including you), an accomplice on the other side of the detector picks up your laptop at the end of the conveyer belt. By the time you get through the metal detector, your laptop is gone—in its unidentifiable black case. So hold on to your laptop at all times.

Tracking your laptop

But what if, despite your best efforts, your laptop gets stolen anyway?

One option to try is an alarm, like the one sold by TrackIt (http://www.trackitcorp.com). Tracking alarms consist of two parts: a sensor attached to your laptop and another sensor carried by you (attached to your keychain or kept in your pocket). The moment your laptop gets separated from you by a fixed distance (such as fifteen feet), an alarm in the laptop screams out. If this doesn't cause the thief to drop the laptop right away, it calls your attention to your laptop and allows you to follow its piercing whine to retrieve it.

REMOTE TRACKING SERVICES

Another protective mechanism is a tracing or monitor program hidden inside your laptop, such as CyberAngel (http://www.sentryinc.com). The moment a thief turns on your computer and connects to the Internet, CyberAngel turns off your modem's speaker and silently dials a CyberAngel's Security Headquarters to report the theft and allow CyberAngel's headquarters to trace the call to track down your laptop computer. You'll find other tracing programs and devices at AlertPC (http://www.alertpc.com), CompuTrace (http://www.computrace.com), and PC PhoneHome (http://www.codexdatasystems.com).

If all else fails and your machine is stolen, consider listing its serial number (have you made a note of it yet?) at the Stolen Computer Registry Web site (http://www.stolencomputers.org). And, if you're in the market for a used machine, you might visit this site just to be sure you don't buy a stolen one.

PASSWORD PROTECTING YOUR COMPUTER

Besides physically locking your machine or using tracking devices and alarms, you should also consider password protecting it. If you use a real password protection program (not Microsoft Windows), you can make it tough for a thief to do much with your machine, even if they nab it.

Posum Software's Workstation Lock (http://posum.com) will let you password protect your system at startup without using a screensaver. Clasp2000 (http://www.claspnow.com) is a good choice if you simply want to block access to Windows.

COVERING YOUR TRACKS

If you use the Internet, you may not want others to know which Web sites you've been visiting. Unfortunately, anyone with access to your computer can find this type of information just by looking at the Internet cookies and browser cache stored on your computer, so if you want to cover your tracks, start here.

Stopping cookies

When you visit some Web sites, they may store information on your computer in a "cookie" file, which contains the address of the Web site along with any additional information you may have typed, such as your name or email address.

When you return to that site, the cookie sends the information stored on your machine to the Web site computer. Cookies allow the Web site to customize or personalize its Web pages, such as displaying the message, "Welcome back, John Doe!" at the top of the page.

While cookies themselves are harmless (they cannot spread a virus or delete any of your files), they can reveal your favorite Web sites. Neither teenagers nor employees may want their parents or boss to know they've been visiting the Penthouse Web site during working hours, but no matter how discreet you are, the tell-tale cookie will give the game away.

If you don't like the idea of Web sites hiding cookies on your computer, you can change your browser's preferences to refuse them. To do this in Internet Explorer, follow these steps (See Figure 19-2):

1. Choose **Tools · Internet Options**. An Internet Options dialog box appears.

2. Click on the **Security** tab.

3. Click on the **Custom Level** button. A Security Settings dialog box appears.

4. Click either the **Enable**, **Disable**, or **Prompt** radio button to change the way your browser handles cookies.

5. Click **OK** in this settings dialog, and then in the main Options dialog.

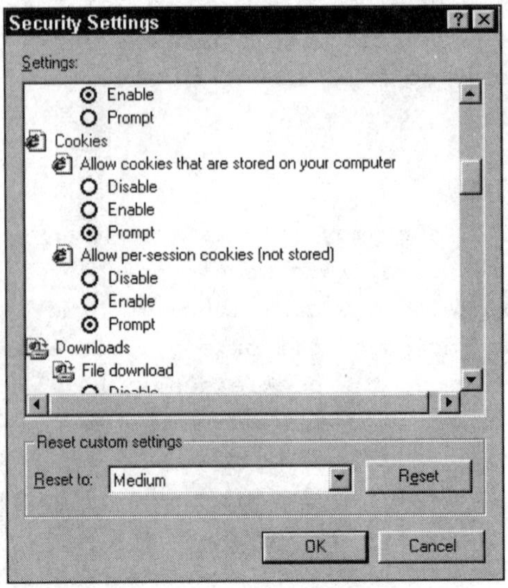

FIGURE 19-2:

Changing the way the Windows version of Internet Explorer handles cookies.

To disable cookies in Netscape, follow these steps:

1. Choose **Edit · Preferences**. A Preferences dialog box appears.

2. Click **Advanced** in the Category group.

3. Click on a radio button such as **Disable cookies**, or in the **Warn me before accepting a cookie** check box.

4. Click **OK**.

To delete existing cookies and filter incoming ones, use a cookie utility program like Cookie Crusher (http://www.thelimitsoft.com), Cookie Pal (http://www.kburra.com), or Magic Cookie Monster (http://download.at/drjsoftware). Cookie programs can filter cookies as you browse, allowing some to pass (like cookies from shopping sites that store your shopping preferences) while blocking others (like cookies from companies that want to track how long you've spent browsing their site). Best of all, these cookie crushers can find and delete existing cookies on your hard disk automatically (See Figure 19-3).

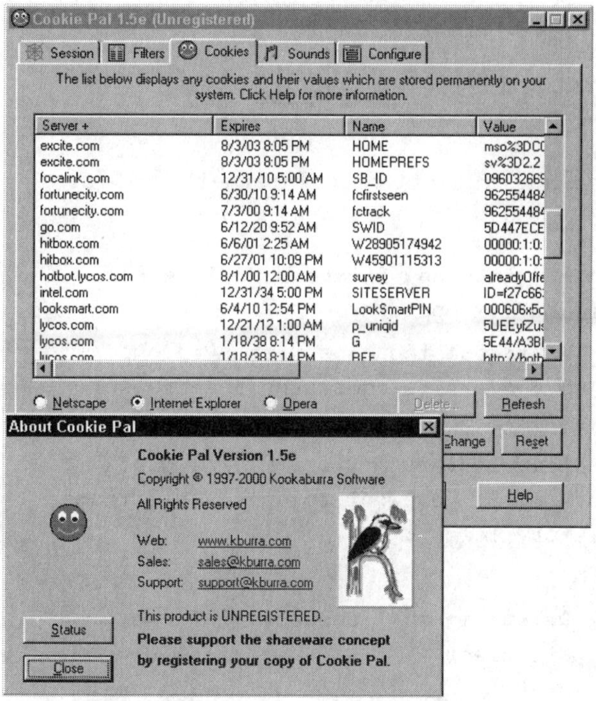

FIGURE 19-3:

Cookie Pal can find all the cookies on your hard disk.

Cleaning out your Web browser cache

Besides storing information about your Web browsing habits in cookie files, your browser may also store pictures, Web pages, and the addresses of the last few Web sites you visited (your "history") in a temporary folder (buried inside the Windows folder) as shown in Figure 19-4.

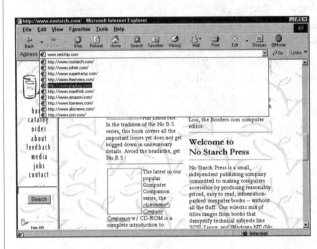

FIGURE 19-4:
You can find the addresses of the last few Web sites someone visited in the Address Bar list box.

To clean out this information in Internet Explorer, follow these steps:

1. Choose **Tools · Internet Options**. An Internet Options dialog box appears.

2. Click on the **General** tab. The History group shows how many Web site addresses the browser stores (such as 20).

3. Click the **Clear History** button. A dialog box appears, asking if you want to delete all items in your history folder.

4. Click **Yes**.

5. Then click **Delete** in the Temporary Internet files group to clear it.

6. Click **OK**.

To clean out temporary Internet files in Netscape, follow these steps:

1. Choose **Edit · Preferences**. A Preferences dialog box appears.
2. Click **Advanced** in the Category group.
3. Click the **Cache** subheading underneath Advanced.
4. Click the **Clear Memory Cache** button.
5. Click the **Clear Disk Cache** button.
6. Click **OK**.

To avoid having to always manually clean up these files, try running CyberClean (http://www.thelimitsoft.com), MacWasher or Window Washer (http://www.webroot.com), or Surf Secret (http://www.surfsecret.com). These programs can automatically clean out your Temporary Internet Files and History folders along with deleting cookies, old email messages, and any downloaded program files at the same time. By running a cleanup program regularly, you can make sure no one can trace your Web browsing usage and violate your privacy (see Figure 19-5).

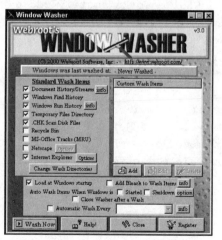

FIGURE 19-5:

Window Washer can delete all traces of your browsing history.

SHIELDING YOUR PRIVACY

Besides protecting your privacy from snoops who can access your computer, you may want to shield your privacy from Web sites, government agencies, and corporations who may be curious about your Internet browsing habits. Don't think others may be interested in knowing what you do on your computer? Think again.

In June 2000, the U.S. District Court in New York received a lawsuit alleging that Netscape's SmartDownload program, distributed with Netscape Communicator, can secretly monitor downloads of .EXE and .ZIP files from Web sites. Although Netscape denied that SmartDownload transmits information about a user's files, the company soon decided to scrap the customer-tracking feature of SmartDownload.

In November 2000, security consultant Richard Smith discovered that information generated from RealNetworks' RealJukebox software could keep tabs on what users play and record. Even more disturbing was that RealNetworks had failed to disclose this practice in its privacy policy, which is certified by the Web privacy seal program Truste (http://www.truste.org), an organization dedicated to pro-tecting users' privacy on the Internet.

Following this revelation, RealNetworks hastily added a section to its privacy policy stating that users are assigned a "Globally Unique Identifier" (GUID) when they download the RealJukebox program.

Besides corporate spying, there are also worrying reports about Echelon, a multinational communications eavesdropping network that can snare email, phone conversa-tions, and faxes for later analysis. The National Security Agency supposedly runs a program called Semantic Forests that uses a feature called Topic Spotting to sort through transcribed speech and search for particular phrases and keywords. The five partners (the United States, the United Kingdom, Canada, Australia, and New Zealand) supposedly use Echelon to detect and prevent international terrorism as well as for spying on other nations for economic espionage.

While it's unlikely that the National Security Agency or Central Intelligence Agency is spying on your computer, the thought of leaving your personal life exposed to others can be as disturbing as trying to disrobe in private while living in a glass house. To protect your privacy, consider browsing the Internet anonymously and encrypt every email you send. Here's how.

Anonymous browsing

Because purging your Internet usage history from your hard disk can be troublesome, most people won't bother doing it. But what if you could prevent your Internet usage information from being stored on your computer in the first place? Or, if you could browse in secret?

Anonymous browsing services, like IDzap.com (http://www.idzap.com), Anonymizer.com (http://www.anonymizer.com), and Rewebber (http://www.rewebber.com), block access to your computer so Web sites can't plant a cookie on your computer, detect which type of browser you're using, or identify your IP address. When you visit them, you simply type in the URL you want to visit, and the anonymizer takes you there—in secret. Best of all, they provide their basic services for free.

One caveat though—anonymous browsing services aren't always reliable. You'll probably run into difficulty with many shopping sites (which rely on cookies), and other sites which want to detect your browser and such. Still, they're a free and a simple way to browse discreetly.

Browsing as someone else—sort of

Bell Labs and AT&T Labs have a really interesting twist on anonymous browsing in their Crowds service (http://www.research.att.com/projects/crowds). The idea is similar to blending in with a crowd in a public place.

When you use Crowds, you're randomly thrown into a crowd of other randomly chosen users. Rather than accessing a Web page yourself, the computer randomly selects another user in the crowd to access the Web page and pass it along to you (which could have the unwanted side-effect of revealing what one individual in the crowd may be doing). By masking any individual's actions within the larger actions of a group, Crowds shields the privacy of everyone since no one can tell which actions any specific individual has taken at any given time.

Freedom software from Zero Knowledge Systems (http://www.zeroknowledge.com) works with your browser and allows you to create several pseudonyms. When you browse the Internet or send email, your request goes through one or more computers, which mask your identity.

Or, if you're a true capitalist, why not sell your personal information instead of giving it away free? Persona (http://www.privaseek.com) and Lumeria's SuperProfile (http://www.superprofile.com) do just that. Not only can you control who gets your personal information, but you can also (theoretically) make some money in the process.

Sending anonymous email

If you want to express your opinion, leak information in secret, or even simply participate in medical or other support groups in confidence, send your email anonymously and securely. One way to do so is to keep opening and closing free email accounts, but anonymous email services, like Subdimension (http://www.subdimension.com/freemail), are a better way. Subdimension is like many free email services except that they don't ask for personal information. Then again, another way to keep your identity private is to use most any free email service and simply fake your personal information.

If these anonymous email services aren't enough, try a secure, encrypted, anonymous email service. Hushmail (http://www.hushmail.com), PrivacyX (http://www.privacyx.com), or ZipLip (http://www.ziplip.com) are three such services. Encryption protects your email from being read and also digitally "signs" outgoing email to verify that it came from you (instead of someone just pretending to be you by spoofing your email address). The whole idea behind encryption is to scramble your data beyond recognition so only you and anyone you choose can access the data. That way even if someone steals or copies your files, they won't be able to read them.

Like other anonymous email services, encrypted anonymous email services don't require a name, address, phone number, or other method of tracing you so your email can remain truly anonymous. And ZipLip will even shred your email after it's been read.

Still a third technique for hiding your identity through email is to use an anonymous remailer, such as Anonymous.To (http://anonymous.to), which sends your email from your computer to a remailer, which is another computer connected to the Internet. The remailer masks your identity by stripping away your real name and address and replacing it with a phony one before sending your email to its final destination.

You can even use multiple remailers to cover your tracks even further. Send your email to the first remailer (which strips out your address), then tell it to send your email to another remailer. Continue this process for two or more anonymous hops, and it will be nearly impossible for anyone to trace or monitor where your email came from.

Although each remailer may work differently, a typical one works as follows:

From: Name@YourAddress.com

To: remailer@RemailerAddress

Subject: Anything

::

Anon-To: destination@address

This is my message.

Your real address appears only when you're sending email to the remailer. Once the remailer gets your message, it ships it off to the address defined by the Anon-To field. (The two colons let the remailer know a destination address will follow. That way the remailer doesn't think the Anon-To field is part of your real message.)

To filter your email through multiple remailers, your message might look like this:

From: Name@YourAddress.com

To: remailer@RemailerAddress

Subject: Anything

::

Anon-To: second@RemailerAddress

::

Anon-To: destination@address

This is my message.

In this example, you're sending your email to the first remailer located at the remailer@RemailerAddress. This first remailer then sends your message to a second remailer located at second@RemailerAddress. The second remailer then sends your email to its final destination at destination@address. For the truly paranoid, you can keep adding remailer addresses indefinitely.

To further protect your privacy, ask an anonymous remailer to hold your email for a random period before forwarding it to its final destination. This delay can prevent snoops from tracing the origin of your email by noting that it arrives at the remailer at 4:00 and then leaves exactly one minute later.

But don't think that anonymous remailers allow you to conduct criminal activities. If you harass others through email, send out death threats, or plot bomb attacks against innocent people, remailer administrators will likely help the police find and prosecute you. Don't abuse the privilege.

The biggest problem with remailers is that they appear and disappear as quickly as democracies in Third World countries. Running an anonymous remailer costs time and money, and most remailers don't charge for their services because asking someone to pay by check or credit card destroys their anonymity. And some anonymous remailers aren't really anonymous. Some require that you open an account with them, which means that whoever runs the remailer has a record of your real email address.

Although anonymous remailers and encryption can help protect your privacy, nothing can guarantee absolute privacy. Anonymous remailers are only as secure as the people running them. Anyone can set up a phony anonymous remailer and read every message that passes through it. Although encryption can protect your email to some extent, the real danger lies in exposing your real email address. For this reason you should use a remailer in another country.

For example, someone living in Communist China should view a Chinese remailer with suspicion. But that same person would probably be safer using an anonymous remailer located in Finland, Canada, or Mexico because its administrators probably won't care about Chinese citizens, and the Chinese authorities are less likely to be able to access the remailer's records.

To learn from people who are using anonymous remailers, browse the Usenet group alt.privacy.anon-server to read the latest developments.

Your own Private Idaho

If the idea of trying to combine anonymous email with encryption seems cumbersome, you might want to try a program designed to simplify this process. Private Idaho (http://www.eskimo.com/~joelm/pi.html) works with the Pretty Good Privacy (PGP) program to encrypt your email. PGP is a highly regarded encryption program that is considered to offer encryption tough enough even to resist cracking by well-funded intelligence organizations such as the CIA and NSA.

Best of all, Private Idaho is free and comes with complete Visual Basic source code so you can modify it or just study the source code to make sure it doesn't contain any back doors that government authorities can use to spy on your email. For a 32-bit version of Private Idaho, visit the Private Idaho Email Web site (http://www.itech.net.au/pi/).

Encryption in pictures

Since few people encrypt their email, those who do use encryption immediately draw attention to themselves. So if you want to use encryption while looking as if you aren't, use *steganography*, a term derived from the Greek words *steganos* (covered or secret) and *graphy* (writing or drawing) to literally mean "covered writing." Steganography is the science of hiding information in an apparently harmless medium, such as a picture or a sound file.

For example, suppose government agents decide to snare every email message sent to and from a particular Web site. With unencrypted email, spying computers could easily search for keywords like "nuclear," "missile," "nerve gas," or "bomb" and store copies of these messages for further analysis. If you encrypt your email, they could just as easily grab copies of your encrypted messages and use their supercomputers to crack them open later.

But, if you use steganography, you can send innocent-seeming graphic files of famous paintings, antique cars, or bikini-clad models that actually contain hidden messages inside. These ordinary files could easily contain underground newsletters, censored information, or simply ordinary text that you want to keep private. If someone intercepts your email, they'll see only a picture. Unless a snoop is certain that the picture contains hidden messages, he'll most likely ignore it.

Steganography programs break up your data (either text or encrypted text) and bury it within a graphics or sound file, such as a .GIF or .WAV file. In the process, the steganography program slightly corrupts the graphic or sound file, so the more data you try to hide, the greater the degradation.

You can use two techniques to prevent total degradation (thus flagging the fact that a graphic or sound file contains hidden information). First, use black-and-white instead of color graphic files, because slight degradation in a black-and-white graphic isn't as noticeable as it is in color. Second, store small files in multiple graphic or sound files rather than cramming one huge file into a single graphic or sound file.

To toy around with other steganography programs and learn more about this relatively obscure branch of encryption, visit the Steganography Archive Web site at http://steganography.tripod.com/stego.html and look for popular steganography programs such as S-Tools, Invisible Secrets, or Hide and Seek (see Figure 19-6).

FIGURE 19-6:

To further mask your data, the Invisible Secrets program can stuff fake files inside a graphic file.

You might also like to visit Stego Online (http://www.stego.com), download the free Java source code, and practice encrypting text files within .GIF files on your own hard disk. If you're serious about encrypting your data and disguising that fact, browse through the steganography newsgroup at alt.steganography.

So let everyone else use ordinary encryption (and broadcast to the world that they're doing it)—for additional security, take encryption one step further and embrace the strange new world of steganography instead. And, to make a snoop's task even more difficult, encrypt your text with PGP and then store the encrypted text inside a graphic image. That way if someone discovers that you're using steganography, he'll still have to crack the encryption.

ENCRYPTING YOUR DATA

Besides encrypting your email, consider encrypting the data on your hard disk as well. Be careful though since not all encryption is the same. Encryption can be classified as weak or strong, depending on the method used. For example, weak encryption might just substitute one letter for another, such as the letter "A" for the letter "B," the letter "B" for the letter "C," and so on. This type of encryption is considered weak because it's fairly easy for anyone to figure out that the message "Uif IBM dpnqvufs jt tnbsu" really stands for "The HAL computer is smart."

Strong encryption uses more complicated methods (algorithms) to encrypt data. Some of the more popular encryption algorithms are the Data Encryption Standard (DES), Blowfish, CAST (Carlisle Adams and Stafford Tavares), International Data Encryption Algorithm (IDEA), Rivest Cipher #5 (RC5), Serpent, Twofish, and Advanced Encryption Standard (AES). Of course, strong encryption algorithms are only as good as your password. If someone steals your password, strong encryption will be as useless as a bank vault without a lock.

Because the weakest link in strong encryption is access to your password, two types of password methods have emerged: private-key encryption and public-key encryption.

Private-key encryption uses a single password to encrypt and decrypt data, which means if you misplace your password, anyone with that password could now decrypt your files. Even more troublesome is that if you want to send people an encrypted file, you have to figure out a safe way to send them the password first so they can decrypt the file when they receive it.

To overcome the flaws of private-key encryption, computer scientists developed *public-key encryption,* which allows you two passwords: a private and a public key. The private key is (hopefully) known only to you. The public key can be given freely to anyone.

You can use your private key to encrypt a file and anyone with your public key can decrypt it. If someone wants to send you data, they have to encrypt it using your public key. Then that encrypted file can only be decrypted using your private key.

Since a weak password can unlock even the strongest encryption, experts recommend choosing passwords consisting of random letters, numbers, and symbols. Ideally after you've chosen a random and lengthy password, don't use that same password for anything else.

Besides choosing a weak password, another flaw is choosing a weak encryption algorithm. Many encryption programs offer a choice of several encryption algorithms. As a general rule, the faster the algorithm, the weaker the security; the slower the algorithm, the stronger the security.

Proprietary encryption algorithms are often the worst since they haven't been tested and examined for flaws. Hiding the way an algorithm works (security by obscurity) doesn't keep it secure. In reality, exposing the way your algorithm works can make sure it's secure because it gives more people a chance to study it for problems. Any program that claims their proprietary encryption algorithm is secure most likely doesn't know anything about encryption in the first place.

The better encryption programs use algorithms that have been published worldwide, allowing others to study and probe them for weaknesses. That doesn't mean that they don't have weaknesses—it's just that no one may have found their weakness yet—or the NSA has and isn't telling. (Studying an encryption algorithm can reveal how that algorithm encrypts data but it won't necessarily show you how to crack it.)

One of the simplest ways to crack encryption is to use a *brute-force attack,* which essentially tries every possible password until it eventually finds the correct one. Brute-force can defeat any encryption algorithm, but the stronger encryption algorithms have so many possible combinations that to exhaustively test each one would take even the fastest computer millions of years, so in practice the encryption is secure.

The faster and more powerful computers get, the easier it will be for brute-force attacks to pry open weaker encryption algorithms. On June 17, 1997, a team of college students used a brute-force attack to crack a DES-encrypted file in a $10,000 contest sponsored by the RSA Corporation. This "cracking" program, code-named DESCHALL (http://www.interhack.net/projects/deschall), was distributed and downloaded over the Internet so volunteers could link thousands of computers together and attack the problem simultaneously. Now, if a team of college students can crack DES using ordinary computer equipment, think what governments can do with their higher budgets and specialized hardware. The moral of this story: If the strongest encryption algorithm a program offers is DES, look elsewhere. Triple-DES (a derivative of the DES encryption standard) is stronger than ordinary DES although many encryption programs prefer the Blowfish algorithm, which is considered even stronger than Triple-DES.

One of the most popular encryption programs is Pretty Good Privacy (http://www.pgp.com and http://www.pgpi.com), written by Phil Zimmerman, who is generally credited with making public-key encryption widely available when he released the source code to his Pretty Good Privacy Program (PGP) over the Internet. When the source code managed to find its way to other countries, the U.S. government began a fruitless five-year criminal investigation to determine if Phil broke any laws that classified encryption technology as a "munition." Eventually the government dropped their charges after realizing they didn't have a case, they were wasting taxpayers' money, and they didn't have a clue what they were doing.

Besides PGP, other encryption software includes Kryptel (http://inv.co.nz), PC-Encrypt (http://www.pc-encrypt.com), Absolute Security (http://www.pepsoft.com), GNU Privacy Guard (http://www.gnupg.org), and DataSAFE (http://www.novastor.com/index.asp). To read a free monthly newsletter covering encryption, visit the Crypt-O-Gram Newsletter (http://www.counterpane.com/crypto-gram.html), written by Bruce Schneier, author of *Applied Cryptography*. Or, to discuss encryption, visit one of these newsgroups: alt.security, alt.security.pgp, comp.security.misc, or comp.security.pgp.discuss.

Hiding files on your hard disk

One problem with encryption is that it can alert someone that you're hiding something important. Because no form of encryption can be 100% secure (someone can always steal the password or crack the encryption method), you might try a trickier method: hide your sensitive files. After all, you can't steal what you can't find.

To do so, visit RSE Software (http://www.pc-magic.com) and download their Magic Folders or Encrypted Magic Folders program. Both programs let you make entire directories invisible so a thief won't even know they exist. Encrypted Magic Folders hides and encrypts your file so that, even if someone finds the directory, they won't be able to peek at its contents or copy any of its files without the proper password. Shetef Solutions (http://www.shetef.com) offers a similar program, Win-Secure-It, which can hide and encrypt folders as well as block access to anyone trying to use your computer without the proper password.

Writing your own encryption programs

Despite protests from nearly everyone in the computer industry, the political might of the technologically igno-rant still reigns in too many governments. For example,

U.S. government officials still insist on cramming encryption export regulations down everyone's throat, despite the fact that strong encryption is readily available overseas.

In case encryption becomes illegal in your country, forget about using any government-approved encryption. Just use a free encryption algorithm (such as Blowfish) and make your own encryption program. To do so, you'll need a programming language compiler for C or C++, although you could use a Pascal, BASIC, FORTRAN, or Modula-2 compiler if you really want. To study the C source code for the popular PGP encryption program, visit http://web.mit.edu/network/pgp.html.

For the really ambitious, buy a copy of the book *Applied Cryptography*, second edition, by Bruce Schneier (John Wiley & Sons, ISBN 0-471-11709-9). (You may be able to find it used at a university bookstore.) Not only does *Applied Cryptography* provide detailed explanations of various encryption algorithms, such as the Data Encryption Standard (DES), but it also provides its own encryption algorithm, called Blowfish. Type, scan, or buy the source code from *Applied Cryptography* (http://www.counterpane.com/scode.html), load it into your favorite C/C++ compiler, and you too can create your own encryption program using a proven encryption algorithm that is not known to have been broken (yet).

Rather than torture yourself by trying to understand and write encryption routines, try using an encryption toolkit instead. A typical encryption toolkit supplies either the actual source code to an encryption algorithm (so you don't have to write it yourself) or a compiled version of an encryption algorithm stored in a .DLL or ActiveX file so you can plug it into your own program.

Many Web sites offer various implementations of encryption algorithms in C, C++, or Pascal absolutely free. If you'd prefer to pay for a commercial encryption toolkit, visit MaeDae Enterprise (http://www.maedae.com), Bokler Software (http://www.bokler.com), Cryptix (http://www.cryptix.org), PGP (http://www.pgp.com), Meganet (http://www.meganet.com), or RSA Data Security (http://www.rsasecurity.com).

For links to dozens more encryption Web sites and software, visit the Cryptography A-2-Z Web site at http://www.ssh.fi/tech/crypto. Here you can find links to free encryption software, companies selling encryption packages, and universities offering encryption course materials, in fact, as much about encryption as you care to learn, provided, of course, that the government hasn't already confiscated your computer.

APPENDICES

Glossary

AES (Advanced Encryption Standard) An encryption standard defined by the United States government. *See* DES.

Anonymous remailer A program or Web site that strips away an email address from a message and then forwards it, allowing you to send email without revealing your identity or location.

Antivirus program A program that detects and removes computer viruses.

AOHell A harassment program designed to cause trouble on America Online by sending fake email, creating fake AOL accounts, kicking people off AOL, and conning people into giving their credit card numbers and AOL passwords.

AOL (America Online) The most popular (and hated) online service in the world.

Assembly language A low-level computer programming language. Each specific family of microprocessors (such as Intel or Motorola microprocessors) has its own assembly language that allows maximum flexibility in controlling the computer. Many viruses are written in assembly language, although a few are written in BASIC, C, or Pascal.

Backdoor A hidden entry-point into a computer or program. Hackers often create backdoors in a computer so they can return later and quickly bypass any security or logging in procedures normally required.

Words are, of course, the most powerful drug used by mankind.

—RUDYARD KIPLING

Back Orifice One of the most popular remote access Trojan Horse programs. *See* RAT and Trojan Horse.

Black hat hacker Term describing a hacker who uses his or her skills for malicious purposes such as deleting files and crashing computers. *See* White hat hacker.

Blowfish Popular encryption algorithm freely available for anyone to use.

Boot sector The part of the disk that identifies its type (floppy or hard), the size of the file allocation table, the number of hidden files, and the number of files in the root directory. Every disk has a boot sector, which makes every disk vulnerable to boot viruses. *See also* Boot virus.

Boot virus A virus that infects the boot sector of a disk.

Brute-force attack A method of discovering a password by exhaustively trying all possible combinations of words and numbers until you find a valid password.

C/C++ Popular programming language.

Censorware Generic term for programs, such as parental control programs, that block or limit access to certain Web sites and Usenet newsgroups. *See also* Parental control software.

Checksum The numeric result of some calculation (e.g., a one-way hash function) that uses the physical contents of a file to uniquely identify that particular file. If the file changes, its checksum also changes. Checksums are often stored in a file that may be encrypted, hidden, or saved on a floppy disk. Antivirus and anti-Trojan Horse programs use checksums to identify when a file may have been altered (and thus possibly infected). Similarly, computer forensics experts often use checksums to verify that a file hasn't been changed from the date that the computer was first seized by the police.

Clusters One or more sectors on a disk, containing all or part of a file. *See* Slack space.

CMOS (Complementary Metal-Oxide Semiconductor) A battery-powered chip that stores information about a computer's configuration. Many viruses target this chip because it can keep your computer from working properly.

Cold boot To turn a computer off and then back on again. *See* Warm boot.

.COM file A program file that ends with the .COM file extension. A .COM file is a non-relocatable file that can be used only to store small programs. Larger programs are always stored as .EXE files. *See* .EXE file.

Companion virus A now obsolete type of MS-DOS virus that stores itself as a separate file, usually as a .COM file. Companion viruses name themselves after an infected program file, such as WP.EXE, but with the .COM file extension.

Compiler A program that converts source code into an executable program. *See* Decompiler.

Cracker 1. A malicious hacker. 2. A type of program that can defeat encryption or copy-protection.

Cracking Defeating a program's copy-protection method or bypassing any password or encryption scheme.

Credit card generator A program that creates credit card numbers using the same mathematical formula used by the credit card companies.

Cross-platform Capable of running on multiple operating systems.

Decompiler A type of program that reconstructs a program's original source code from an executable program file. Decompilers exist for Visual Basic, Clipper, Java and other program languages. *See* Disassembler.

Delphi Rapid-application development tool based on the Pascal programming language. Often used to write remote access Trojan Horse programs. *See* RAT and Visual Basic.

Denial of service attack The tying up of a computer's resources to prevent its use by others. Often abbreviated as DoS.

DES (Data Encryption Standard) An encryption method. DES can be cracked and is thus considered useless for encrypting valuable or sensitive information. *See* AES.

Dictionary attack A way of finding a password by trying a list of common passwords such as Star Trek lingo, names of cars, or titles of popular movies.

Direct action virus A virus that does something immediately each time you run it, such as attack your hard disk or display a message on the screen.

Disassembler A program that generates assembly language source code from an executable program file. *See* Decompiler.

Email bombing Clogging up an email account by sending a large number of email messages, or several huge files. *See* Fax bombing and Phone call flooding.

Encryption A method of scrambling data to make it unreadable by others. *See* AES and DES.

.EXE file A common name for a file that contains a program such as a word processor or a game. An .EXE file is a relocatable program that can be used to store larger programs. Nearly all MS-DOS and Windows programs are stored as .EXE files.

False negative When an antivirus or anti—Trojan Horse program fails to detect a virus.

False positive When an antivirus or anti—Trojan Horse program incorrectly claims that a file is infected by a virus.

Fast infector A type of virus that infects program files whenever the computer loads or examines it.

FAT (File Allocation Table) Part of the disk that contains information about the size and location of all the other files on the disk. Each time you format a disk, it creates two identical FATs, which store information on the clusters used by each file stored on the disk. If your disk's FAT gets messed up, the files are still on the disk, but your computer will no longer be able to find or use them.

Fax bombing Sending multiple messages to a fax machine to prevent others from using it. *See* Phone call flooding.

File infector Another name for program infectors.

Firewall Utility designed to keep intruders out of a network or individual computer.

Flooder A malicious program designed to overwhelm a target computer with more data than it can handle.

Forensics Computer forensics is the recovery of deleted files for evidence.

Fortress phone Slang name for a pay phone, referring to its extensive defenses to keep people from breaking into it.

Freeware Software that can be copied, distributed, and given away without payment or legal restrictions of any kind. *See* Shareware.

Gnutella Program designed to allow people to "share" audio and video files with each other over a distributed network. *See* Napster.

Hacker Slang name given to someone extremely knowledgeable about computers. Pejorative in some circles—but not here.

Hacktivism Form of protest that uses computer skills, mostly Web site defacing, to spread a message.

Hate group An organization or collection of people who advocate violence and discrimination against another group of people. Usually motivated by religious or racial differences.

Heuristic analysis Sometimes called rule-based or artificial intelligence analysis, it uses intelligent guesswork, which more often than not finds the solution faster than a standard algorithm. Antivirus programs use heuristic analysis to examine a file, and based on typical virus characteristics, make an educated guess whether a file is infected or not.

Hex editor A program that can directly examine and modify the contents of a file or disk.

Honey pot A phony target used to tempt hackers. Often used to keep hackers logged on to a system long enough to trace their location, or to lure a hacker into a harmless part of a network so he or she can't get out and cause real damage. Also called a *goat file*.

ICQ Popular instant messaging program.

Information warfare Popular term to describe hacking on an individual, commercial, and international level.

Integrity checker An antivirus program that examines each file and calculates a numeric result based on that file's size, time, and date stamp. If the integrity checker notices that the file's size, time, or date has changed, it assumes the file may be infected by a virus. *See* Checksum.

IRC (Internet Relay Chat) A loosely structured network where people can type and read messages to each other in real time.

Java Cross-platform programming language used to create Web page applets and full-blown applications.

Keystroke monitor A program that records keystrokes and/or mouse clicks on a computer, usually without the user's knowledge.

Linux A free version of UNIX designed for personal computers. Although Linux can be copied and distributed without restriction, many companies sell their own versions of Linux that include technical support, software, or other value-added services.

Logic bomb A type of program, often buried within another program, that is set to go off on a certain date or event, erasing data or crashing the computer. Logic bombs are often inserted by disgruntled programmers willing to sabotage their own programs to get back at their employers.

Macro virus A virus written using the macro programming language of a particular program. The most common macro viruses are written in WordBasic or Visual Basic for Applications, although a few macro viruses have been written in the macro programming language for Ami Pro (now called WordPro) and Lotus 1-2-3.

Master Boot Record (MBR) The information stored on a hard disk that tells the computer how the hard disk is partitioned. Most hard disks have only one partition, but can usually be divided into up to four partitions.

Michelangelo virus A virus that made headlines in all the major newspapers worldwide in 1992. The Michelangelo virus isn't as common as many other viruses.

MP3 Acronym that stands for MPEG-1 Layer 3 (Moving Pictures Expert Group), a file compression format for storing digital audio. *See* Napster and Gnutella.

Multipartite virus A type of virus that can infect both files or boot sectors.

Mutation engine A programming toolkit designed to help virus writers create polymorphic viruses, which can modify themselves to avoid detection by antivirus scanners. *See* Polymorphic virus.

Napster Program designed for "sharing" MP3-compressed audio files over the Internet. *See* Gnutella and MP3.

Newbie Slang term to describe a novice or beginner.

Nuker A malicious program designed to crash another computer.

Online harassment program A special program designed to harass a specific online service such as America Online. Typical features of an online harassment program include the ability to kick people off the online service, engage in email bombing, and phish for credit card numbers and passwords in a chat room. *See* AOHell.

Online service A privately run computer network that allows members to chat, swap files, and read text files.

The most popular online services are America Online and
CompuServe.

Overwriting infector A type of file-infecting virus that
erases part of a file while infecting it.

Packet sniffer A program that surreptitiously captures
information flowing through the Internet. Often used to
intercept credit card numbers and passwords.

Parasitic infector A type of file-infecting virus that
attaches itself to the front or back of a file.

Parental control software Programs that block access to
certain Internet resources (such as Web sites or FTP sites)
that may contain adult-oriented material. Can also filter
email, chat rooms, and control access to certain programs
stored on the computer. *See* Censorware.

Partition table The part of a hard disk's boot sector that
defines the size and partition of the hard disk, the operating system each partition uses, and the partition the
computer uses to boot from.

PGP (Pretty Good Privacy) One of the most popular and
effective encryption programs used on the Internet.

Phishing To trick or fool chat room attendees into revealing their passwords, credit card numbers, or other valuable
information. Often a special feature provided in an online
harassment program. *See* Online harassment program.

Phone call flooding Dialing a single phone number over and
over again. Often used to harass a specific company or
individual, such as a company or individual that sent
unwanted email. *See* Fax bombing.

Phreaking Manipulating the phone system.

Pirated software Illegally copied software. Check any computer in any organization, and you'll probably find at
least one pirated program somewhere.

Polymorphic virus A virus that modifies itself each time it spreads to avoid detection by antivirus scanners. *See* Mutation engine.

Ponzi scheme A con game where early investors only receive their money when others invest money into the scheme. Similar to Social Security. *See* Pyramid scheme.

Port An "opening" in your computer used to send and receive data. When a computer connects to the Internet, it opens several ports where each port performs a specific function such as sending and receiving Web pages or email.

Private-key encryption Method of encrypting and decrypting data that uses a single key. *See* Public-key encryption.

Program infector A virus that infects program files, such as word processors or spreadsheets.

Public-key encryption Method of encrypting and decrypting data that uses two separate keys: a private key (known only to you) and a public key that anyone can use. Data encrypted with one key can only be decrypted using the other. *See* Private-key encryption.

Pyramid scheme A con game where one person receives money from two or more other people in exchange for the promise that they can make money if they recruit others to give them money too.

RAT (Remote Access Trojan) A program that allows hackers to access your computer from a remote location. *See* Trojan Horse.

Rollback program Utility that restores a hard disk's contents back to a previous state. Often used to repair damage caused by erratic software installations but can also be used to repair damage caused by hackers, viruses, or Trojan Horses.

SATAN An acronym that stands for Security Administrator for Analyzing Networks. SATAN is a program designed to probe a Web site for security weaknesses.

Scanner   1. A program that contains a database of known virus or Trojan Horse characteristics. By comparing files to this database, a scanner can determine the type of virus or Trojan Horse that may be infecting your computer. 2. A type of program that searches the Internet or a network for computers.

Script kiddie   Derogatory term used to describe hackers who use programs written by other people without understanding the technical details.

Shareware   A method of software distribution that lets you freely copy and try the program without payment. If you use the program regularly, you must pay for it. *See* Freeware.

Signature   The unique structural characteristic of a virus or Trojan Horse, much like a fingerprint on a person. Every virus and Trojan Horse has a unique signature, which antivirus and anti-Trojan Horse scanners use to detect and identify it.

Slack space   The unused space in a cluster, which often contains keystrokes or other fragments of a file that can be recovered and used as evidence. *See* Clusters.

Slow infector   A virus that only infects files when they are created or modified to avoid detection by antivirus programs such as integrity checkers.

Source code   The commands that make up a program. If you have the source code of a virus, you can modify its behavior. Virus source code is usually written in assembly language or VBA, online harassment programs are usually written in Visual Basic, and Trojan Horses are usually written in C/C++ or Delphi.

Spam   Slang name for unwanted email.

Sparse infector   A virus that infects files only occasionally to avoid detection by antivirus programs.

'sploit   Slang term for "exploits." Often used by hackers to identify the latest vulnerabilities found in a particular program such as an operating system or firewall.

Spyware Programs that retrieve information off a hard disk and send that information to another computer. Often used by advertiser-sponsored shareware programs.

Stealth A virus that tries to avoid detection by antivirus programs.

Steganography The science of hiding information like text in another medium, such as a graphic file, sound file, or another text file. *See* Encryption.

Tiger team A group of hackers who get paid to test the security and vulnerability of computers.

Trigger The event that causes a virus to act. The trigger can set off the virus on a certain date (Friday the 13th or April 15) or when certain conditions have been met (such as when the hard disk is 80% full).

Trojan Horse A type of program that pretends to be a useful (usually well-known) program while it really does something else, such as erase files from your computer. Unlike computer viruses, Trojan Horses can't duplicate themselves.

TSR (Terminate and Stay Resident) A program that stays in memory after it has finished, so that it can be restarted quickly.

UNIX Operating system originally developed at Bell Laboratories in the early 1970s. UNIX is one of the most popular operating systems in the world, developed primarily for larger computers such as mainframe and minicomputers, although a free version of UNIX, called Linux, has been gaining popularity on personal computers. *See* Linux.

Vaccine A type of antivirus program that claims to protect files from virus infection.

Virus monitor A program that hides in your computer's memory and watches for signs of a virus infection.

Visual Basic A program sold by Microsoft that lets you visually design a program and then write BASIC commands to make the program work.

Visual Basic for Applications A special version of Visual Basic, often abbreviated as VBA, designed for creating programs within Microsoft applications such as Word, Excel, PowerPoint, and Access.

War dialer A program that can dial a range of phone numbers, searching for a modem on the other line. Can also be used to repetitively dial a single phone number, thereby harassing the recipient. Also called a *Demon dialer*.

Warez Slang term for pirated software, usually games. Also called *Appz*.

Warm boot To restart a computer without turning it off and on again. Most computers have a restart or reset button, or you can press CTRL-ALT-DEL.

Web spoofing To intercept a user's request to view one Web site and display a different Web site with the intent to deceive.

White hat hacker Term used to describe a hacker who uses his or her skill for constructive purposes such as hunting down pedophiles or guarding against malicious (black hat) hackers. *See* Black hat hacker.

Worm A type of program that copies itself from computer to computer. Unlike a virus, a worm doesn't infect a file or disk but simply reproduces itself.

Wrapper A program that can combine two separate programs into a single file, most often used to combine a Trojan Horse installation program with an installation program for a legitimate program. Also called a *binder* or *joiner*.

A **Hacker's** Gallery

**WITH SO MANY HACKER TOOLS AVAILABLE ON THE INTERNET, IT'S QUITE POSSI-
BLE THAT YOUR COMPUTER MAY BE ATTACKED ONE DAY.** Since most people
aren't likely to see, let alone use, these hacker tools,
this appendix contains screenshots from a selection of
recent and previously popular hacker tools. This will give
you a historical and present-day perspective of the tools
that hackers use when they attack someone (maybe even you)
over the Internet.

AOHell

Released around 1995, AOHell defined the standard for online
harassment programs and quickly spawned numerous copycats
for harassing other online services including CompuServe,
Prodigy, and the Microsoft Network (see Figure B-1). Written
in Visual Basic 3.0, AOHell was a relatively simple program
that helped hackers send spoofed email, create phony credit
card numbers for making fake AOL accounts, con AOL users out
of passwords and credit card numbers, and send insulting
messages to others in chat rooms.

Although AOHell initially caused problems for AOL, the
program is now obsolete. Few hackers are currently developing AOHell copycat programs, preferring to channel their
energy towards creating more sophisticated Internet hacking
tools such as port scanners or harassment tools that cause
chaos on IRC or in ICQ chat rooms.

B02K — Back Orifice

With a name deliberately chosen to mock Microsoft's Back
Office program, Back Orifice caused a sensation when
released in 1998 as one of the first remote access Trojan
Horse programs that could remotely control another computer
over a phone line or through the Internet (see Figure B-2).

Developed by a hacker group calling themselves the Cult
of the Dead Cow, Back Orifice made headlines again in 1999
when released at DefCon 7.0 with improvements, including
the option of adding plug-in programs written by others,
and the complete C/C++ source code so anyone could study
and modify the program. Ironically, when introduced at
DefCon, the Back Orifice 2000 CD was infected by the
Chernobyl (CIH) virus.

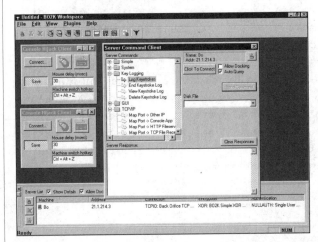

FIGURE B-2:

*Back Orifice 2000 is
the latest incarnation
of the popular and
groundbreaking remote
access Trojan Horse.*

Although Back Orifice still poses a threat to computers, the buzz surrounding BO2K has faded. Still, the program has spawned numerous and trickier copycats while the Cult of the Dead Cow has turned their programming skills towards less destructive projects such as Hacktivismo, which plans to develop software to circumvent censorship on the Internet.

Crack Whore

One of the new breed of Web site hacking programs, Crack Whore uses a brute force/dictionary attack against a Web site to find the password to a legitimate account (see Figure B-3). Since so many people use weak, easy-to-guess passwords, programs like Crack Whore are surprisingly successful far more often than they should be.

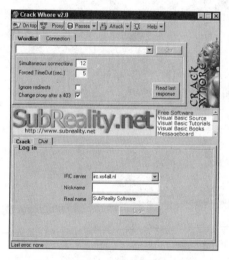

FIGURE B-3:

Crack Whore probes a Web site for easily guessed passwords to give a hacker access to a system.

Once hackers have access to a legitimate account, they can either modify Web pages and other data directly or attempt to burrow through the system and either gain access to additional accounts or elevate the current account to get greater access to the rest of the system.

Death 'n Destruction

One of the simplest denial-of-service (DoS) hacking tools, Death 'n Destruction sends endless streams of useless data to a victim's computer port (usually port 139), effectively overwhelming the target computer and causing it to crash or disconnect from the Internet (see Figure B-4).

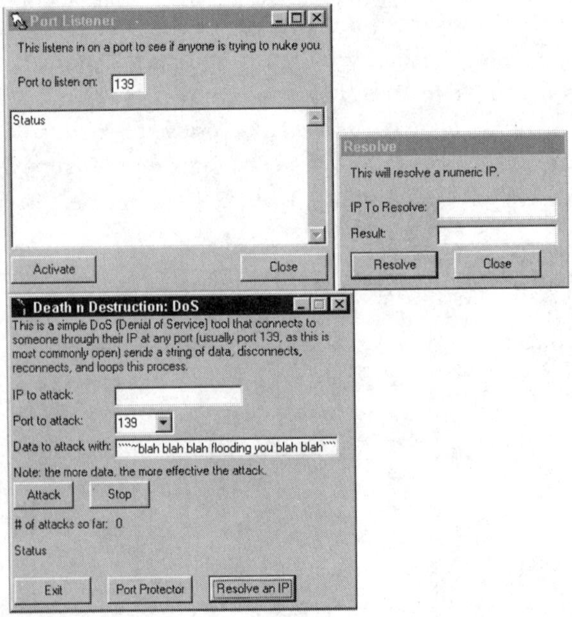

FIGURE B-4:

Death 'n Destruction can flood a computer with useless data as a primitive, but effective, form of a denial-of-service attack.

Donald Dick

A Russian remote access Trojan Horse similar to Back Orifice, Donald Dick offers a unique twist by including a server generating program that allows it to disguise its appearance on a target computer (see Figure B-5). Disguising the server program prevents (theoretically) antivirus and anti–Trojan Horse programs from recognizing the unique "signature" they need to identify and remove Donald Dick from a computer. Like Back Orifice, Donald Dick also comes with C/C++ source code so you can examine the program and make any modifications yourself.

Donald Dick is a remote
access Trojan Horse,
presented to the world
from Russia with love.

ICQ War 2000

With the popularity of instant messaging services (and the
dwindling popularity of online services), hackers quickly
turned their attention from writing online harassment programs such as AOHell clones and started writing ICQ
harassment tools instead (see Figure B-6).

FIGURE B-6:

ICQ War 2000 provides
multiple features for
harassing someone (and
protecting yourself)
while using ICQ.

ICQ War 2000 is one of many multipurpose ICQ harassment programs that can flood a victim with messages, track
down a person's IP address, and disrupt chat rooms with
insults and obscenity.

John the Ripper

One of the more popular password-cracking programs available, John the Ripper runs under UNIX and MS-DOS to crack
weak UNIX passwords and systems such as Linux, FreeBSD,
OpenBSD, Solaris, Digital UNIX, AIX, HP-UX, and IRIX.

```
John the Ripper Version 1.6 Copyright (c) 1996-98 by Solar Designer

Usage: //E/TEMP/JOHN-16/RUN/john [OPTIONS] [PASSWORD-FILES]

-single                  "single crack" mode

-wordfile:FILE -stdin    wordlist mode, read words from FILE or
                         stdin

-rules                   enable rules for wordlist mode

-incremental[:MODE]      incremental mode [using section MODE]

-external:MODE           external mode or word filter

-stdout[:LENGTH]         no cracking, just write words to stdout

-restore[:FILE]          restore an interrupted session [from
                         FILE]

-session:FILE            set session file name to FILE

-status[:FILE]           print status of a session [from FILE]

-makechars:FILE          make a charset, FILE will be overwritten

-show                    show cracked passwords

-test                    perform a benchmark

-users:[-]LOGIN|UID[,..] load this (these) user(s) only

-groups:[-]GID[,..]      load users of this (these) group(s) only

-shells:[-]SHELL[,..]    load users with this (these) shell(s)
                         only

-salts:[-]COUNT          load salts with at least COUNT passwords
                         only

-format:NAME             force ciphertext format NAME (DES/BSDI/
                         MD5/BF/AFS/LM)

-savemem:LEVEL           enable memory saving, at LEVEL 1..3
```

FIGURE B-7:

John the Ripper is a command-line program that can find weak passwords on UNIX-based systems.

John the Ripper can automatically detect DES, MD5, and Blowfish encrypted UNIX passwords and use a brute force attack to uncover easy-to-guess passwords (see Figure B-7). Once hackers have a password, they can log in to a valid account and establish a foothold on a computer.

NetBus

Originally developed as a remote access Trojan similar to Back Orifice, NetBus version 2.0 and later is now being marketed as a legitimate remote access administrative tool (see Figure B-8). Despite this change of focus by the NetBus programmers, hackers continue to use earlier versions of NetBus to secretly access other computers. In addition, many hacker Web sites provide the original Delphi source code so anyone can make modifications to create a new version of NetBus or write an entirely different remote access Trojan Horse.

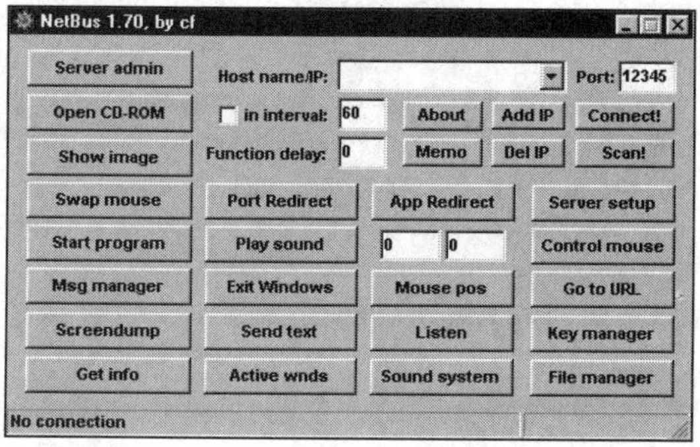

FIGURE B-8:

NetBus originally started as a remote access Trojan Horse.

Nmap

Considered one of the best scanning tools for probing a system, Nmap incorporates almost every scanning technique known into one single program (see Figure B-9). Depending on the scanning option you use, Nmap can offer you speed or stealth (to prevent a target computer from knowing it's being probed) using a variety of different protocols (ICMP, UDP, TCP, etc.). You can safely assume that given enough time, Nmap can find an opening in practically any computer.

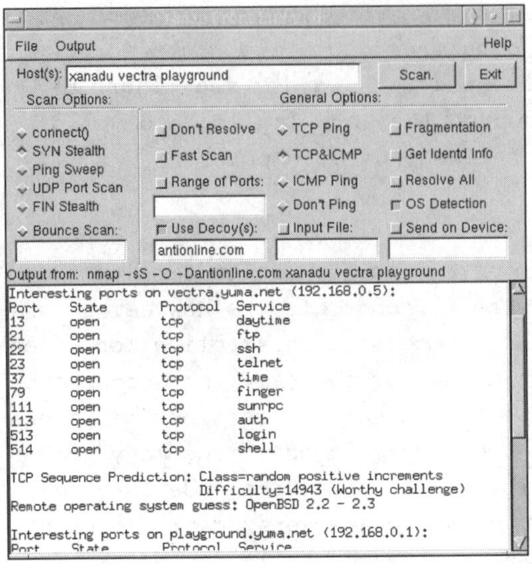

FIGURE B-9:

Nmap provides a variety
of scanning techniques
to help you probe the
vulnerabilities of a
computer.

Nmap runs on UNIX-based operating systems such as Linux and FreeBSD, and comes with full C/C++ source code that you can study and modify. With an active programming community behind it, Nmap is likely to continue for some time as the most powerful scanning tool available to both system administrators and hackers.

Senna Spy Internet Worm Generator 2000

In much the same way as hackers tried to create special programs for mass-producing viruses and Trojan Horses, hackers have now created the Senna Spy Internet Worm Generator 2000 for mass-producing worms that use the VBScript language (see Figure B-10).

While the program can create worms quickly and easily, the worms it creates are not necessarily malicious; they simply provide a skeleton program that can retrieve addresses stored in Microsoft Outlook to email themselves to other people. If you want to customize the worm to add a malicious payload of some sort, you'll still need to understand the VBScript language. Still, this program is likely to help an aspiring worm programmer understand the basics of retrieving Outlook addresses and getting the worm to email itself to others.

Senna Spy Internet Worm Generator 2000 Version 1.00

Senna Spy Internet Worm Generator 2000 Version 1.00

The first Internet-Worm Generator in the World!

Brazilian Hacker Group

http://sennaspy.cjb.net   ICQ UIN: 3973927

Worm Name: Type the Worm's name here

Subject: Type the message's subject here...

E-Mail Message: Type the message's body here...

☑ Crypt Code ?   ☐ Network Compatible ?

Choose:
◉ English   ○ Português

Make   Exit

FIGURE B-10:

Senna Spy Internet Worm Generator 2000 simplifies the creation of VBScript worms.

SubSeven

While development of Back Orifice has slowed to a crawl, a new Trojan Horse named SubSeven has taken its place as the most popular Trojan Horse to use (see Figure B-11). SubSeven's programmers continue to add new features to the program, such as a text-to-speech module, a spy program for retrieving passwords and other data used by instant messaging programs, and the ability to retrieve a variety of information from an infected computer such as the user's name, address, and even Windows CD key number.

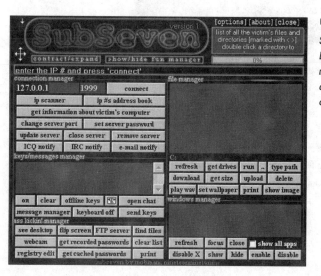

FIGURE B-11:

SubSeven has surpassed Back Orifice as the most popular remote access Trojan Horse currently in use.

To help stay in touch with other users, SubSeven's programmers even offer a mailing list and IRC chat room. With the popularity of SubSeven, more computers could eventually be infected by SubSeven than other remote access Trojan Horses.

TakeAdvantage

As its name implies, the TakeAdvantage program is designed to take advantage of the AllAdvantage Internet service that uses advertising revenue to pay people to go online (see Figure B-12). The only catch with AllAdvantage is that you have to view advertising and the service automatically cuts you off after a certain amount of inactivity.

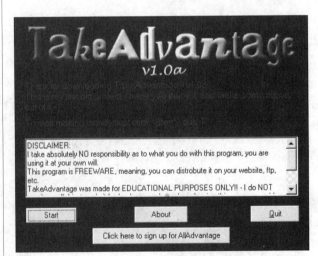

FIGURE B-12:

TakeAdvantage targets Internet services that pay people to stay online as long as possible to view advertisements.

To stop this cut-off, the TakeAdvantage program simply moves the mouse randomly around the screen, giving the illusion that someone's actually using the computer. By running the TakeAdvantage program all night, hackers have been able to scam thousands of dollars from AllAdvantage and get paid to surf the Internet while they sleep.

ToneLoc

An old MS-DOS—based wardialer that's still used by hackers today, ToneLoc provides a variety of options for hunting out a modem (see Figure B-13). Despite the growing use of the Internet, many corporations and organizations still provide phone modems for connecting to their network, particularly for sales people who need to use remote access programs like PCAnywhere or Carbon Copy to access a computer through the phone lines.

```
ToneLoc 1.10 by Minor Threat & Mucho Maas (Sep 29 1994)

ToneLoc is a dual purpose wardialer. It dials phone numbers using a mask
that you give it. It can look for either dialtones or modem carriers.
It is useful for finding PBX's, Loops, LD carriers, and other modems.
It works well with the USRobotics series of modems, and most Hayes-
compatible modems.


USAGE:

ToneLoc [DataFile] /M:[Mask] /R:[Range] /X:[ExMask] /D:[ExRange]
/C:[Config]

/#:[Number] /S:[StartTime] /E:[EndTime] /H:[Hours] /T /K

[DataFile] - File to store data in, may also be a mask      Required

[Mask]       - To use for phone numbers    Format: 555-XXXX  Optional

[Range]      - Range of numbers to dial    Format: 5000-6999 Optional

[ExMask]     - Mask to exclude from scan   Format: 1XXX      Optional

[ExRange]    - Range to exclude from scan  Format: 2500-2699 Optional

[Config]     - Configuration file to use                    Optional

[Number]     - Number of dials to make     Format: 250      Optional

[Number]     - Number of dials to make     Format: 250      Optional
```

FIGURE B-13:

ToneLoc is a DOS-based wardialer that can search a range of phone numbers to determine which ones are connected to a modem.

```
[StartTime] - Time to begin scanning      Format: 9:30p      Optional

[EndTime]   - Time to end scanning        Format: 6:45a      Optional

[Hours]     - Max # of hours to scan      Format: 5:30       Optional

              Overrides [EndTime]

/T = Tones, /K = Carriers (Override config file, '-' inverts) Optional
```

FIGURE B-13 (continued)

Once a hacker has found a connected modem to attack, the last line of defense is usually a password, which can often be guessed. As a result, many hackers use wardialers to connect to a network and bypass any firewalls that may be in the way.

UpYours

For a brief period, email bombs surged in popularity. The idea was to flood a single email account with multiple messages or to subscribe a victim to multiple mailing lists, usually to topics that included child pornography, sexual bondage, or necrophilia.

In 1996, a hacker named "johnny xchaotic" made the headline news when on two separate occasions he email bombed various organizations and prominent people including Bill Gates, the Ku Klux Klan, Pat Buchanan, Bill Clinton, the Church of Scientology, and Newt Gingrich.

Email bombing quickly faded as ISPs shut down their mail forwarding services and removed Web sites that offered email bombing programs. While still an effective tool, email bombing programs like UpYours can reveal an attacker's IP address, further reducing the appeal of attempting a large-scale email bombing attack (see Figure B-14).

VBS Worm Generator

This is a sophisticated worm generator that offers pull-down menus for mass-producing custom worms that can start infecting the Internet as soon as you release them into

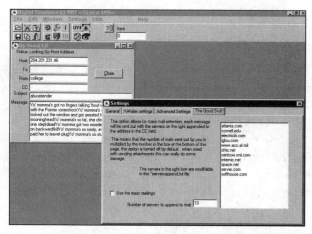

FIGURE B-14:

UpYours provides a variety of options for email bombing a victim.

the wild (see Figure B-15). Some of its replication methods include sending itself to email addresses stored in Microsoft Outlook and through IRC by infecting the mIRC or Pirch IRC programs.

To avoid detection, the VBS Worm Generator tries to encrypt its VBScript code. For payloads, the program allows a hacker to display a message and picture, crash the computer, or gain access to a Web site. Since the VBS Worm Generator provides the complete VBScript source code to a worm, hackers

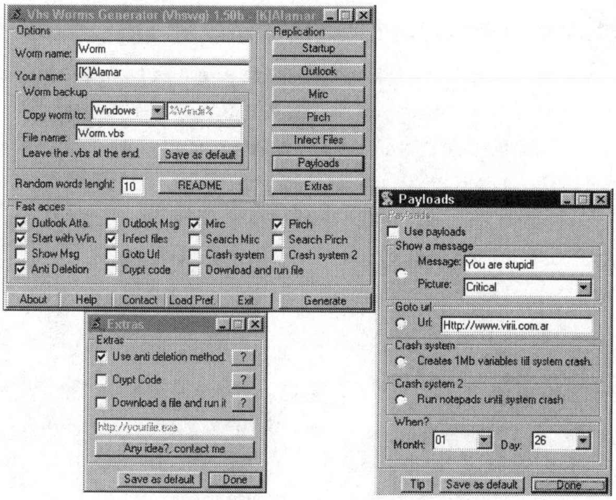

FIGURE B-15:

The VBS Worm Generator can mass-produce custom worms for spreading to your enemies.

can just modify the code and create custom worms nearly as fast as the VBS Worm Generator can produce them.

Virus Creation Laboratory (VCL)

Released in 1992, the Virus Creation Laboratory (VCL) was written by a hacker dubbed the Nowhere Man (see Figure B-16). VCL provides pull-down menus so users with little or no knowledge of programming can customize a virus. In theory, VCL sounds formidable, but in reality, bugs and its limited features kept VCL from creating any new viruses that could seriously threaten anyone.

```
 UNTITLED.UCL          [- Virus Creation Lab]
 ≡ File  Options  Effects  Make  Configuration                    Help
        ┌──────────────────┐
        │ Appending        │
        │ Infect EXE ( )   │
        │ Infect COM (·)   │
        │ Go TSR     ( )   │
        │ Stop trace ( )   │
        │ Encryption (·)   │
        │ Virex-Prot ( )   │
        │ Search type...   │
        │ Virulence...     │
        │ Note...          │
        └──────────────────┘

 [ F1 Help  F2 Save  F3 Open  F4 Boss  F8 Create .ASM  F9 Create .COM ]
```

FIGURE B-16:

The Virus Creation Laboratory offered a graphical user interface for mass-producing computer viruses.

Most of the viruses VCL creates either don't work or don't spread. On top of that, VCL viruses are easily identi-fied by nearly all antivirus programs. Although the threat that hackers could mass-produce viruses using VCL initially panicked the antivirus community, the limited capabilities of VCL have guaranteed the program a place as an interesting but unsuccessful footnote in computer virus history.

What's on the CD

NOTE Neither No Starch Press nor the author of this book offer any warranty or technical support for these programs. Use them entirely at your own risk, according to the license terms for each program, and according to the CD License Agreement printed on the last page of this book. Should you need help with any of these programs please contact the software publisher directly.

> See the README.PDF file on the CD (readable on all platforms) for hyperlinks to all the Web sites listed in this appendix. Clicking on the Web addresses will launch your browser and take you directly to the software pubishers' Web sites, where you can find installation information, troubleshooting help, and any updates to the programs.

To help protect your computer against the many hostile threats on the Internet, the CD bundled with this book includes a range of freeware, shareware, free trials, and demos of defensive programs. Just browse through this list, find the program you think you need, and run it on your computer. (Don't worry, we've checked and double-checked all of these programs for viruses. They're guaranteed to be free of viruses.)

PROGRAM TYPES

This CD-ROM includes three types of programs: Freeware, Shareware, and Demoware/Trialware.

→ *Freeware* programs are free for you to use, copy, and distribute without license restrictions.

(In some cases, they even include source code that you can study and modify.)

→ *Shareware* programs are "try before you buy." You get the full program but if you continue to use it you must pay for it.

→ *Demoware* and *Trialware* are time limited or "crippled" versions of a piece of software. If you like the program you must buy the full version to continue to use it.

To save money, try the many freeware programs on this CD first. Many freeware programs offer equal (or better) protection than shareware or commercial software. For example, Aladdin Knowledge Systems and Computer Associates are lesser-known names in the antivirus world, yet their products, eSafe and InoculateIT, are just as effective as McAfee or Norton. Both companies have released these programs as freeware to penetrate the market, in hopes that satisfied users will buy site licenses for their program to protect their corporation's computers. Similarly, while BlackICE is a well-regarded (and excellent) firewall program, ZoneAlarm offers similar protection for free.

INSTALLATION SUPPORT

Since installing many of these programs may be tricky, we've made no attempt here to tell you how to install or troubleshoot them. **Before you install a program, you should visit the program's Web site (listed with each program) and follow the software publisher's installation instructions.**

UNCOMPRESSING, UNZIPPING, UNSTUFFING, AND SO ON

Many of the programs on the CD are compressed; you'll recognize the compressed files by their extensions.

→ **.zip** files are Windows files which may be "unzipped" with Stuffit Expander or WinZip.

→ **.exe** files are program files; double-click them from within Windows to extract them and run the application.

→ **.sit** and **.sea** files are Macintosh stuffit files which may be "unstuffed" with Stuffit Expander.

→ **.gz** and **.tar** are gzipped or tarred Linux files which may be uncompressed with LinZip or tar.

You must expand or uncompress these programs before you can run them. In the "Utilities" folder, you'll find the free Stuffit Expander from Aladdin Systems for both Macintosh and Windows, tar for Linux, and some useful shareware for this purpose.

UTILITIES

Programs to help you read Acrobat PDF files or expand compressed files.

Windows

→ Adobe Acrobat Reader (**ar405eng.exe**). Open, print, and display Acrobat PDF files. Freeware. (*http://www.adobe.com*)

→ Aladdin Expander (**alex50.exe**). Decompress, decode, convert and access the most popular compression archive formats, including StuffIt (.sit), Zip (.zip), UUencode (.uu), MacBinary (.bin), BinHex (.hqx), and more. Freeware. (*http://www.aladdinsys.com*)

→ Visual Basic 6 Runtime files (**vbrun60.exe**). Includes the necessary DLLs and support files to run programs written in Microsoft Visual Basic 6.0. Freeware. (*http://www. microsoft.com*)

→ WinZip (**winzip80.exe**). A straightforward zipping and unzipping utility. Shareware. (*http://www.winzip.com*)

Macintosh

→ Adobe Acrobat Reader (**Reader Installer**). Open, print, and display Acrobat PDF files. Freeware. (*http://www.adobe.com*)

→ Aladdin Expander (**Aladdin Expander 5.5 Installer**). Decompress, decode, convert and access the most popular compression archive formats, including StuffIt (.sit), Zip (.zip), UUencode (.uu), MacBinary (.bin), BinHex (.hqx), and more. Freeware. (*http://www.aladdinsys.com*)

→ Aladdin DropStuff (**dropstuff55.sit**). Compress, encrypt, and make self-extracting archives. Shareware. (*http://www. aladdinsys.com*)

Linux

→ Adobe Acrobat Reader (**linux-ar-40.tar.gz**). Open, print, and display Acrobat PDF files. Freeware. (*http://www.adobe.com*)

- → LinZip (**linzipv1_1.tgz**). A full-featured compression utility. Shareware. (*http://www.linzip.com*)
- → tar (**tar-1.13.10.tar.gz**). Compress and manipulate tar archives. Freeware.

ANONYMITY

Hide your identity with these programs.

Windows

- → No Referrer (**NoReferrer.zip**). Helps you surf anonymously by stripping out identifying information normally sent out by your computer. Unzip **NoReferrer.zip** and run **setup.exe**. Freeware. (*No installation support.*)
- → Privacy Companion (**privacy_companion.exe**). Protects your privacy by alerting you when a Web site is trying to give your computer a cookie, which could be used to gather information about your computer. Works with Internet Explorer only. Freeware. (*http://www.idcide.com/*)
- → Private Idaho (**pi28b3.exe**, **pisource.zip**, and **pi32g.exe**). Email utility program to help you encrypt your email using PGP and anonymous remailers. The pi28b3.zip file contains the original 16-bit version of Private Idaho. The pisource.zip file contains Visual Basic 3.0 source code. The pi32g.exe file contains a 32-bit version of Private Idaho with additional features and support for the latest anonymous remailers. Freeware. (*http://www.eskimo.com/~joelm/pi.html*)

Macintosh

- → Cone of Silence (**Cone of Silence 1.0b2 f.sit**). Prevents keystroke capturing programs from recording anything you type. Shareware. (*http://www.parkbenchsoftware.com/*)
- → Free Guard (**Free_Guard.sea**). Hides files and folders. Freeware. (*http://www.msrwerks.com/applications.html*)
- → VSE My Privacy (**VSE My Privacy 1.2.1.sit**). Encrypts private information, such as credit card numbers, passwords, confidential names and addresses, and so on, to keep it safe from prying eyes. Shareware. (*http://www.vse-online.com*)

ANTI-CON GAMES

Protects you from falling for Internet con games.

→ MegaHack (**megahack.zip**). Cracks the Mega$Nets online pyramid scheme. Includes Visual Basic 3.0 source code. Freeware. (*No installation support.*)

ANTI—SPYWARE

These programs block or disable advertiser-sponsored programs that could secretly transmit information about your computer over the Internet.

Windows

→ Ad-Aware (**aaw_35.zip** and **alist86.zip**). Helps detect and block advertiser-sponsored software (spyware) from retrieving information from your hard disk. The file alist86.zip lists advertiser-sponsored shareware programs that you may want to avoid. Freeware. (*http://www.lavasoft.de*)

→ Aureate/Radiate Remover (**remove.exe**). Removes the Radiate/Aureate spyware DLL files from your computer to prevent them from retrieving information from your hard disk. Advertiser-supported freeware. (*http://www.radiate.com/privacy/remover.html*)

→ Flow Protector (**setup_flowprotector_us.exe**). Blocks cookies, spyware, and Internet connections that could send data from your computer without your knowledge. Freeware. (*http://www.flowprotector.com/usa*)

→ OptOut (**optout.exe**). Removes the Aureate/Radiate DLL files that turn shareware into spyware. Freeware. (*http://grc.com/optout.htm*)

→ Silencer (**silencer.zip**). Blocks communication between spyware and the server that the spyware is trying to send your data to. Freeware. (*http://radsoft.net/bloatbusters/*)

ANTI—TROJAN HORSE

These programs can help you detect, block, and remove remote access Trojan Horse programs.

Windows

→ BODetect (**BoDetect_StandAlone.zip**). A comprehensive Trojan Horse detection and removal program. Shareware. (*http://www.cbsoftsolutions.com/*)

→ The Cleaner (**cleaner3.exe**). Scans your system for Trojans. Shareware. (*http://www.moosoft.com*)

→ Jammer (**jammer.exe**). Protects you against NetBus, Back Orifice 1.x and BO2K. (*http://www.agnitum.com*)

→ NetBus Remover (**nobus.exe**). Finds and removes the NetBus Trojan that affects Windows 95/98/NT. Freeware. (*No installation support.*)

→ NetBuster (**netbuster1_31.zip**). Detects and removes the NetBus Trojan Horse. Will also create a fake NetBus connection to help you fool any hackers trying to access your computer using NetBus. Freeware. (*http://surf.to/netbuster*)

→ Startup Monitor (**StartupMonitor.zip**). Monitors all programs that automatically start up when you boot up Windows. Use this to detect Trojan Horse programs that may be secretly starting when you boot up. Freeware. (*http://www.mlin. net/StartupMonitor.shtml*)

→ Sub-Net 2.0 (**subnet2.zip**). Trojan Horse port scanner useful for analyzing and securing your Internet connection. Freeware. (*http://www.sub-seven.com*)

→ SubSeven Server Sniper (**s7sniper.zip**). Detects and removes the SubSeven Trojan Horse; can also trace an attacker over the Internet. Freeware. (*http://subseven.slak.org*)

→ Tauscan (**tauscan.exe** and **ttutor.zip**). Detects and removes remote access Trojans installed on your hard disk. The ttutor.zip file contains a tutorial for using Tauscan. Trialware. (*http://www.agnitum.com/products/tauscan*)

→ TDS-2: Trojan Defence Suite (**tds2.zip** and **tds2help.zip**). Detects and removes hundreds of Trojan Horses from your computer. The tds2help.zip file contains the help file for the program. Trialware. (*http://www.diamondcs.com.au*)

→ Trojans Database (**tlibrary.zip**). Describes the most popular Trojan Horses including their features and the ports they use to attack a computer. Freeware. (*No installation support.*)

→ Trojans First Aid Kit (**tfak40.zip**). Detects and removes hundreds of Trojan Horses. Freeware. (*http://www.coderz. net/Snakebyte*)

→ Win Trinoo Server Sniper (**trinooss.zip**). Detects and removes the Trinoo Trojan, which can use your computer to launch a distributed denial-of-service attack against another computer. Freeware. (*http://www.diamondcs.com.au*)

ANTIVIRUS

These programs can detect, remove, and block viruses from infecting your computer.

Windows

→ eSafe Protect Desktop (**esd22.exe**) and eSafe Protect Desktop user's manual (**espd.pdf**). Multipurpose program that provides content filtering (so you can selectively block certain Web sites from users), an antivirus program, a desktop lockdown program (to prevent unauthorized access to your computer), and an anti-vandalism program to keep malicious worms and viruses from attacking your hard disk. Trialware. (*http://www.ealaddin.com*)

→ F-Prot (**fp-307b.zip**). DOS-based antivirus program. Freeware. (*http://www.f-secure.com/*)

→ InoculateIT (**IPESetup.exe**). Free antivirus program (for personal use only) from Computer Associates. Freeware. (*http://antivirus.cai.com*)

→ Mail Cleaner (**MCSetup.exe**). Scans your Outlook or Outlook Express email for viruses hidden as file attachments. If it finds one, the program deletes the suspect email and notifies you of its action. Freeware. (*http://www.mailcleaner.com*)

→ Norton Antivirus 2000 (**ZLContainer.exe**). Well-known leading antivirus program. Running this file will take you online to download the actual program which is quite large. Trialware. (*http://shop.symantec.com*)

→ ScripTrap (**strap.exe**). Blocks the running of malicious scripts, such as viruses written with VBScript. Freeware. (*http://members.home.net/rkeir/index.html*)

→ Script Defender (**sdefendi.exe**). Protects against all forms of malicious code (such as macro viruses) that run scripting languages such as VBScript or JavaScript. Freeware. (*http://www.analogx.com*)

→ SurfinGuard (**SurfinGuard_Setup.exe**). Monitors programs for suspicious behavior; if malicious behavior is detected, SurfinGuard kills the suspect program. Freeware. (*http://www.finjan.com*)

→ Virus Trap (**vtrap.exe**). Helps detect and capture viruses by offering "bait" files for viruses to infect. Once a "bait" file has been infected, the program alerts you so you can send the trapped virus to an antivirus company for further analysis. Freeware. (*http://www.diamondcs.com.au/vtrap.htm*)

Macintosh

→ Agax (**Agax v1.3**). An expandable, free antivirus program that offers both standard virus-scanning and more advanced background protection. Freeware. (*http://www.cse.unsw.edu.au/~s2191331/agax/agax.html*)

→ Disinfectant (**Disinfectant 3.7.1**). Adds basic virus protection by scanning files when opened and monitoring your system for unusual activity. Freeware. (*http://macinfo.its.queensu.ca/MacSDistribution/Disinfectant.html*)

→ McAfee VirusScan (**Virex 6.1 Demo.sit**). One of the most popular antivirus programs in the world. Shareware. (*http://www.mcafee.com*)

BULK EMAILERS

This program is typical of the type of programs that spammers use to flood email accounts with their advertisements.

Windows

→ Express Mail Server (**emsdemo.exe**). A bulk emailing program. We don't like these any more than you do but here's an example of one. Demoware. (*http://www.homeuniverse.com*)

CACHE AND COOKIE CLEANERS

Clean your browser's cache and wipe out any cookies with these programs.

Windows

→ AdSubtract SE (**ad-setup.exe**). Selectively blocks unwanted ads or cookies. Free for personal use. (*http://www.adsubtract.com*)

→ Complete Cleanup (**cleanup.exe**). Deletes temporary files, cookies, and Web cache files to guard your privacy. Trialware. (*http://www.softdd.com*)

→ Cookie Crusher (**ccrusher.exe**). Automatically accepts or rejects cookies for you. Trialware. (*http://www.thelimitsoft.com*)

→ Cookie Pal (**cp1setup.exe**). Manages your cookies. Shareware. (*http://www.kburra.com*)

→ CyberClean (**cybrinst.exe**). Removes cookies, history files, bookmarks and cache files, and registry entries that refer to recently visited Web sites. Trialware. (*http://www. thelimitsoft.com*)

→ Surf Secret (**trial.exe**). Removes cookies and Internet surfing debris. Trialware. (*http://www.surfsecret.com*)

→ Window Washer (**wwinstall.exe**). Cleans up any files created by your browser, such as cookies or lists of recently visited Web sites, to prevent others from tracking your Internet usage. Trialware. (*http://www.webroot.com*)

Macintosh

→ AOL3CacheCleaner [**AOL3CC(PPC)** and **AOL3CC(68K)**]. Cleans the cache in AOL 3.0. Shareware. (*http://www.whitecrest.com*)

→ MacWasher (**mw20demo.sit**). Cleans up cookies or lists of recently visited Web sites to prevent others from tracking your Internet usage. Trialware. (*http://www.webroot.com*)

→ MagicCookie Monster (**MagicCookieMonster.img**). A free (Emailware) utility to help you manage your Netscape Navigator or Communicator cookies. Freeware. (*http:// download.at/drjsoftware*)

→ WCCacheCleaner [**WCCC1.8.2(68K).sit** and **WCCC1.8.2(PPC).sit**]. Cleans your Netscape Navigator or Communicator cache. Trialware. (*http://www.whitecrest.com*)

DESKTOP SECURITY

Generate secure passwords and protect your computer while you're away with these programs.

Windows

→ Benjamin Password Generator (**PasGen11.zip**). Generates random passwords. Freeware. (*http://benjaminsoftware. hypermart.net/*)

→ Fake DOS (**fakedos.zip**). Protects your computer by displaying a fake DOS prompt to keep unauthorized users out. Freeware. (*http://www.nerc.com/~aharvey/fakedos.html*)

→ ISS Complock II (**isscmp20.zip**). Password-protects your computer to prevent someone from booting it up without your knowledge. Shareware. (*http://www.techniclabs.com/software.htm*)

→ Magic Folders (**mfd.exe**). Hides files and folders from view to keep a thief from finding them. Shareware. (*http://www.pc-magic.com/*)

→ Quicky Password Generator (**qpassgen.exe**). Helps you create a unique and difficult-to-guess password (which may also be difficult to remember). Freeware. (*http://www.quickysoftware.com*)

→ Password Checker (**password.zip**). Lets you type in a password and then evaluates how secure that password would be against a hacker trying to guess it. Freeware. (*http://www.tidave99.cjb.net*)

→ PGP Desktop Security (**PGP_Desktop_Security_6[1].5.3_Eval.zip**). Protects your data across your network and the Internet by encrypting information in email, hard drives and more. Trialware. (*http://www.mcafee.com*)

→ Security Officer 2000 (**SecurityOfficerPro.zip**). In addition to monitoring the programs run on your computer, this program can also protect your files from being modified or deleted. Shareware. (*http://www.compelson.com*)

→ System Lock (**systemlock.zip**). Protects your computer so nobody can use it without the correct password. Freeware. (*http://zucchinisoft.cjb.net*)

→ WinGuardian (**wg20.exe**). Logs all programs run along with keystrokes typed in each program. Trialware. (*http://www.webroot.com*)

DISASSEMBLERS

These programs can tear a program apart and reveal its assembly language source code so you can see how the program works.

Windows

→ IDA Pro Disassembler (**demo410.zip**). Shows you the assembly language source code of an executable file. Demoware. (*http://www.datarescue.com*)

→ Letun Disassembler (**LetunD101.zip**). Disassembles Windows executable files. Shareware. (*http://users.gazinter.net/letun*)

DNS LOOKUP

Verify a domain's existence with these tools.

→ Cyberkit (**cyber25.zip**). Ping, TraceRoute, WhoIs, Finger, and more in one easy-to-use utility. Postcardware. (*http://www.cyberkit.net*)

→ DNS Workshop (**dns_ws.exe**). Converts between IP addresses and Internet host names. Trialware. (*http://www.evolve.co.uk/dns*)

→ Domain Searcher (**dsearch.exe**). Searches for and investigates domain names. Trialware. (*http://www.igsnet.com/igs/dsearch.html*)

ENCRYPTION CRACKER

Crack files encrypted with DES.

→ BrydDES (**bryddes.zip**). Brute force cracker for the DES encryption algorithm. Freeware. (*No installation support.*)

FILE ENCRYPTION

These programs will scramble your data using a variety of algorithms, to keep your files safe.

Windows

→ Absolute Security (**absecurity.zip**). Protects the confidentiality of sensitive information. Shareware. (*http://www.pepsoft.com*)

→ Blowfish-C (**bfsh-koc.zip**). C source code implementation of the Blowfish encryption algorithm. Freeware. (*http://www.counterpane.com*)

→ Blowfish-Java (**blowfish-java.zip**). Java source code implementation of the Blowfish encryption algorithm. Freeware. (*http://www.counterpane.com*)

→ CuteZip (**cutezip10.exe**). Compression utility that includes 128-bit encryption using the Twofish algorithm. Trialware. (*http://www.cuteftp.com/products/cutezip/*)

→ Encrypted Magic Folders (**emf.exe**). Hides files and folders and protects them with encryption. Shareware. (*http://pc-magic.com/*)

→ GNU Privacy Guard (**gnupg-w32-1.0.2.zip**). A complete and free replacement for PGP. Freeware. (*http://www.gnupg.org*)

→ Kryptel Lite (**krlite.exe**). A free version of Kryptel, a file encryption program. Freeware. (*http://inv.co.nz*)

→ PC-Encrypt (**PC-Encrypt.exe**). Encrypts and compresses any type of file used in Windows 95/98 and NT. Shareware. (*http://www.pc-encrypt.com*)

→ PGP (**PGPfreeware651int.exe** or **PGPFW658Win32.zip**; **pgp651i-win-src.zip** contains the source code; **PGPWinUsersGuide.pdf** contains the user guide). The popular PGP encryption program for protecting your files. Freeware. (*http://www.pgpi.org*)

→ PGP Personal Privacy (**PGP_Personal_Privacy_6[1].5.3_Eval.zip**). Protects your email, files, folders, disk volumes, and network communication from prying eyes with one integrated product. Trialware. (*http://www.mcafee.com*)

→ ScramDisk (**SD301r3c.zip** and **sdfullsource202h.zip**). Encrypts your hard disk with various encryption algorithms including IDEA, Blowfish, DES, and Square. (sdfullsource202h.zip includes Visual C++ source code.) Freeware. (*http://www.scramdisk.clara.net/*)

→ Twofish-C (**twofish-optimized-c.zip**). C source code implementation of the Twofish encryption algorithm. Freeware. (*http://www.counterpane.com/twofish.html*)

→ Twofish-Java (**twofish-java.zip**). Java source code implementation of the Twofish encryption algorithm. Freeware. (*http://www.counterpane.com*)

→ Twofish-VB (**twofish-vb.zip**). Visual Basic source code implementation of the Twofish encryption algorithm. Freeware. (*http://www.counterpane.com/twofish.html*)

Macintosh

→ PGP (**PGP651IntFreeware**; **pgp651i-mac-src.zip** contains the source code; **PGPWinUsersGuide.pdf** contains the user guide). The popular PGP encryption program for protecting your files. Freeware. (*http://www.pgpi.org*)

→ Tresor (**Tresor GPPC E.sit**, **Tresor G3 E.sit**, and **Tresor G4 E.sit**). File encryption program for protecting individual files and entire folders using IDEA. Shareware. (*http://warlord.li/*)

→ VSE My Privacy (**VSE My Privacy 1.2.1.sit**). Encrypts private information, such as credit card numbers, passwords, confidential names and addresses, and so on, to keep it safe from prying eyes. Shareware. (*http://www.vse-online.com*)

Linux

→ GNU Privacy Guard (**gnupg-1.0.2.tar.gz**). A complete and free replacement for PGP. Freeware. (*http://www.gnupg.org*)

→ PGP (**PGPcmdln_6.5.8.Lnx_FW.tar.gz; PGPWinUsersGuide.pdf** contains the user guide). The popular PGP encryption program for protecting your files. Freeware. (*http://www.pgpi.org*)

FILE INTEGRITY CHECKERS

These programs can help you detect changes in your files that could indicate a hacker has gotten into your computer.

Windows

→ Veracity (**veracity_v201_win32.zip**). A network intrusion detection tool that uses cryptography to detect unauthorized changes to files. Trialware. (*http://www.veracity.com*)

Macintosh

→ Veracity (**veracity**). A network intrusion detection tool that uses cryptographics to detect unauthorized changes to files. Trialware. (*http://www.veracity.com*)

Linux

→ Tripwire (**Tripwire_221_for_Linux_x86[1].tar.gz**). Monitors and protects your data against changes. Freeware. (*http://www.tripwire.com*)

→ Veracity (**veracity_v300_linux386.tar.gz**). A network intrusion detection tool that uses cryptographics to detect unauthorized changes to files. Trialware. (*http://www.veracity.com*)

FILE SHREDDERS

These programs can securely delete files to prevent all but the best-funded authorities from recovering your data.

→ DoD 5220.22-M (**DoD 5220.22-M.pdf**). The DoD 5220.22-M National Industrial Security Program operating manual that includes government standards for shredding and destroying files.

Windows

→ ASL File Wiper (**aslfw.zip**). Securely deletes your files by overwriting them several times. Freeware. (*http:// alstonlabs.pair.com/aslfw.htm*)

→ Assure (**AssureSetup.exe**). Permanently deletes files from your computer. Shareware. (*http://www.alienseed.com*)

→ BCWipe (**bcwipe.exe** and **bcwipehelp.zip**). Shreds your files and disks to eliminate traces of your data. The file bcwipehelp.zip contains the help file for using the BCWipe program. Free for non-commercial use. (*http://www.jetico. com*)

→ CyberScrub (**CyScrb_E.exe**). Securely shreds and deletes confidential files beyond recovery. Shareware. (*http://www. cyberscrub.com*)

→ Eraser (**eraser41.zip** and **eraser41s.zip**). File shredder with Visual C++ source code in the eraser41s.zip file. Freeware. (*http://www.tolvanen.com*)

→ Evidence Eliminator (**insteelm.zip**). Securely shreds files and disks. Defeats forensic analysis software. Trialware. (*http://www.evidence-eliminator.com*)

→ Shredder 95 (**setup.exe**). Completely destroys files and even free space beyond any hope of recovery. Shareware. (*http:// www.gale-force.com/shredder*)

→ Shred-It (**ShredItPC.exe**). Shreds your files and folders beyond recovery. (*http://www.arccom.bc.ca*)

→ Shred-X (**shredx10.zip**). Removes all traces of your files. Shareware. (*http://www.bsoft.ic24.net*)

Macintosh

→ Burn (**Burn 2.5**). File shredder to keep your deleted files from being recovered. Freeware. (*http://www.thenextwave. com/burnHP.html*)

→ NetShred (**NetShred.PPC.sit**, **NetShred.68K.sit**, and **NetShred. FAT.sit**). Shreds your Web cache and other related files to prevent someone from tracking your Internet usage. Shareware. (*http://www.arccom.bc.ca*)

→ Shred-It (**ShredIt.PPC.sit**, **ShredIt.68K.sit**, and **ShredIt. FAT.sit**). Shreds files and folders beyond recovery. Shareware. (*http://www.arccom.bc.ca*)

Linux

→ Wipe (**wipe-0.16.tar.gz**). Includes C source code. Freeware. (*http://gsu.linux.org.tr/wipe*)

FORENSICS

These programs can retrieve information from deleted files and formatted disks.

Windows

→ Directory Snoop (**dirsnp.zip**). Recovers erased files and data from individual clusters. Can also wipe sensitive data from a disk to prevent recovery. Shareware. (*http://www. briggsoft.com/dsnoop.htm*)

→ Disable (**disable.zip**). Turns off a keyboard to prevent accidental damage while examining a computer. Freeware. (*No installation support.*)

→ Disk Drive Analysis (**dd.exe**). Reads sectors from a disk and displays or prints their contents. Freeware. (*No installation support.*)

→ DM, Database Analysis Tool (**dm.zip**). Used by law enforcement. Freeware. (*No installation support.*)

→ File Scavenger (**32fs140.exe**). Scans a disk to find previously deleted files that can still be recovered. Shareware. (*http://www.quetek.com/*)

→ NTIDoc (**ntidoc.zip**). Lists all files and creation dates and times stored in a directory. Freeware. (*http://www. secure-data.com*)

→ Omniquad Detective (**detectv.zip**). Searches and examines a hard disk for information. Shareware. (*http://www. omniquad.com*)

→ Space Detective (**sd23.zip**). Identifies all disk space used by every directory on a hard disk. Shareware. (*http://www. bwsoft.com*)

HACKER INFORMATION

These files provide additional information for learning the latest about the hacker underground community.

→ Hacker Links (**HackerURL.txt**). Last-minute additional hacker Web site addresses that didn't appear in the book.

→ Online Security Ticker (**osticker2.zip**). Provides up-to-the-minute news about computer security.

HEX EDITORS

Programs that peek inside files and disk sectors so you can see what's inside them or so you can modify their contents.

Windows

→ ASL HexView (**aslhv.zip**). Allows you to examine the contents of a file without changing anything. Freeware. (*http://www. alstonlabs.pair.com/aslfw.htm*)

→ Frhed (**frhed155.zip**). Windows-based hex editor with Microsoft Visual C++ source code. Freeware. (*http://www. tu-darmstadt.de/~rkibria*)

→ Hex Editor (**hexedit.zip**). Hex editor for peeking inside files and disk clusters. Freeware. (*http://www.geocities. com/SiliconValley/Campus/9680/*)

→ Hex Workshop (**hw32v31.exe**). A powerful hex editor for examining the contents of files and disk clusters. Shareware. (*http://www.bpsoft.com*)

→ UltraEdit (**uedit32.zip**). Hex editor with a dictionary for spell-checking. Trialware. (*http://www.idmcomp.com*)

→ VEDIT (**vpwt32.exe** and **vm-pdf.zip**). Hex editor that can edit files up to 2 gigabytes in size. Includes a manual, stored as an Acrobat PDF file, in the vm-pdf.zip file. Trialware. (*http://www.vedit.com*)

HONEY POT TRAPS

Programs to help you catch and counterattack hackers.

Windows

→ NetBuster (**netbuster1_31.zip**). Detects and removes the NetBus Trojan Horse. Will also create a fake NetBus connec-

tion to help you fool any hackers trying to access your
computer using NetBus. Freeware. (*http://surf.to/netbuster*)

➔ Tambu UDP Scrambler (**tambuudp.zip**). Watches ports for
hacker probes and floods attackers with a flurry of messages. Freeware. (*http://www.xploiter.com/tambu*)

HOWTOS

These files contain information about hacking written by hackers.

➔ The Complete Social Engineering FAQ (**social_eng.
txt**). Basic introduction to social engineering, a
technique used by hackers to convince others to
give them what they want.

➔ Countermeasures (**counter.txt**). Tips for protecting yourself on your computer and in the everyday
world.

➔ The Ethics of Hacking (**hacethic.txt**). Short essay
explaining that the real purpose of hacking is
not to hurt others but to learn.

➔ An Introduction to Computer Security (**Handbook.
pdf**). Produced by the National Institute of
Standards and Technology, this handbook provides
tips and general information for corporations to
guard their systems against all forms of attack.

➔ Introduction to Denial of Service (**denial.txt**).
Explains different denial-of-service attacks, how
they work and how to defend against them.

➔ The Neophyte's Guide to Hacking (**Hacking_guide.
txt**). Short introduction explaining how to become
a hacker.

➔ A Novice's Guide to Hacking (**noviceguide.txt**).
Introductory text explaining the basics of hacking.

➔ SecureLinux for Newbies (**SecureLinux.txt**).
Information to help a system administrator
tighten up security on a server running Linux.

➔ The Ultimate Beginner's Guide to Hacking and
Phreaking (**starthack.txt**). Introduction to hacking and phreaking with plenty of resources for
beginners to learn from and study.

INTRUSION DETECTION

These programs can help you block or monitor the ports on your computer to determine if a malicious hacker is trying to access or probe your computer.

Windows

→ Anti-Hack (**setup.exe**). Monitors your open ports to detect unauthorized access attempts. Shareware. (*http://www. carbosoft.com*)

→ AntiSniff (**as-101.zip**). Detects port sniffing on a network. Freeware. (*http://www.10pht.com/antisniff*)

→ Attacker (**attacker.zip**). Monitors your ports for suspicious behavior and notifies you when someone tries to connect to your computer through a Trojan. Freeware. (*http://www.keir. net/*)

→ BlackICE Defender (**blackice21.zip**). Intrusion detection and a personal firewall. Demoware. (*http://www.networkice.com/*)

→ Jammer (**jammer.exe**). Monitors ports on your computer to detect attempted break-ins. Shareware. (*http://www. agnitum.com*)

→ McAfee Personal Firewall (**Mf0210ad.exe**). Secures your computer from hackers. Trialware. (*http://www.mcafee.com*)

→ Netmon (**netmon12.exe**). Monitors your ports for suspicious behavior and detects the more common Trojan Horses. Freeware. (*http://members.tripod.com/circlet*)

→ NukeNabber (**nn29b.exe**). Monitors your computer ports to alert you when someone may be trying to access your computer using a Trojan Horse. Freeware. (*http://www.dynamsol.com/ puppet/*)

→ Port Blocker (**pblocki.exe**). Blocks open ports on your computer to prevent them from being used by hackers or Trojan Horses. Freeware. (*No installation support.*)

→ ProtectX (**protectx.exe**). Monitors your ports to detect and remove any Trojan Horses that could be used to access your computer. Shareware. (*http://www.plasmateksoftware.com/*)

→ Rainbow Diamond Intrusion Detection (**intrusiondetectorV1. exe**). Detects suspicious activity through your ports. Demoware. (*http://www.brd.ie/*)

→ SuperScan (**superscan.exe**). Port scanner that probes your computer to detect any open ports that could be vulnerable to a remote attack, such as through a Trojan Horse. Freeware. (*http://www.keir.net/*)

→ ZoneAlarm (**zonalarm.exe**). Firewall that protects your computer from port scanners and remote access Trojans. Freeware. (*http://www.zonelabs.com/*)

Macintosh

→ TrashScan (**TrashScan f.sit**). Monitors the ports on your Macintosh to make sure an intruder isn't secretly accessing your computer over a network or the Internet. Freeware. (*http://trashscan.hypermart.net*)

IRC CLIENTS

These programs connect you to Internet Relay Chat (IRC) rooms so you can chat in real time with people all over the world.

Windows

→ mIRC (**mirc58t.exe**). Very popular Windows IRC client. Shareware. (*http://www.mirc.co.uk/*)

→ Pirch98 (**pirch98s.exe**). Shareware. (*http://www.pirchat.com*)

→ Visual IRC (**virc97_100.zip**). Easy-to-use IRC program. Donationware. (*http://www.megalith.co.uk/*)

Macintosh

→ Ircle (**ircle 3.0.4 US.sit**). Popular Macintosh IRC client. Shareware. (*http://www.ircle.com*)

→ ShadowIRC (**shadowIRC-1.1b1.sit**). Open source IRC client. Shareware. (*http://www.shadowirc.com*)

Linux

→ Bitch-X (**BitchX75p1-glibc.tar.gz** and **BitchX75p1-libc5.tar.gz**). The most popular Linux IRC client. Free (GPL). (*http://www.bitchx.com/*)

→ IRCIT (**ircit-0.3.1.tgz**). IRCIT (IRC for the Information Terrorists) is a full-featured, text-mode, macro-extensible modern IRC client. Free (GPL). (*http://www.alphalink.com.au/~aayman*)

KEYSTROKE LOGGERS

See what others are doing with your computer in your absence.

Windows

→ 2Spy (**2spy.exe**). Logs all activity on your PC so you can see what others may be doing on your computer in your absence. Shareware. (*http://www.zoranjuric.com*)

→ AppsTraka (**appstraka310.exe**). Records all programs run, when they were used, and all keystrokes typed to help you detect unauthorized users on your computer. Shareware. (*http://appstraka.hypermart.net*)

→ Key Interceptor (**ky9x.zip** for Windows 95; **kynt.zip** for NT). Logs all typed keys. Freeware. (*http://www.ultrasoft.ro/*)

→ KeyKey 2000 (**kk2000.zip**). Records keystrokes in Windows or a DOS box. Shareware. (*http://mikkoaj.hypermart.net*)

→ Key Logger (**keylog1a.zip**). Logs keystrokes and mouse clicks. Freeware. (*http://www.starindo.net/~nono/index.htm*)

→ Omniquad Desktop Surveillance (**spy32.zip**). Runs as an invisible agent, which unobtrusively captures keystrokes and records screen contents for replay. The program also compiles activity reports that include all user activities: Web sites, chat rooms, newsgroups, games, files, and folders. Trialware. (*http://www.omniquad.com*)

→ RedHand Pro (**red600.exe**). Secretly monitors your computer to determine which programs someone may be using without your knowledge or permission. Can also limit users to performing only certain functions on a computer. Shareware. (*http://www.harddrivesoftware.com*)

→ Security Setup II (**ssu20I.zip**). Restricts different users from accessing certain features, such as disabling the Control Panel and limiting users to running only certain programs. Shareware. (*http://www.security-setup.dk*)

→ STARR (Stealth Activity Recorder and Reporter) (**007starr_ setup.exe**). Monitors the use or abuse of your PC. Shareware. (*http://www.iopus.com/*)

→ Stealth Keyboard Interceptor Auto Sender (**skin982.zip**). Records keystrokes to help you monitor what people are doing on a computer without your knowledge. Shareware. (*http:// www.geocities.com/SiliconValley/Hills/8839/index.html*)

→ SureShot Ghost Keylogger (**gkldemo.zip**). Secretly records keystrokes so you can see what someone may have been doing on your computer. Demoware. (*http://www.keylogger.net*)

→ WinWhatWhere Investigator (**w3i2.exe**). Quietly monitors and reports date, time started, time elapsed, program captions, and keystrokes. Shareware. (*http://www.winwhatwhere.com*)

Macintosh

→ Cone of Silence (**Cone of Silence 1.0b2 f.sit**). Prevents keystroke capturing programs from recording what you type. Shareware. (*http://www.parkbenchsoftware.com*)

→ Free Guard (**Free_Guard.sea**). Hides files and folders. Freeware. (*http://www.msrwerks.com/applications.html*)

→ Keystroke Recorder (**Keystroke Recorder2.0.1.sea**). Records each keystroke into a file for later viewing. Shareware. (*http://www.campsoftware.com/camp*)

→ SuperLock Pro (**InstallSuperLock45Pro** and **InstallSuperLock4 Lite**). Prevents unauthorized access to your Macintosh by recording any break-in attempts, sounding an alarm, automatically going into sleep mode, and stopping someone from rebooting your computer. Shareware. (*http://www.trivectus.com*)

MP3 TOOLS

These programs allow you to play or record MP3 files.

Windows

→ Audiograbber (**agfreesetup.exe**). Grabs music from CDs digitally. Freeware. (*http://www.audiograbber.com-us.net/*)

→ Audiocatalyst (**acw21t.exe**). Transforms your CD files to MP3s. Shareware. (*http://www.xingtech.com/mp3/audiocatalyst/*)

→ CD'n'Go (**cdngo.zip**). Extracts and encodes digital MP3s. Freeware. (*http://www.cdngo.com*)

→ HyCD Play & Record (**HYCDPR0809.exe**). Lets you create your own MP3 audio CDs. Demoware. (*http://www.hycd.com*)

→ MP3 JumpGate (**mp3setup.exe**). Lets you play, create, decode, and mix MP3s. Freeware. (*http://www.worldusa.com/mp3/mp3studio.shtml*)

→ MuzicMan (**mzminstall.exe**). Organizes and plays MP3 files. Shareware. (*http://www.muzicman.com*)

→ Rosoft CD Extractor (**RosoftCDExtractorFree.exe**). Creates WAV and MP3 files. Advertiser-supported freeware. (*http://www.theripper.com-us.net/*)

→ Simple (**smp3plyr.exe**). Plays MP3s or creates them from audio CDs or WAV files. Freeware. (*http://simple.audiogalaxy.com/*)

→ Winamp (**winamp265.exe**). Popular MP3 player. Freeware. (*http://www.winamp.com*)

Macintosh

→ Macast Lite (**MACAST Lite 2.1.smi.sit**). Plays MP3 files on your Macintosh. Shareware. (*http://www.macamp.net*)

→ SoundJam MP Free (**SoundJam MP Free 2.1.1.sea**). MP3 player (encoding features are time-limited). Shareware. (*http://www.soundjam.com*)

Linux

→ CD Paranoia (**cdparanoia-III-alpha.9.7.src.tgz**). MP3 ripper. Freeware. (*http://www.xiph.org/paranoia*)

→ MPG123 (**mpg123-0.59r.tar.gz**). A real-time MPEG audio player. Freeware. (*http://www.mpg123.de/*)

→ ripperX (**ripperX-2.0.tar.gz**). Extract CD audio and encode it to MP3 format. Freeware. (*http://www.digitallabyrinth.com/*)

OPERATING SYSTEMS

Free operating systems that you can use instead of or in addition to Microsoft Windows.

→ Phat Linux (**PhatLinux32.zip**). A complete Linux distribution that Windows users can run while preserving their Windows partition. The files must be unzipped to \phat\ or Phat Linux will not function. Freeware. (*http://www.phatlinux.com/*)

→ PicoBSD (**pb_en-D.bin** and **README.en**). A one-floppy version of FreeBSD 3.0-current, which allows you to have secure dialup access, all on only one standard 1.44MB floppy. It runs on a minimum 386SX CPU with 8MB of RAM (no HDD required!). Freeware. (*http://people.freebsd.org/~picobsd/picobsd.html*)

→ Trinux (**trinux-070.tgz**). A complete Linux-based operating system and suite of security tools that can boot up and

run from a single floppy disk. Freeware. (*http://trinux.*
sourceforge.net/)

PACKET SNIFFERS

Analyze information traveling across a network with these
programs.

Windows

→ Network Sniffer (**sniffer_setup.exe**). Intercepts and analyzes packets transmitted over a network. Network Sniffer
can take plug-ins for different protocols, including IP,
TCP, and UDP. Shareware. (*http://www.ufasoft.com/*)

→ TraceWolf Packet Sniffer (**twolf181.zip**). Opens all packets
passing through your modem or Ethernet card and displays
header and data fields. Unzip **twolf181.zip** and run **trace-
wolf.exe**. Demoware.

PARENTAL CONTROL

Limit and monitor Internet access and program use on your
computer.

Windows

→ ChatNANNY (**nanny.exe**). Filters what your kids can access on
the Internet. Demoware. (*http://www.chatnanny.com*)

→ Enuff (**enuff-pc.exe**). Limits and monitors computer use.
Shareware. (*http://www.akrontech.com*)

PASSWORD RECOVERY

These programs can recover forgotten passwords from password-
protected files.

Windows

→ 007 Password Recovery (**007pwd11_setup.exe**). Retrieves passwords hidden behind asterisks. Freeware. (*http://www.iopus.
com*)

→ Access Data (**prtkdemo32.zip**). Retrieves passwords from
password-protected files created by programs such as
Quattro Pro, Microsoft Money, Excel, and Windows NT.
Demoware. (*http://www.accessdata.com*)

→ Advanced Zip Password Recovery (**azpr.zip**). Retrieves a password from a password-protected ZIP file using bruteforce, dictionary, and plain text attacks. Shareware. (*http://www.elcomsoft.com/azpr.html*)

→ Fast Zip Cracker (**fzc105c.zip**). Executes a brute force attack to retrieve a password from a password-protected ZIP file. (*http://www.netgate.com.uy/~fpapa/*)

→ John the Ripper (**john-16w.zip** and **john-1.6.22-dev.tar.gz**). Password cracker to help you detect weak UNIX passwords. The john-1.6.22-dev.tar.gz file contains the C source code. Freeware. (*http://www.openwall.com/john*)

→ Password Converter (**passconv.zip**). Peeks behind asterisks to reveal the password underneath. Freeware. (*http://metroforecast.com/storm-2000/*)

→ Password Recovery Toolkit (**kitd.exe**). Helps recover passwords from password-protected files created by a variety of popular programs including Quicken, Lotus 1-2-3, WordPerfect, and Outlook. Demoware. (*http://www.lostpassword.com*)

→ Peek-a-Boo (**peekaboo.exe**). Retrieves a password hidden behind asterisks. Freeware. (*http://www.corteksoft.com*)

→ Revelation (**revel11.exe**). Displays passwords hidden behind asterisks. Freeware. (*http://www.snadboy.com*)

→ The Ultimate Zip Cracker (**uzcsetup.exe**). Retrieves the password for any password-protected ZIP, ARJ, Excel, or Word file. Shareware. (*http://www.home.ru/vdg/uzc.htm*)

Unix/Linux

→ John the Ripper (**john-1.6.tar.gz** and **john-1.6.22-dev.tar.gz**). Password cracker to help you detect weak UNIX passwords. The john-1.6.22-dev.tar.gz file contains the C source code. (*http://www.openwall.com/john/*)

PORT SCANNERS

Analyze ports on your network and detect vulnerabilities with these programs.

Windows

→ AA Tools (**aat40a.zip**). Scans a network for vulnerable computers and open ports. Shareware. (*http://www.glocksoft.com*)

→ AntiSniff (**as-101.zip**). Detects port sniffing on a network. Freeware. (*http://www.10pht.com/antisniff*)

→ Internet ports (**Internet_Ports.zip**). Text file that lists all Internet ports and their functions. Freeware.

→ NetView (**nview10.exe**). Searches for shared resources, detects open ports on a computer or network, and tests a Web site for password security. Freeware. (*http://www.rawlogic.com/products.html*)

→ Port Blocker (**pblocki.exe**). Blocks open ports on your computer to prevent them from being used by hackers or Trojan Horses. Freeware. (*No installation support.*)

→ SATAN (Security Administrator Tool for Analyzing Networks) (**satan.zip**). Recognizes several common networking-related security problems and reports the problems without actually exploiting them. Freeware. (*No installation support.*)

→ TJ Ping (**tjping.zip**). Ping, traceroute, and lookup utility. Freeware. (*http://www.topjimmy.net/tjs*)

→ Ultra Scan (**uscan12.zip**). Port scanner that searches for vulnerable computers and open ports on a network. Freeware. (*http://www.point1.com/UltraScan*)

Linux

→ Nmap (**nmap-2.53.tar**). Linux-based port scanner regarded as the most comprehensive port scanner currently available. Freeware. (*http://www.insecure.org*)

→ Snort (**snort-1.6.tar.gz**). A lightweight network intrusion detection system, capable of performing real-time traffic analysis and packet logging on IP networks. C/C++ source code available. Freeware. (*http://www.snort.org*)

READERS

Disguise what you're reading by displaying the entire text of an ASCII document on your screen in large letters, one word at a time, at speeds up to 1,000 words per minute, so that it's virtually impossible for anyone to see at a glance what you're reading.

→ AceReader (**acerd.exe**). Read or skim text on your computer. Demoware. (*http://www.stepware.com*)

→ Vortex (**VIV_SHIP.exe**). Machine-assisted reading software that allows you to read at up to 2000 words per minute in fonts as large as 1000 points. Free for personal use. (*http://www.vallier.com/*)

REMOTE MONITORING

These programs can help you remotely monitor a computer (such as your own) without the knowledge of anyone using it.

Windows

→ NetBus Pro (**nbpro210.zip**). A remote access program that has moved away from its original remote access Trojan Horse roots. The current version of the program allows you to control another computer from a remote location. Shareware. (*http://www.netbus.org*)

→ PC Spy (**pcspyt.exe**). Monitor your computer while you are away by capturing and saving screen images. Shareware. (*http://www.softdd.com*)

→ QPeek (**qpeek121.exe**). View the desktop of a computer from anywhere on the Internet or on your local network using a standard Web browser. Shareware. (*http://www.qpeek.com*)

ROLLBACK PROGRAMS

These programs can return your computer to a previous state to help you recover from all types of malicious attacks such as virus, Trojan Horse, or hacker attacks.

Windows

→ Aladdin FlashBack (**flashWTW.EXE**). Saves all previous versions of your files so you can retrieve previously created or deleted data at any time. Trialware. (*http://www.aladdinsys.com*)

→ ConfigSafe (**Cfgsafe3.exe**). Tracks changes in your computer so you can return to a previous state at any time. Demoware. (*http://www.imagine-lan.com*)

Macintosh

→ Aladdin FlashBack (**flashback_macdemo.sit**). Saves all previous versions of your files so you can retrieve previously created or deleted data at any time. Trialware. (*http://www.aladdinsys.com*)

SPAM FIGHTERS

These programs block or filter email to reduce or eliminate spam from clogging your email account.

→ Spam Buster (**spambu32.zip**). Advertiser-supported freeware. Filters your email to remove spam. (*http://www.contactplus. com/*)

→ Spam Hater (**spamh.exe**). Helps track down spammers. Freeware. (*http://www.cix.co.uk/~net-services/*)

→ Spam Killer (**SpamKiller280.exe**). Filters your email to remove spam from known spamming addresses, while allowing email from a list of addresses that you define. Shareware. (*http://www.spamkiller.com/*)

→ SpammerSlammer (**spammerslammer.exe**). Tags suspected spam so you can delete or read it if you choose. Freeware. (*http:// www.n2plus.com/*)

→ WebCrypt (**webcrypt-trial.exe**). Unique program that encrypts your HTML code so spammers can't retrieve email addresses from your Web site. Shareware. (*http://www.moonlight-software.com*)

STEGANOGRAPHY

Hide data in graphics or sound files with these programs.

Windows

→ Contraband (**contrabd.exe**). Hides data in bitmap files. Copy contrabd.exe to your PC and then run it. (*No installation support.*)

→ dc-Steganograph (**dc-stego.zip**). A very small DOS-based program that hides data in PCX images. Freeware. (*http:// members.tripod.com/~Nikola_Injac/stegano/*)

→ Gif-It-Up (**setupex.exe**). Hides data in GIF files. (*No installation support.*)

→ Hide and Seek (**hdsk50.zip**). Encrypts data using Blowfish then hides it in GIF files. Freeware.

→ Hide4PGP (**H4pgp20w.zip** and **H4pgp20s.zip**). Works with PGP to encrypt and hide data in bitmap or sound files. (H4pgp20s. zip contains the ANSI C source code.) Freeware. (*http:// www.heinz-repp.onlinehome.de/Hide4PGP.htm*)

→ Hide in Pictures (**hip.zip**). Hides and encrypts data in a bitmap file. Unzip **hip.zip** and run **winhip.exw**. Freeware. (*No installation support.*)

→ Invisible Secrets (**etispro.exe**). Hides files in other files not usually suspected of encryption, including JPEG, PNG, and BMP. Freeware. (*http://www.east-tec.com*)

→ MP3Stego (**MP3Stego_1_1_15.zip**). Hides data in MP3 audio files. (Includes C source code.) Freeware. (*http://www.cl. cam.ac.uk/~fapp2/steganography/mp3stego/*)

→ Simple Personal Privacy (**sppdemo.exe**). Encrypts email by disguising it to look like an email containing jokes. Demoware. (*http://www.tiac.net/users/hlynka/privacy/*)

→ S-TOOLS4 (**s-tools4.zip**). Hides data in bitmap, GIF, or WAV files. Unzip **s-tools4.zip** and run **s-tools.exe**. Freeware.

→ Steganos II Security Suite (**s2et.exe**). Encrypts email using ordinary encryption or steganography to hide your email from prying eyes and can shred files beyond recovery. Trialware. (*http://www.demcom.com*)

→ wbStego (**wbs99351.zip**). Hides data in graphic, ASCII, HTML, or Adobe Acrobat files. Trialware. (*http://www.wbailer.com/ wbstego*)

Java

→ EZStego (**source.zip**). Hides and recovers encrypted data in GIF files. Free (Open Source). (*http://www.stego.com/*)

SYSTEM LOCKS

These programs can keep unauthorized users from accessing your computer in your absence.

Windows

→ DesktopShield 2000 (**desktopshield2000.zip**). Secures your PC when you're not using it. Freeware. (*http://www. crosswinds.net/~steff3/index.htm*)

→ Klik-Lok (**klk600.zip**). Locks your desktop when you walk away from your computer or when your computer starts up. Freeware. (*http://www.geocities.com/SiliconValley/Peaks/ 6799/index.htm*)

→ Workstation Lock (**Wrklocki.exe**). Password-protects your system at startup without using a screensaver. Shareware. (*http://posum.com*)

Macintosh

→ SuperLock Pro (**InstallSuperLock45Pro**), and SuperLock Lite (**InstallSuperLock4Lite**). Prevents unauthorized access to your Macintosh by recording any break-in attempts, sounding an alarm, automatically going into sleep mode, and stopping someone from rebooting your computer. Shareware. (*http://www.trivectus.com/*)

SYSTEM RESTORER

This program can help your computer recover from an accident, malfunction, or malicious attack.

Windows

→ System Safe (**ss2k.EXE**). Automatically detects and repairs corrupted system files so you can restore your computer after an accident or hacker, virus, or Trojan Horse attack. Shareware. (*http://systemsafe.now.nu/*)

VOICE ENCRYPTION

Use this program to encrypt voice transmissions over the Internet or other networks.

Windows

→ PGPFone (**PGPfone21-win.zip**; **pgpfone10b7.pdf** is the manual). Encrypts voice transmissions over the Internet or other networks. (Includes C/C++ source code.) Freeware. (*http://www.pgpi.org/*)

Macintosh

→ PGPFone (**PGPfone10b7.sit**; **pgpfone10b7.pdf** is the manual). Encrypts voice transmissions over the Internet or other networks. (Includes C/C++ source code.) Freeware. (*http://www.pgpi.org/*)

VULNERABILITY SCANNERS

Vulnerability scanners combine the features of an ordinary scanner with a database of all known weaknesses that hackers commonly exploit. The scanners list weaknesses that they find in a network and then offer suggestions for closing these possible openings.

Windows

→ Kane Security Analyst (**Ksant461.zip**). A network security assessment tool that provides a fast, thorough analysis of network security for Windows NT and Novell NetWare. Trialware. (*http://www.intrusion.com*)

→ Retina (**retina.exe**). Scan, monitor and fix vulnerabilities within a network's Internet, Intranet, and Extranet. Windows NT. Trialware. (*http://www.eeye.com*)

Linux

→ The Security Administrator's Integrated Network Tool (SAINT) (**saint-2.2.tar.gz**). An updated and enhanced version of SATAN, designed to assess the security of computer networks. Freeware. (*http://www.wwdsi.com/saint*)

WEB SITE PROTECTION

These programs can help protect your Web site from getting attacked or abused.

→ WebAgain (**setup.exe**). Automatically fixes vandalized Web pages. Trialware. (*http://www.lockstep. com*)

→ WebCrypt (**webcrypt-trial.exe**). Helps stop linkbacks to your Web pages that eat up your bandwidth, and blocks spammers who use spiders to get email addresses from your site. Trialware. (*http://www.moonlight-software.com/*)

Index

455

Updates

This book was carefully reviewed for technical accuracy, but it's inevitable that some things will change after the book goes to press. Visit **http://www.nostarch.com/ stcb_updates.htm** for updates, errata, and other information.

CD-ROM LICENSE AGREEMENT FOR *STEAL THIS COMPUTER BOOK 2*

Read this Agreement before opening this package. By opening this package, you agree to be bound by the terms and conditions of this Agreement.

This CD-ROM (the "CD") contains programs and associated documentation and other materials and is distributed with the book entitled *Steal This Computer Book 2* to purchasers of the book for their own personal use only. Such programs, documentation and other materials and their compilation (collectively, the "Collection") are licensed to you subject to terms and conditions of this Agreement by No Starch Press, having a place of business at 555 De Haro Street, Suite 250, San Francisco, CA 94107 ("Licensor"). In addition to being governed by the terms and conditions of this Agreement, your rights to use the programs and other materials included on the CD may also be governed by separate agreements distributed with those programs and materials on the CD (the "Other Agreements"). In the event of any inconsistency between this Agreement and any of the Other Agreements, those Agreements shall govern insofar as those programs and materials are concerned. By using the Collection, in whole or in part, you agree to be bound by the terms and conditions of this Agreement. Licensor owns the copyright to the Collection, except insofar as it contains materials that are proprietary to third party suppliers. All rights in the Collection except those expressly granted to you in this Agreement are reserved to Licensor and such suppliers as their respective interests may appear.

1. Limited License. Licensor grants you a limited, nonexclusive, nontransferable license to use the Collection on a single dedicated computer (excluding network servers). This Agreement and your rights hereunder shall automatically terminate if you fail to comply with any provision of this Agreement or the Other Agreements. Upon such termination, you agree to destroy the CD and all copies of the CD, whether lawful or not, that are in your possession or under your control. Licensor and its suppliers retain all rights not expressly granted herein as their respective interests may appear.

2. Additional Restrictions. (A) You shall not (and shall not permit other persons or entities to) directly or indirectly, by electronic or other means, reproduce (except for archival purposes as permitted by law), publish, distribute, rent, lease, sell, sublicense, assign, or otherwise transfer the Collection or any part thereof or this Agreement. Any attempt to do so shall be void and of no effect. (B) You shall not (and shall not permit other persons or entities to) reverse-engineer, decompile, disassemble, merge, modify, create derivative works of, or translate the Collection or use the Collection or any part thereof for any commercial purpose. (C) You shall not (and shall not permit others persons or entities to) remove or obscure Licensor's or its suppliers' or licensor's copyright, trademark, or other proprietary notices or legends from any portion of the Collection or any related materials. (D) You agree and certify that the Collection will not be exported outside the United States except as authorized and as permitted by the laws and regulations of the United States. If the Collection has been rightfully obtained outside of the United States, you agree that you will not reexport the Collection, except as permitted by the laws and regulations of the United States and the laws and regulations of the jurisdiction in which you obtained the Collection.

3. Disclaimer of Warranty. (A) The Collection and the CD are provided "as is" without warranty of any kind, either express or implied, including, without limitation, any warranty of merchantability and fitness for a particular purpose, the entire risk as to the results and performance of the CD and the software and other materials that is part of the Collection is assumed by you, and Licensor and its suppliers and distributors shall have no responsibility for defects in the CD or the accuracy or application of or errors or omissions in the Collection and do not warrant that the functions contained in the Collection will meet your requirements, or that the operation of the CD or the Collection will be uninterrupted or error-free, or that any defects in the CD or the Collection will be corrected. In no event shall Licensor or its suppliers or distributors be liable for any direct, indirect, special, incidental, or consequential damages arising out of the use of or inability to use the Collection or the CD, even if Licensor or its suppliers or distributors have been advised of the likelihood of such damages occurring. Licensor and its suppliers and distributors shall not be liable for any loss, damages, or costs arising out of, but not limited to, lost profits or revenue; loss of use of the Collection or the CD; loss of data or equipment; cost of recovering software, data, or materials in the Collection; the cost of substitute software, data, or materials in the Collection; claims by third parties; or other similar costs. (B) In no event shall Licensor or its suppliers' or distributors' total liability to you for all damages, losses, and causes of action (whether in contract, tort or otherwise) exceed the amount paid by you for the Collection. (C) Some states do not allow exclusion or limitation of implied warranties or limitation of liability for incidental or consequential damages, so the above limitations or exclusions may not apply to you.

4. U.S. Government Restricted Rights. The Collection is licensed subject to RESTRICTED RIGHTS. Use, duplication, or disclosure by the U.S. Government or any person or entity acting on its behalf is subject to restrictions as set forth in subdivision (c)(1)(ii) of the Rights in Technical Data and Computer Software Clause at DFARS (48 CFR 252.227-7013) for DoD contracts, in paragraphs (c)(1) and (2) of the Commercial Computer Software Restricted Rights clause in the FAR (48 CFR 52.227 - 19) for civilian agencies, or, in the case of NASA, in clause 18-52.227-86(d) of the NASA Supplement to the FAR, or in other comparable agency clauses. The contractor/manufacturer is No Starch Press, 555 De Haro Street, Suite 250, San Francisco, CA 94107.

5. General Provisions. Nothing in this Agreement constitutes a waiver of Licensor's, or its suppliers' or licensors' rights under U.S. copyright laws or any other federal, state, local, or foreign law. You are responsible for installation, management, and operation of the Collection. This Agreement shall be construed, interpreted, and governed under California law. Copyright (c) 2000 No Starch Press. All rights reserved. Reproduction in whole or in part without permission is prohibited.